Evergreens

THE TIME-LIFE LIBRARY OF BOATING

HUMAN BEHAVIOR

THE ART OF SEWING

THE OLD WEST

THE EMERGENCE OF MAN

THE AMERICAN WILDERNESS

THE TIME-LIFE ENCYCLOPEDIA OF GARDENING

LIFE LIBRARY OF PHOTOGRAPHY

THIS FABULOUS CENTURY

FOODS OF THE WORLD

TIME-LIFE LIBRARY OF AMERICA

TIME-LIFE LIBRARY OF ART

GREAT AGES OF MAN

LIFE SCIENCE LIBRARY

THE LIFE HISTORY OF THE UNITED STATES

TIME READING PROGRAM

LIFE NATURE LIBRARY

LIFE WORLD LIBRARY

FAMILY LIBRARY:
   HOW THINGS WORK IN YOUR HOME
   THE TIME-LIFE BOOK OF THE FAMILY CAR
   THE TIME-LIFE FAMILY LEGAL GUIDE
   THE TIME-LIFE BOOK OF FAMILY FINANCE

Evergreens

by
JAMES UNDERWOOD CROCKETT
and
the Editors of TIME-LIFE BOOKS

Watercolor Illustrations by
Rebecca A. Merrilees and John Murphy

TIME-LIFE BOOKS, NEW YORK

THE AUTHOR: James Underwood Crockett is an eminent horticulturist and writer on gardening subjects. A graduate of the University of Massachusetts' Stockbridge School of Agriculture, he has lived in—and cultivated a wide variety of plants in—California, New York, Texas and New England and has served as a consultant to many nurseries and landscapers. His monthly bulletin, "Flowery Talks," is distributed to more than a million customers annually through florists' shops. Mr. Crockett lives in Massachusetts.

THE ILLUSTRATORS: Unless otherwise credited, the watercolor paintings of evergreens on pages 90 to 148 were provided by Rebecca A. Merrilees and John Murphy. Mrs. Merrilees studied at the American School of Design and Pratt Institute; she resides in Vermont. Mr. Murphy, who lives in Philadelphia, received his training there at the Hussian School of Art.

GENERAL CONSULTANTS: Staff of the Brooklyn Botanic Garden: Robert S. Tomson, Assistant Director; Thomas R. Hofmann, Plant Propagator; George A. Kalmbacher, Plant Taxonomist; Edmond O. Moulin, Horticulturist; Frank Okamura, Gardener. John E. Bryan, Director, Strybing Arboretum, San Francisco, California. William Flemer III, Princeton Nurseries, Princeton, N.J. Alfred J. Fordham, Propagator, Arnold Arboretum, Harvard University. Albert P. Nordheden, Morganville, New Jersey. George H. Spalding, Botanical Information Consultant, Los Angeles State and County Arboreta, Los Angeles, California. Dr. Donald Wyman, Horticulturist Emeritus, Arnold Arboretum, Harvard University.

THE COVER: New spring-green shoots contrast with the deep green of older foliage on a Canada hemlock. A graceful and versatile evergreen, this tree thrives in sun or light shade; if left to grow to its natural height, it may reach 50 feet or more, but it can easily be kept much smaller by pruning.

Portions of this book were written by Joseph Kastner. Instructional drawings are the work of Matt Greene. Valuable assistance was provided by the following departments and individuals of Time Inc.: Editorial Production, Norman Airey; Library, Benjamin Lightman; Picture Collection, Doris O'Neil; Photographic Laboratory, George Karas; TIME-LIFE News Service, Murray J. Gart; Correspondents Jane Estes (Seattle), Martha Green (San Francisco), Joyce Leviton (Atlanta), Holland McCombs (Dallas), Mary Quisenberry (Wetumpka, Ala.), Jessica Silvers (Los Angeles), Sue Wymelenberg (Boston).

CONTENTS

An evergreen for every use 1

Mention the word evergreen to the average man and he will probably think of a pine tree. When I was a nursery boss I often had a customer ask me for "an evergreen." And when I responded by asking what sort of evergreen, he would be astonished to learn what a variety there actually is. Pine and spruce are evergreens, of course. So are live oaks and camellias, not to mention eucalyptus and magnolia, azalea, abelia, olive and oleander. There is an enormous range of evergreens available for your garden, no matter what part of the country you live in.

There are evergreens tall enough to shield your house from winter winds or shade it from summer sun, and others so low that they carpet the bare ground with a low-growing mat, often flourishing in places where grass will not grow. Some stand slim and straight like sentries at your doorway, and others spread their shadows over half your yard. Some form a modest green background for your perennials, and others upstage everything else in your garden with a dramatic display of blossoms.

Evergreens grow gigantic enough to make your home a neighborhood landmark or, as miniature varieties of these same giants, snuggle into pockets in your rock garden. They invite your friends to linger under their shade or, with branches and foliage and even thorns, they keep out intruders both human and animal. On the open plains they offer respite from constant wind, and in crowded suburbs they screen out headlights and noise. They come in all shades of green, some so dark as to seem almost black and some so light as to look almost white. Even the plainest of them carry natural decorations: in much of the country they are frosted with snow in December, and everywhere they are covered with pollen in spring and hung with cones or berries in summer and fall. And they bring a wide world into your garden—pines from the South Pacific and firs from the Himalayas, cypresses from China and azaleas from Japan, spruces from Siberia and monkey puzzle trees from Chile, heathers from Scotland and yews from Ireland, laurels from the

Looking like a gigantic Christmas tree, this 50-foot-tall white spruce dominates the view from a waterfront terrace in Maine—and at the same time provides shade and shelter from the winds that sweep in off the bay.

AN INTREPID PLANT HUNTER

The Douglas fir was named for David Douglas, an astonishing young Scot who discovered scores of trees, shrubs, flowers, birds and animals on several perilous expeditions through the Northwest between 1823 and 1834. Born at Scone in Perthshire in 1798, Douglas went to school when he was three, got himself expelled for devilry before he was seven and started work as an apprentice gardener at 10. Educating himself, he became so expert a botanist that what is now the Royal Horticultural Society engaged him as a collector when he was 24 and sent him to North America. Traversing thousands of miles of what is now British Columbia, Washington and Oregon, he faced down Indians, survived canoe wrecks, incapacitating injuries and starvation, and shipped home case after case of specimens. He died in 1834 while climbing Mauna Loa in Hawaii: slipping into a pitfall, he was gored to death by a wild bull that was caught in the same trap.

Appalachian Mountains and scented cedars from the Sierras.

One type or another of the many kinds of evergreens can be grown anywhere in America, even in the harshest climates. To find out which types do best in the area in which you live, look at page 149. The map on that page identifies the areas where various kinds of evergreens grow and is keyed to the encyclopedia *(pages 89-148)*, where each is described.

The term evergreen can be somewhat misleading, simply because not all plants included in this category are green. Depending on age, variety and season, they can be shades of yellow, blue, gray, bronze or even deep purple. But the term has been used for so long that it persists. The easiest definition of an evergreen is a plant that holds its foliage even when it is dormant, or resting, in winter. This characteristic sets evergreens apart from deciduous trees and shrubs, which lose their leaves in autumn.

Evergreens themselves are divided into two large classes: the narrow-leaved ones, whose leaves are needlelike, as in pines and spruces, and the broad-leaved ones, whose leaves are wider, as in rhododendrons and magnolias. The narrow-leaved ones are also called conifers because they carry their seeds in cones. This last name leads to some confusion, for the conifers also include a few trees that are *not* evergreen, such as the larch, the bald cypress and the dawn redwood. Unlike true evergreens, these conifers lose all their needles each fall, as oaks and maples lose their leaves, so they are properly called deciduous conifers.

Although narrow-leaved and broad-leaved varieties share the name of evergreen, they are very different types of plants. The difference, in fact, is one of the sharpest and most significant in the plant world. In the warmth of the preglacial eras, palm trees grew in Greenland, and all plants were green all year round. The first trees and shrubs to emerge on earth, about 345 million years ago, were of the family called gymnosperms. The gymnosperms bore what botanists call "naked" seeds, unprotected by any fleshy covering. The conifers, which belonged to this family, gathered their seeds into cones to facilitate their dispersal. All gymnosperm blossoms were fertilized with the help of the wind, which carried male pollen to the female flowers.

In later geological eras a new family of plants gradually evolved. These were the angiosperms, which carried their seeds in a capsule of fruit. Their flowers were fertilized by insects, which did a much more efficient job than the wind. The deciduous trees of today are angiosperms.

Almost everywhere that gymnosperms and angiosperms met in competition for growing space, the gymnosperms lost out. The cold of the advancing glaciers killed many of them off. But the most successful of the survivors were the conifers; of the 700 gymnosperms still alive today, over 500 are conifers. Even these are retreating, however. If it weren't for the help of man, they would be disappearing even faster, being pushed off the earth by the 250,000 kinds of angiosperms.

Among these 250,000 angiosperms are all of the handsome broad-leaved evergreens that grace American gardens. For the most part, conifers are trees that prosper in cold climates because their needles lose moisture at a slow rate during cold weather. Most broad-leaved evergreens do better in warm areas where winter moisture is more available and frost does not damage their fibrous roots. So American gardeners in the North have a wider choice of conifers, while the southern gardener has a better selection of broad-leaved evergreens.

Both kinds of evergreens have so many special virtues for your garden that a catalogue of their unique qualities could go on and on. Many affect us subjectively. During a northern winter it is comforting to see green plants in a frozen garden, perhaps as a sort of assurance that spring will return. They suggest warmth and cheer and even security at a time when the land seems forbidding and hostile. In warmer regions evergreens offer the solace of cooling shelter from the heat and eye-soothing relief from the glare of the sun. Wherever they are planted they add a feeling of richness and elegance to a garden and grounds.

Because of the evergreens' great variety of sizes, shapes and uses, your choice can be as bewildering as it is tempting. The first thing you have to decide, if you decide to plant an evergreen, is what use you will make of it. Use largely determines the size you need, and for this reason size provides the most convenient way of grouping evergreens for systematic choice.

As a general guide, evergreens are divided into six categories that describe the plants and indicate their best uses. These categories are: (1) tall trees, (2) small trees and large shrubs, (3) medium-sized shrubs, (4) small shrubs, (5) low-growing shrubs and (6) ground covers. The chart beginning on page 152 summarizes the specific sizes and characteristics of the 132 evergreens illustrated in the encyclopedia. You can find the size, shape and other traits of a particular plant you are looking for in this chart, then turn to the encyclopedia for a more detailed description and how-to-grow advice.

TALL TREES grow 30 to 50 feet high in the garden, sometimes even higher, spreading their branches over an area 20 to 40 feet in diameter. They are planted primarily as specimen trees—that is, trees used singly for their individual beauty or drama. On a large property, they can also be used in rows to screen out wind, noise or

GETTING THE PROPER FIT

9

an unpleasant view. By their very size, they become the dominant element in your garden and should be planted only if your grounds are big enough to accommodate them easily. A tree with a 30-foot spread would push almost everything else out of a narrow lot—to say nothing of pushing into the house itself. So be prudent about planting a giant in your suburban backyard. Many a potential giant is worth planting because it is handsome when young; but remember that the day may come, in 20 years or so, when you may have to remove it.

In suggesting specific kinds of trees, I will dwell on those few which I think represent the best qualities of the trees in each group —not to persuade you that these trees are the only ones to be considered but to suggest the qualities you should look for. Among the many tall, handsome and useful conifers, my favorite for the northeastern quarter of the country is the white or eastern white pine. Almost any soil suits it, and once it is properly planted it makes few demands on you. The long needles, which come in clusters of five, are deep blue-green and soft to the touch. As a specimen tree it is impressive—conical in shape with main branches held horizontally outward from the trunk. As a windbreak or as a boundary marker, it has the virtue of fast growth.

The white pine is native to North America; my favorite tall conifer for the West Coast and South is an immigrant, the deodar cedar. It comes from the Himalayas and has had a romantic quality for me ever since I read Rudyard Kipling's *Under the Deodars*. It is used exclusively as a specimen. Its shape is broadly conical. Its branches droop gracefully at the tips. Spaced widely, they give an airy quality to the whole tree—so ethereal, in fact, that I am always surprised at the deodar's toughness. It will survive both the dry seasons of the West Coast and the rainy months along the Gulf and in the Northwest. Its needles are blue-green and soft to the touch. (I have been accused, with some reason, of being partial to evergreens with soft needles. This bias probably comes from my days working in a nursery when, all too often, I would find myself backing into the painfully stiff needles of a spruce or mugo pine. People say that a stiff-needled tree has character. I agree—but so does a cactus.)

Most tall broad-leaved evergreens do not grow in the cold regions of the northern United States, but they do thrive elsewhere —the eucalyptus in California, the live oak throughout the South. The broadleaf that thrives best in most mild climates is the magnolia, more precisely a species called *Magnolia grandiflora*. It is a round tree whose branches spread wide and, if they are left unpruned, sweep the ground. When the lower ones are pruned out, the tree provides a dense and comforting shade. And it has some-

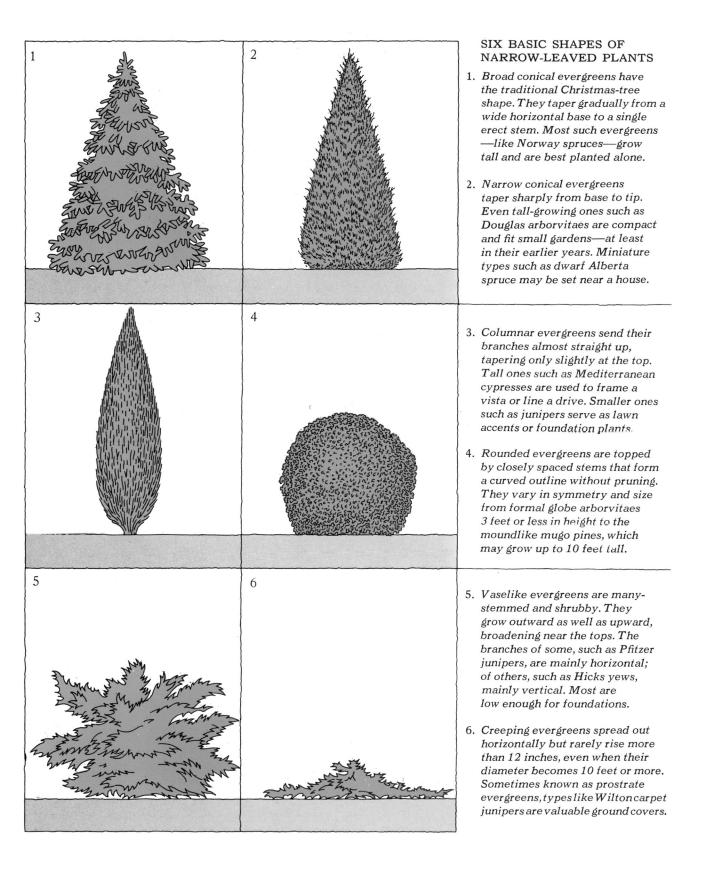

SIX BASIC SHAPES OF NARROW-LEAVED PLANTS

1. *Broad conical evergreens have the traditional Christmas-tree shape. They taper gradually from a wide horizontal base to a single erect stem. Most such evergreens —like Norway spruces—grow tall and are best planted alone.*

2. *Narrow conical evergreens taper sharply from base to tip. Even tall-growing ones such as Douglas arborvitaes are compact and fit small gardens—at least in their earlier years. Miniature types such as dwarf Alberta spruce may be set near a house.*

3. *Columnar evergreens send their branches almost straight up, tapering only slightly at the top. Tall ones such as Mediterranean cypresses are used to frame a vista or line a drive. Smaller ones such as junipers serve as lawn accents or foundation plants.*

4. *Rounded evergreens are topped by closely spaced stems that form a curved outline without pruning. They vary in symmetry and size from formal globe arborvitaes 3 feet or less in height to the moundlike mugo pines, which may grow up to 10 feet tall.*

5. *Vaselike evergreens are many-stemmed and shrubby. They grow outward as well as upward, broadening near the tops. The branches of some, such as Pfitzer junipers, are mainly horizontal; of others, such as Hicks yews, mainly vertical. Most are low enough for foundations.*

6. *Creeping evergreens spread out horizontally but rarely rise more than 12 inches, even when their diameter becomes 10 feet or more. Sometimes known as prostrate evergreens, types like Wilton carpet junipers are valuable ground covers.*

thing that conifers do not have: large fragrant blossoms that cover the tree profusely throughout the month of June and keep blooming sporadically for the rest of the summer.

SMALL TREES AND LARGE SHRUBS are more useful than the taller types in the average garden. They usually grow to 20 feet or so at maturity and spread 10 to 20 feet; old plants in ideal locations may grow 30 feet high. They are fine specimen trees. When planted close together they make good screens. Pruning can keep them relatively small without thwarting their natural growth habits. For the taller specimen tree, nurserymen prune away the stems so as to concentrate all the growth into the main trunk. To make a screen of shorter, denser evergreens, they sometimes cut back the main trunk almost to the ground and thus encourage several stems to grow up at once.

My favorite conifer in this category is one of the most reliable and accommodating of all trees, the juniper, particularly the upright varieties of Chinese juniper. It is the universal evergreen. It grows fast in virtually every part of the U.S. and under any conditions—hot climate and cold, dry and wet, in good soil and on rocky ledges or at the desert's edge. It will withstand salt that is blown in by the sea or left by highway trucks to melt winter snow and ice. For all its toughness it is a good-looking tree, forming a column of dense foliage that ranges from dark green to blue-green throughout the year. The needles are prickly when young, but soften with age—as so many of us do.

The hard blue-gray berries of juniper are actually tightly packed cones in disguise, and in some varieties they have a practical use: they give gin its flavor. Crush and smell one and you immediately think of a martini.

Broad-leaved evergreens of the small-tree–large-shrub category will grow only in warmer parts of the country. The cherry laurel, for example, is a sturdy plant, its rounded shape covered with dark glossy leaves. It grows up to 18 feet tall, spreading out if planted as a specimen but becoming very dense if pruned as a screen. In fact, it responds to shearing so well that you can make it almost any shape you want.

On the West Coast as well as in the South the loquat grows quickly to its full height of 20 feet, often becoming as wide as it is high. It has stunning pointed leaves, 8 or more inches long and very glossy. To show them off, it is often trained to grow flat against a wall—espaliered *(page 77)*. It also has small cream-colored blossoms that develop into small yellow or orange fruits. The fruits can be made into very good jam.

In both the South and the West you can grow one of the most dramatic of all evergreens, the Italian cypress, whose slender columns provide emphatic exclamation-point accents in the landscape. You will recall them as the stiff, dark green trees that dot the landscape in Italian Renaissance paintings.

The trees that I have been describing grow in geometric, contained shapes, but I would like to mention one that does not—the Japanese black pine. A very hardy tree that grows throughout most of the country, it generally sends its branches out horizontally but every once in a while it bends one up almost vertically, creating a picturesque look. It also ages rapidly in appearance and by the time it is 10 it already looks quite old. This show of distinctive maturity makes it a uniquely decorative tree.

MEDIUM-SIZED SHRUBS make up the bulk of garden evergreens and are, all in all, the most widely useful. Most reach a height, and often a spread, of 8 to 10 feet at maturity. Planted singly or in small groups they make handsome specimens. As low screens and hedges they can be pruned to an impenetrable thickness. Planted along a foundation they can improve the proportions of a house and cover unsightly foundations. As borders and backgrounds they set one part of the grounds off from another. Their size, in fact, accommodates them to almost any part of your yard. They grow slowly enough when mature so that they can keep their places and fill their roles for years. Yet they grow fast enough when they are young so that a nursery dealer can afford to sell a good-sized plant at a relatively low price.

For me the finest of the medium-sized conifers is the yew, which, in one variety or another, grows almost everywhere in the country except where winters are quite warm. I prize yews most for their elegance; they lend a richness to any garden. The very dark green needles make it the classic background for flower beds—any color is enhanced by a yew backdrop. Yew needles are soft and the wood is tough. As you remember from the tales of Robin Hood, yew was the wood used by the archers of medieval England for their bows. In warm areas of the South and parts of the West, where yews do not thrive, the podocarpus is a reasonable facsimile—it so resembles the yew that it is often called the yew podocarpus.

The broad-leaved types of medium-sized shrubs include the two finest of all flowering shrubs: the rhododendron, which grows in much of the North, and the camellia, which thrives in the South and West. Both serve most roles assigned to the medium-sized evergreens, although as hedges they are not dense, and their soft outlines indicate a boundary rather than define it emphatically. But their special glory is their flowers—of an astonishing range of color, purity of tone and delicacy of shading. The rhododendron grows along the East Coast as far north as Maine and as far west as Ohio. The camellia grows all through the South and along the West Coast in Cal-

HOW TO CURE AN OLIVE

If you have a backyard olive tree that produces table-sized fruit, you know you cannot eat it directly off the tree because it is too bitter. But all you need is patience, a few staples and a little effort to make the harvest edible. To prepare green olives, tap each one with a wooden mallet (the tapping speeds the curing process 12-fold by breaking the skin); soak them in water for three days, changing the water daily. Then pack the olives into jars with small quantities of one or several of the following: bay leaves, lemon leaves, lemon slices, garlic, peppercorns or chili peppers. Make a brine using 1 cup of coarse salt for every 12 cups of water; pour the brine into the jars. Leave the jars uncovered but keep the olives immersed for a month while fermentation takes place. When fermentation stops, skim the brine and eat the olives, or add a little olive oil to the top of the brine—this layer of oil will seal the olives for use later.

13

ifornia. And in the Northwest, beyond the Cascades, rhododendrons and camellias grow magnificently side by side.

SMALL SHRUBS generally reach a height of 4 to 6 feet and have a spreading nature. They are quite versatile and are small enough to fit in almost anywhere yet big enough to fill an important space comfortably. They are often planted in front of larger evergreens to give the billowing appearance of a gradual stepping down of height—an effect called "facing down" by landscape architects. Small shrubs make the most practical outline hedges, neatly defining the edge of the property or the various sections inside —separating, for example, a walk from the lawn or a rose bed from the vegetable plot. And their attractive shapes and flowers also make them admirable specimens.

The most widely useful of these small shrubs is a broadleaf, the evergreen azalea. In regions where winter is cold, most azaleas are deciduous, but there are several evergreen species that will withstand winter cold as far north as St. Louis inland and Rhode Island along the Atlantic Coast. Many more evergreen varieties in this category are grown farther south. Their flowers have a lovely color range from white to many shades of pink to sharp red, and they bloom before the new leaves arrive, hiding the plant in color in early spring. Then the young leaves grace the shrubs with that delicate soft color known as spring green. For formal borders another broadleaf is better: the convexleaf holly *(Ilex crenata convexa)*. Its leaves are not long and prickly like those of English or American hollies, but small, round, convex and so glossy that each one seems to have been given a wax polish.

Curiously, most plants in this group cost more than the medium-sized shrubs. The reason is simple—they grow slowly, and nurserymen wait until they make some kind of show before offering them for sale. This investment in time, up to 10 years, means higher prices. Even so, these shrubs are a sound investment: they rarely outgrow their space or need to be replaced.

LOW-GROWING SHRUBS are generally 1 to 3 feet high and of wide-spreading character. Small as they are, they have many uses: at the very front of a foundation planting, as marker borders within the grounds, as plants to fill any awkward gap and as miniature specimens, especially in a rock garden. A few of the plants in this group are naturally small—the Heller Japanese holly, for example, which makes a low but very emphatic edging for a lawn or garden, or the hardy mountain andromeda, which bears white flowers similar to those of the lily of the valley on gracefully drooping branches. But most low-growing evergreens are genetic dwarfs, the freaks of nature. A perfectly normal spruce, for example, may produce a mutation, a plant that is radically different from the parent.

A 100-foot tree may have a 1-foot offspring. Such aberrations occur rather frequently. In a forest, unable to reach up to the sunlight, the dwarfed seedlings would die. But horticulturists have propagated thousands of dwarfs from almost all of the towering coniferous evergreens.

Many of those mutations are propagated from the so-called witches'-brooms—the ragged clusters of twigs and branches that you see growing along the trunks and boughs of big trees; they sometimes look like huge, sloppily built birds' nests. They are apparently caused by insect wounds or a virus attack. Seeds that grow in them produce unexpected offspring, and horticulturists have found them a rich and fascinating source of mutations. In the Arnold Arboretum in Boston there is a plot in which seeds from a single white pine's witches'-broom have been sown. The seeds have produced a whole sideshow of plant freaks—small floppy pines, tiny compact ones, spreading ones, skinny ones—in a variety of colors, and all from a single clump. If any seem unique and truly useful, they will be propagated and tested, and perhaps a brand-new dwarf pine will be made available for your garden.

Dwarf plants grow very slowly, an inch or two a year, perhaps less, and require no pruning at all. They should be planted away from large shrubs to maintain a sense of scale. I have a 15-year-old Sargent's weeping hemlock on my lawn; it still is only 18 inches tall and makes a delightful conversation piece. Such a dwarf is ideal in a rock garden, where it helps create a toylike landscape.

There is one group of low-growing evergreen shrubs that is too often overlooked—the heathers and the closely related heaths. If you are seeking a low-growing evergreen plant that will withstand wind, drought and winter cold and still provide several months of lovely summer bloom, carpeting any sunny area with masses of white, pink, lavender or reddish purple flowers, you would be well advised to try a heather or heath.

GROUND COVERS, the lowest-growing category of all, hug or creep over the ground. They rarely grow more than 10 inches high. They are invaluable where grass will not grow, as under a dense and shallow-rooted tree such as a maple or beech. They cannot be walked on as a lawn can but they provide a green carpet as grass does; what is more, they have interesting flowers, berries and textures. Properly planted on banks, they can slow or stop erosion and they add beauty to a shrub border.

The ground covers include one of my favorite evergreens—I like it for its name as much as for its other qualities—the kinnikinnick, or bearberry. It grows thick, spreads readily, stays green through most of the year (it becomes bronze in cold weather) and sports bright red berries in fall. It is a circumpolar plant, thriving in

WHAT MAKES CORK FLOAT

Each cubic inch of cork, the bark of the cork oak (Quercus suber), contains more than 200 million individual 14-sided cells with impermeable walls that trap air. That is why it "bobs like a cork" in water—the Romans used cork in floats 2,000 years ago—and why it can serve as insulating material even in spacecraft. Unlike other evergreen trees, the cork oak survives without injury the periodic stripping of its bark and sets about growing a new outer cover. Native to Spain and Portugal, it now thrives in California gardens.

climates up to the Arctic, as well as down to Tennessee and all around the world. And only recently has it been domesticated to make it grow in the garden.

I remember my frustration as a nurseryman at not being able to offer bearberry for sale. I would find large healthy clumps in the woods or along the beaches. I would dig them up and give them the best of care only to find that the kinnikinnick stubbornly refused to be tamed. Domestication has finally been achieved by growing the plants in clay, plastic or metal containers, a method described in detail in the next chapter.

Among the conifers there is a juniper that serves as a fine ground cover—the Wilton carpet juniper, which does well everywhere but in the Deep South. It raises its gray-green foliage just off the ground; a single plant can become as much as 10 or 15 feet wide and still be no more than 4 inches tall.

GETTING THE RIGHT EFFECT

Within each of these broad groups of evergreens are so many different kinds that gardeners find it difficult to select the types they need for the effects they desire. But size again is a good starting point. It depends on rate of growth.

I realize that it is all very well to caution you about planning carefully where to put "fast-growing" or "slow-growing" evergreens; but what do such terms mean? I am repeatedly asked how fast a tree or shrub will grow. And I admit that my answers are not really satisfying. The trouble is that an evergreen's growth depends on so many things. Consider two identical Chinese junipers, one growing in Illinois, the other in Texas. The Illinois juniper has a frost-free season of 180 days in which to put out and consolidate new growth; it can grow about 8 inches in that time if weather conditions are favorable. The Texas plant has a frost-free season of 240 days and can grow 16 inches—double the height of its Illinois counterpart —in that time. Climate and growing season are predictable, but there are many unpredictables: the vagaries of weather within the same climate zone, the fertility of the soil, the health of the particular plant and the diligence of its owner. Besides all this, evergreens, somewhat like people, grow rather slowly in childhood, shoot up rapidly in adolescence, then grow slowly as they near maturity. Yet you cannot make an intelligent choice of a plant without some notion of its rate of growth. The encyclopedia chapter gives some indication of how many years a plant takes to reach maximum height; just remember that these estimates are broad averages and that the evergreen you plant may turn out to be very different from average.

When you are considering size remember that an evergreen does not grow in your garden as it does in the wild. The pines you see in a forest have to reach up for life-giving sunlight. And since each pine is surrounded by other pines, the only way it can get sunlight is to grow up and up. Forest trees eventually have thrust all their useful branches up near the top where sunlight can reach them. In the open space of your garden a tree can reach sunlight by growing outward as well as up. So the narrow 80-foot-high pine of the forest would probably be a spreading 50-footer on your lawn.

You should also remember that some of the sizable evergreens, such as the beautiful Colorado blue spruce, for example, do not grow old gracefully. When young they have a symmetrical conical shape. But at the age of about 20 they begin to lose branches, especially at the bottom. The tree will never recover its youthful beauty, so plan to replace it when it becomes unsightly.

The sideways growth of trees also applies, of course, to shrubs. To avoid gaps in a border a gardener may plant shrubs close together; in a few years he will have to take some out. Or he will plant a spreading shrub too close to the edge of his walk, and the branches will get in the way if he does not prune constantly. There is almost nothing that irritates me more than going down a garden walk on a wet day and having to choose between getting my trouser legs soaked by an out-of-bounds juniper on one side or tiptoeing through a tulip bed on the other. An equally important consideration in choosing an evergreen is the variety of colors and textures. Too much of this variety can give a spotty effect to a home landscape, while a good selection will blend beautifully. And color can perform some useful tricks for you—if your grounds seem small, plant a border of light-colored evergreens at the far end; because it is light, the border will seem to recede and, by an optical illusion, make the place look bigger. Some evergreens have such definite colors that they must be used cautiously. A blue spruce is usually at its best when set off by itself for its own beauty. And there is a juniper called Gold Coast whose golden color is spectacular. But I would use it only in a rock garden where its theatrical quality is matched by large boulders.

Evergreens appear so durable, so permanent in character—it is one of their major attractions—that when you plant them you feel that you are planting them to remain forever. But after you have lived in your home for several years, your needs and tastes can change. You do not have to have those rhododendrons screening off the sandbox because the children are grown up, or have the row of junipers hiding the clothesline because now you have a dryer. Besides, you want something that requires a lot less work to maintain. Go ahead and redecorate your grounds. With careful planning, it is not all that difficult or expensive. Plant your evergreens as if they were to remain in place forever. But don't let that keep you from doing it all over again later on.

The first steps: choosing and planting 2

When you are ready to plant your evergreens, the first thing you should do is go for a walk. Start if you can at an arboretum or a botanical garden, even if it means traveling a couple of hours to get there. Stroll around looking at evergreens to see what catches your eye in color and texture and what suits your needs in size and shape. In most arboretums the trees are individually labeled; if they aren't, ask about any trees that appeal to you. Write down their names and study up on their characteristics as described in the encyclopedia chapter starting on page 89.

Then take another walk; meander around your neighborhood. Take note of what seems to be both popular and thriving. You may get bored by the unimaginative repetition of landscaping but at least this will tell you what kinds of trees and shrubs will do well for you. Ask the owners if you can't identify some of them.

Armed with a set of sensible and attractive possibilities, go next to a plant nursery or garden center. You may be completely confused by the available varieties of each kind of evergreen, but take your time. Compare the foliage of that mugo pine with that of the red pine, and see if you really prefer something thick and stubby or something airy and tall.

By keeping your eyes open you can judge the quality of the nursery's wares. A good evergreen should be thickly branched and densely clothed with foliage of healthy color. Deep green is usually a sign of health (though some evergreens are by nature pale green or even yellow-green; the encyclopedia chapter will tell you what the natural color is). If the color seems questionable or the foliage is not thick, forget about that tree or shrub. If the tips of many plants are yellowing, that means an ailment or a neglect of proper watering; forget about that nursery. Don't be alarmed, however, if the tips of some branches seem to be drooping; new growth in healthy plants often acts this way.

On a narrow-leaved evergreen pay particular attention to the distance between the branches as they go up the trunk. If the spaces

A sturdy ladder and a rope-operated cutter on a long pole are two pieces of essential equipment for maintaining the trim of this 40-foot-high magnolia hedge, which is a living wall for a Washington, D.C., garden.

between the branches of a 4-foot spruce, for example, measure more than 6 inches, don't think of buying that tree. No branches will ever grow in those gaps. It is normal for trees to grow rapidly upward to reach toward the sunshine in the forest. But in the garden they should be pruned to keep them from becoming spindly and sparsely branched. Look for trees that have short spaces between the branches, almost hidden by thick growth; this indicates that the nurseryman has been paying proper attention to the control of natural but wayward tendencies. A good nurseryman prunes new growth on evergreens to make them bushier. (For details on pruning narrow-leaved evergreens, see pages 51-54; for broad-leaved evergreens, see pages 85 and 86.) The plant compensates for this loss by throwing out extra growth along the sides of the branches. This is what makes a shrub or tree thick and compact.

These qualities can also be achieved by pruning the roots. The nurseryman cuts the roots off near their tips by pushing his spade through them. By depriving a plant of some of its roots, he limits its capacity for taking up food and water, and this drastically shortens the length of the new branches a plant produces. So when you see a narrow-leaved evergreen with short spaces between its branches or a broad-leaved evergreen with short heavy branches, it invariably signifies that the nursery is conscientiously employing good root-pruning practices.

It is likely that the nurseryman has transplanted the tree or shrub several times. When plants are small they are grown close together to save space. As they crowd each other they are dug up—incidentally being root-pruned in the process—and are moved to more spacious quarters. A 10-year-old yew has probably been moved at least four times. Each time it is moved its shape is checked to see if it is lopsided (this can happen if the sides have not been getting equal sunlight). If so, the skimpy side is given the best exposure in the new location. Turning the tree this way assures a symmetrical plant—and symmetry is another thing to watch for.

EVERGREENS IN CONTAINERS

As you go around the nursery, you will see rows of evergreens with their roots wrapped in burlap or set in containers. What you are seeing is the result of a horticultural revolution.

Not too many years ago, nurserymen could not sell their trees except when they were dormant, between periods of active growth. Then the nurseryman would go out into his field and dig up an evergreen, being careful to keep a ball of soil around its roots. He would place the ball in a square of burlap, pin the corners together with nails, tie it up and take it to the customer, who would plant it quickly. It was assumed that transplanting could only be done at this time because new growth demands large amounts of moisture, putting a heavy burden on the roots, and if the roots were disturbed by being dug up and cut off they could not meet the demand. The foliage would wilt and the plant would go into a kind of shock from which it might never recover. So evergreens could never be moved after new growth started in the spring, nor during the growing season, which lasted through most of the summer.

Then nurserymen discovered that if they dug up dormant evergreens, wrapped the roots in burlap and kept them alive through the growing season by giving them light shade and plenty of moisture, the plants would survive without being replanted for some time. In fact, they could be replanted without shock even after new growth was underway.

This discovery led in turn to what is called container culture. A young tree could be dug up and, with its ball of soil, put in a container of wood, metal or plastic. Because the container restrained the roots, the top growth was slowed, just as if the roots were pruned. With a little foliage pruning the plant became stocky and thick. And when taken from the container and set in the ground, it suffered little shock.

This revolution has made things better and easier for you, but there are still things to watch out for. The burlap around the roots of a balled-and-burlaped tree (called a "B&B") should be as tight as a drumhead; if it is loose the roots will tear away from the soil. The ball should be the soil the tree was growing in. It is easier to dig a tree up, put it on a piece of burlap and then throw dirt around the roots—this is called a "manufactured ball"; but it isn't much better than moving the tree bare rooted, which might be fatal to an evergreen. You can spot a manufactured ball—the soil inside the burlap is loose and the roots wobble around inside the ball. Don't buy the tree. If you are considering a container-grown tree, check to make sure the soil is firmly packed, indicating that the tree has been growing in the container for a year or more.

But a plant that has been in its container for a very long time may not be a wise choice either. There is always the danger that roots may become constricted. With no chance to spread naturally, the roots will fill the container, doubling back to wind around one another until the plant becomes root-bound. In extreme cases it will choke itself to death. The way to tell is to look at the top growth of a container-grown evergreen—either needled or broad-leaved; if the top seems sparse and unhealthy, the plant may be root-bound; in any event, pass it by. Do not try to handle a container larger than a 5-gallon size by yourself; it will be too heavy.

Never buy a plant whose branches are tied up without first taking off the twine to make sure the branches are reasonably full and symmetrical. And if the nurseryman trusses up the branches to make the plant easier for you to transport home, first check to see which is the fullest or prettiest side and tie a bit of string to it. It will come in handy later.

Evergreens are almost never sold with their roots bare. A deciduous plant in its dormant period can be sold with bare roots because it has no leaves to make demands on the roots for moisture. But evergreens always have leaves or needles and their roots need to be encased in moist soil at all times. There is one exception. Very small evergreens, each with only a few clumps of needles, can survive brief periods without soil. These are usually sold by mail-order nurseries to gardeners who want to plant a great many for hedges or windbreaks, and are willing to wait an extra year or so in order to save money. When the plants are bought in quantity the prices are low, and if a few plants are lost it does not matter very much. Balled-and-burlaped or container-grown plants weigh so much and cost so much to ship that few are sold by mail. One reputable mail-order nursery sells narrow-leaved evergreens up to 20 inches high by taking them out of their containers and shipping them with roots and soil wrapped in plastic. Customers are warned to expect a loss of 5 per cent with such plants and 10 to 15 per cent with smaller bare-root seedlings. So you should compare costs; it might prove cheaper ordering by mail, even if you lose a few plants, than paying more at the nursery.

One thing you should be precise about, whether you buy from a nursery or by mail, is the name of the plant you want. Many evergreens have similar names, with only minor variations. Knowing the correct name would have been a great help to a neighbor of mine. He told me he had seen a garden with a pair of globular evergreens that gave it a delightful look. They were arborvitaes, the owner had told him, so my friend bought a couple of arborvitaes and then spent season after season pruning them into a round shape. But the trees kept stubbornly trying to grow tall and straight. I sympathized with him but told him that he should have gotten the full name of those round shrubs in the first place—they were Woodward globe arborvitaes, which need little pruning to achieve the round shape he desired. What he had bought were conical American arborvitaes, which have a natural upright form. My friend had simply been fighting nature. The encyclopedia chapter of this book gives both the popular and the Latin botanical names of 95 evergreens; it is wise to consult this to make sure you are asking for what you want by its full and proper name.

PLANTING A NEW EVERGREEN   Once you get the plant home, the rest is up to you. The first thing you have to do is plant it properly. You start this process by digging a proper hole—and by that I mean one that is at least twice

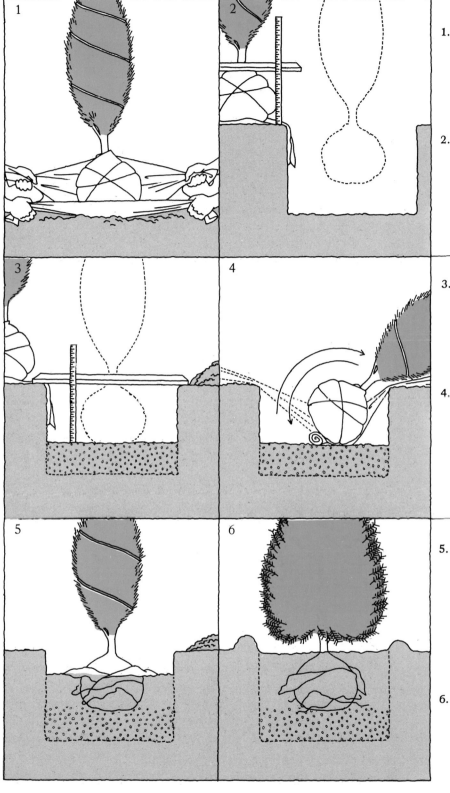

HOW TO PLANT A BALLED-AND-BURLAPED TREE

1. *To move a sizable tree with burlap-wrapped roots, slide a large piece of canvas beneath the soil ball to form a two-man sling, then lift. A shrub may be lifted by its ball, but never grasp its trunk lest you loosen the ball or damage the bark.*

2. *After measuring the width of the ball, hold a board at the soil line on the trunk and measure the depth (left). Then dig a hole twice as wide and one and a half times as deep as the ball as shown by the dotted outline. Mix 1 part of peat moss into every 2 parts dug-out soil.*

3. *Mix 2 or 3 inches of additional peat moss into the loose soil at the bottom of the hole with a spading fork, then add the dug-out soil mix until the board and rule show that the hole is the depth of the ball. Firm the added soil with your feet as you fill.*

4. *Spread out the sling as indicated by the dotted lines on the left, solid lines on the right, and lower the tree gently into the hole. Rock the tree to one side so you can roll half of the sling under the soil ball, then rock the tree in the opposite direction and pull the canvas free. Set the tree upright in its hole.*

5. *Pack more of the soil-and-peat-moss mixture around the bottom two thirds of the soil ball, tamping it down with your feet to eliminate air pockets. Cut the ropes around the top of the soil ball and fold the burlap down from the trunk; leave the burlap as it falls—it will rot away. Then fill the hole with water and wait for it to soak away.*

6. *Finish filling the hole to the level of the old soil mark on the trunk. Form a saucer with a 2-inch-high rim around the edge of the hole. Fill the saucer with water and cut away the twine around the branches.*

the width of the soil ball or container and one and one half times its depth. Digging is dull business, but those extra inches around or at the bottom of the hole can make a great difference to the roots. I always find that when I think I have dug enough, I had better dig just a little more.

At this point practice a simple bit of soil improvement. Pick out and discard any rocks or construction debris that might be in the soil you have removed from the hole; then mix the clean soil with peat moss—2 parts soil to 1 part peat moss. In addition, mix a 3- to 4-inch layer of peat moss into the loose soil at the bottom of the hole. (You can buy peat moss by the bale; it is far cheaper that way.) Peat moss is not a fertilizer but a soil conditioner. It absorbs up to 10 times its weight in water and, when mixed with the soil, holds moisture where the roots can get at it. The peat moss lightens heavy clay soils, making it easier for roots to grow, and it gives substance to light sandy soils, keeping the water from running right through. Some broad-leaved evergreens require an especially acid soil, which may call for additional soil treatment, as detailed in Chapter 4, but virtually every kind of evergreen will benefit from the peat-moss addition described above.

In some parts of the Southwest, treated ground redwood is used by some gardeners instead of peat moss. It does a better job of opening up the heavy adobe soil of the region than peat moss and it lasts longer. In addition it helps to convert the alkaline soil of the region to the level of acidity that evergreens prefer, just as peat moss does. It too should be mixed with the planting soil, 1 part ground redwood to 2 parts soil.

Now you are ready to plant your evergreen. A good way to accomplish this is shown in the step-by-step drawings on page 23 for balled-and-burlaped trees and at right for trees that have been grown in containers.

I cannot emphasize too strongly that you should never pick up an evergreen by its trunk. It shakes up the soil ball, separating the roots from the soil and letting the air get at them. Lift the plant by the ball or container or, if it is too heavy to lift that way, use the burlap sling shown on page 23.

Before you lower the plant into the hole, make sure you are putting its best face forward. This is why you tied that piece of string to the tree at the nursery. It is much easier to keep the branches of the tree trussed up with twine while you are planting it. With the piece of string you know which is the tree's best side and you can make certain it is the side you will see from the windows of the house. I don't know how many marriages have been strained because a wife, summoned by her husband to admire a new tree —untrussed, all spread out and installed—has innocently suggest-

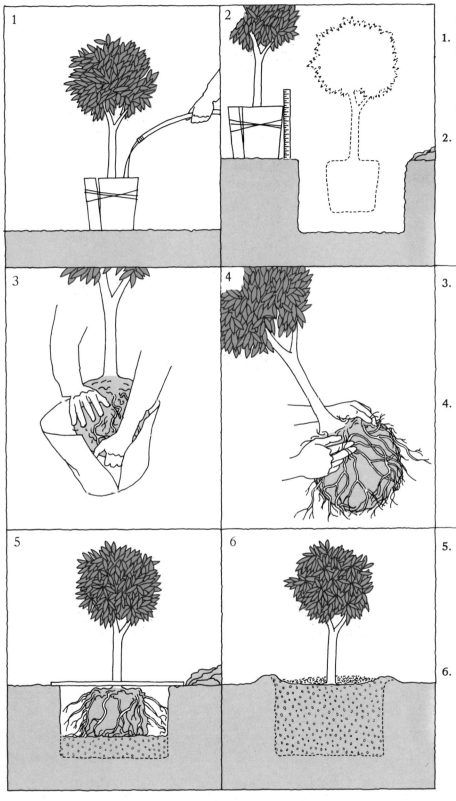

HOW TO PLANT A CONTAINER-GROWN EVERGREEN

1. *When you get your new evergreen home, moisten the ball of earth around the roots, but do it gently so that soil is not flushed off. The plant will be easier to remove if the dealer slits the container down the sides and ties it up.*

2. *Determine the root ball's size by measuring the container's width and depth, less the distance from the rim to the soil level inside. Dig a hole twice as wide and once and a half as deep for the plant (dotted outline). Work 1 part peat moss into 2 parts soil.*

3. *Cut the twine at the planting site and push back the container's sides, then ease out the root ball slowly so that you do not loosen the soil around the tender roots. If the container is metal, wear heavy gloves so that you do not cut your hands on the sharp edges.*

4. *Loosen roots that are coiled around the ball of soil or that are tangled together; they might eventually grow to the point where they would strangle the plant. Gently pull the roots free from the ball and straighten them out to their full length.*

5. *Fill the hole one third full with the soil and peat moss, tamp it down, then stand the plant upright with its roots spread. Lay a board across the hole. The soil level on the trunk should touch the board so the plant will grow at the same depth as before.*

6. *Fill the hole, firming the soil mix gently. Build a watering saucer with 2-inch-high walls around the plant just beyond the ends of its branches and drench the plant. Then fill the saucer to a depth of about 3 inches with a permanent mulch such as wood chips.*

ed that it be turned around so that its nicest side can be seen from the living room.

At all times, be very careful of the roots. They are both tremendously strong and very delicate. Almost everyone has seen how roots of trees crack big boulders apart and buckle concrete sidewalks. Yet the tiny root hairs near the tips of the roots are very fragile—and they are the most important part of the system. By the process of absorption they pull water and nutrients from the soil and send them up to the rest of the plant. A few moments of exposure to the air will dry them out and rough handling can break them off. If the root hairs cannot take up moisture, the plant will wilt—and no amount of extra water will help.

If even after you have followed these instructions you find yourself with an evergreen whose branches are limp and wilting, there are emergency steps you still can take. One is to cover the plant with a temporary sun shield made of burlap supported by stakes to reduce moisture evaporation through the foliage. Another, of great benefit, is to mist the foliage with a fine spray from the garden hose; this also slows down evaporation.

If your plant is tall—say 5 feet or more—or if you plant it in a windy place, it must be held securely in place for a year or two until the roots have anchored firmly. Do not drive a stake down along the trunk and tie the tree to it. The stake will only go through the root ball instead of into the firmer ground, and the support will shift when the upper part of the tree does. Instead, drive a triangular arrangement of three stakes into the ground a few feet away from the tree and tie the tree to them with guy wires as shown in the drawings at right.

When you are anchoring the tree you will want to make sure the trunk is vertical (unless, of course, it is a picturesque twisted plant). Don't trust your eye, especially if you have planted the tree on a slope. Use a carpenter's level, checking the bubble at the end that indicates when the trunk is exactly vertical.

One last thing—and I've come to believe that this is as important as anything else: put a covering of coarse material, a mulch, on the ground around the tree, covering a little more than the area of the hole as shown on page 29. Garden centers offer a choice of mulches. I recommend a 3- to 4-inch layer of wood chips or ground bark; both are unobtrusive and efficient. If you are planting pines, you might prefer a 2- to 3-inch layer of pine needles. A mulch conserves moisture in the ground by warding off sun and wind and reducing evaporation. It will save you a great deal of future watering as well as weeding.

I can almost hear you say, "But you have forgotten something: the fertilizer." I haven't. You don't give an evergreen any fertilizer at planting time. It would simply encourage the upper part of the plant to grow, forcing extra work on the limited number of roots. The plant needs a little time to recover from the transplanting operation before it is ready for a normal diet.

What the newly planted evergreens do require, however, is plenty of water. If rainfall is light, soak the ground around the plant thoroughly at least once a week in addition to the initial heavy watering. If you don't want to lug water by the pailful, let the hose trickle slowly into a little saucer of dirt built around the plant. Or use a soaking hose made of canvas or one with tiny pinhole perforations along its length (both are great time- and back-savers). How much watering is enough? The soil should be moist at least to the depth of the soil ball. How fast that happens depends on your water pressure, the diameter of your hose and how porous the soil is. About the best you can do is water for a measured length of time, wait a couple of hours for the water to soak in and then dig a small hole (outside the perimeter of the roots) to see how deeply the moisture has penetrated. Once you determine how many minutes or hours it takes to moisten the soil to the required depth you can water the trees for that length of time thereafter.

If you live in a region of winter frost, slacken up on watering in the late summer for a few weeks. Water encourages new growth

HOW TO WIRE AN EVERGREEN UPRIGHT

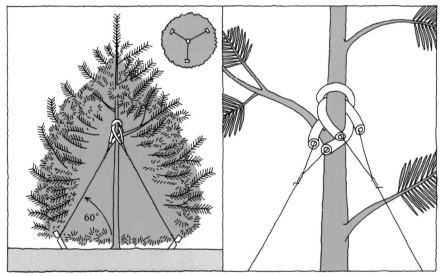

To hold a newly set evergreen upright against the wind, drive long 2-inch-square notched stakes into the ground on three sides of the tree (inset). Attach wires to the stakes and loop each wire around the trunk at a 60° angle with the ground; stack the wires above a strong branch (above, left). Short lengths of garden hose (above) keep the wires from cutting the bark. Leave them in place two or three years.

and at this point you want the plant to stop growing and get ready for winter. By midautumn the new growth should have matured completely. You can tell when this stage is reached because the light, soft new growth has deepened in color and the new stems and branches, which were as succulent as tender asparagus, have become darker and tougher. At this point, if fall rains do not supply adequate moisture, watering should be resumed so the plant goes into winter well prepared for the months when its moisture supply will be at a minimum.

It is hard, under normal conditions, to give an evergreen plant too much water but sometimes there is that danger. Roots need a supply of air as well as water and if water stands around the roots instead of seeping off, the roots will drown. This can happen if the soil is not porous enough—if, for example, it is largely clay through which the water will not pass. You generally can improve the porosity of the soil with peat moss, as already described. But in extreme circumstances this measure can make things worse—which is just what happened when I planted a grove of large live oaks at the city hall in Houston some years ago.

The soil there was a dark Texas gumbo, slippery when wet and as hard as adobe brick when dry. With what I considered great foresight, I dug oversized holes, filled them with a rich mixture of topsoil and peat moss and planted 20-foot-tall live oaks. The city soon had a heavy rain and I recall that at the time I felt the trees were lucky in being so well watered. But to my horror one by one they began to sicken and die.

What had happened is that the carefully prepared holes had become in effect underground pools. Unable to penetrate the gumbo, the runoff rain had poured into the spongelike soil in the holes and filled them, drowning the roots. I dug up the trees and installed an elaborate drainage system, then planted new trees. They prospered and today are a lovely sight, but I still remember the experience with a shudder.

If you are in doubt about the porosity of your soil, dig a hole a foot and a half deep and a foot and a half square and fill it with water. If it hasn't drained away in an hour or so, you probably have impenetrable soil. One solution that often works in such soils is to plant your evergreens in a raised bed, with the soil 4 to 6 inches higher than its original level. To keep the soil superstructure from washing away, surround it with planks, metal edging or concrete blocks. And in such an area try to choose those plants that do not mind what nurserymen call wet feet—an arborvitae instead of a pine, for example, or a sweet bay magnolia instead of an oleander. The evergreens that will thrive in soggy spots are identified in the encyclopedia chapter.

On the other hand, if your soil is very sandy, put in an extra measure of peat moss and choose plants that can tolerate dryness —juniper, sun rose, cotoneaster and broom are good for such areas.

When I am asked how to plant a hedge or windbreak, I say, "First have a talk with your neighbor." Even if you don't plant right on the property line—and I don't advise this since you will have to go to the other side to do the pruning—the branches will eventually spread over the line. Your neighbor may have an unreasoning dislike of arborvitae, which you were proposing to use, and you might just as happily settle for hemlock. Remember that good windbreaks, like good fences, make good neighbors.

In planting a hedge of needled evergreens, plan to set the trees or shrubs about 2 to 4 feet apart, depending on how wide they will eventually grow. Dig a trench the whole length of the row, one and one half times as deep as the root ball and at least a foot wider, so the plant will have 6 inches of prepared soil on each side of the root ball. Follow the soil-peat moss mixing procedure already described. And even though you are planning to put the plants a certain distance apart, don't try to save work by digging separate holes instead of a trench; in this case you can outsmart yourself. It is far easier to place the plants in a trench. The depth,

HEDGES AND SCREENS

HOW TO MULCH EVERGREENS

Isolated evergreens planted as lawn ornaments (left) benefit from a 3-inch mulch beneath the full spread of their branches. Use organic material such as wood chips, pine needles or chunky peat moss. An edging of metal or a row of bricks may be used to keep the mulch in its place. In a border of evergreens (center and right), supplement the 3-inch mulch under the trees with a 5-inch mulch in the spaces between plants—where the sun beats down. Maintaining the mulch at the proper depth ensures its effectiveness in conserving moisture, eliminating weeds and keeping the ground at a seasonally constant temperature.

for one thing, will be more uniform than that of holes and easier to adjust. When you set the plants in the ground you may find they are more crowded than you expected; you can take out two or three and use them at the other end of the yard to conceal the garbage cans. Or you may find you have bought too few and will have to get a couple more. With a trench you can easily make such adjustments as you feel are needed. If you dig individual holes, you may dig a lot more than you planned.

Hedges are usually planted in a straight line, but trees in windbreaks and screens should be staggered and two or three rows deep. Hedges are solid structures intended as barriers to wall everything out. A windbreak should be more open, designed not to block the prevailing wind but to diminish its force by slowing it down and deflecting it up and over the trees. Usually windbreaks require larger, stronger trees than hedges; black pines and black spruces are good choices for this purpose.

Increasingly, evergreens are also being used as a screen against noise. The ideal way to plant an antinoise barrier is in three sections. First, close to the source of the noise—perhaps a busy road—put a strip of grass. This will absorb sound waves instead of reflecting them as a hard surface does. Next plant a row of small shrubs to muffle noise that is traveling toward you close to the ground. Behind them plant tall shrubs or trees, preferably a variety with soft thick foliage. Hemlocks, arborvitaes and tall yews are noise absorbent. The whole screen should be as close to the source of the noise—that is, the road—as you can place it. The noise that is thus blocked out is the irritating high-pitched noise such as the whine of tires as an automobile goes by at high speed.

PLANTS AND CLIMATE   The kinds of evergreens that will do well in your garden are partly determined by their resistance to winter cold and summer heat —but only partly. Several other factors must be considered: the amount of rainfall, soil conditions, altitude and proximity to bodies of water. All of these are taken into account in the area map on page 149 and in the plant descriptions in the encyclopedia chapter, so you can easily determine what grows well where.

As far as rainfall is concerned, most evergreens will grow wherever the rainfall measures at least 25 inches a year, fairly evenly distributed. I can give a conclusive illustration of how important rainfall is to evergreens. At the base of the Rocky Mountains, where the rain falls sparingly, no evergreens grow and the land is taken over by grass. Part of the way up the mountainside, where there is more rain, there are shrubs, including some evergreens. But higher up the mountainside, where rain clouds drop their loads and heavy snows sink slowly into the ground, keeping the soil almost constantly moist—that is where the great spruce and fir forests thrive.

The pattern of rainfall has odd effects. In Southern California the rains come in fall and winter, while the summer months are very dry. This is the pattern in much of Australia. As a result many of the evergreens now cultivated in California gardens—eucalyptuses, acacias and tea trees, for example—are native to Australia. Similarly, many of the evergreens grown in the northeastern United States originated in Japan and along the east coast of Asia, where the rainfall pattern is similar.

Insofar as altitude is concerned, every 1,000 feet higher you go above sea level is the equivalent, in terms of average temperature, of going 300 to 400 miles farther north at sea level. A large body of water will of course moderate temperatures both in winter and in summer. This explains why many evergreens will survive near the Great Lakes and along both coasts but cannot be grown on the great plains of the upper midwest.

Your choice of plants can be a matter not of large areas like climate zones but of small ones like your own grounds, where climate can vary significantly depending on exposure. The west side of your house in summer, what with the afternoon sun and the heat reflected from the house, can get as hot and dry as a desert and bake an evergreen to death. A south side may create a heat trap in winter, a place so pleasant that you might sit out there on a February afternoon as if it were spring. But an evergreen planted there might also be fooled into thinking it was spring, start its growth cycle and be damaged by the next cold wave. The way your house is set on your lot may create very windy spots. A golden larch or a Douglas fir, for example, cannot tolerate such wind, while a juniper would be a better choice for such a location. (In fact, it is a good practice never to plant junipers in a place that is not well ventilated by wind, since they are attacked by spider mites that flourish in stagnant air.)

The location of your garden can create its own miniature climate—a microclimate, as the scientists call it. Under unusual conditions you may be able to grow plants not generally recommended for your area, and it is always fun to try. Only a couple of blocks away from my garden a friend has two fine sequoias growing vigorously. I have tried several times to grow sequoias in my yard, but when I plant them they promptly fade. The reason for this difference is that my garden is in a rather low, level spot along the Concord River; my friend's garden is above mine on a hillside. In winter the cold air rolls down the hillside through his garden, settles in my garden and stays there. His trees never get within 25° as cold as mine do; that little hill creates its own climate zone. And like all gardeners, I am subject to envy.

THE CEDARS OF THE LORD
Of the huge forests of cedars that blanketed the mountains and valleys of Lebanon in ancient times, only 375 trees remain today; of these, 10 are more than 2,000 years old and two are more than 3,000 years old. These 12 cedars of Lebanon—Cedrus libani in Latin, arz al-Rabb or "Cedars of the Lord" in Arabic—have special meaning for people of three religions: Jews consider them to represent the Twelve Friends of Solomon, Christians the Twelve Apostles and Muslims their saints. Yet it is ironic that the esteem in which cedars are held helped to bring about the destruction of the forests. Thousands of trees were felled to roof the Temple of Solomon, to build churches and palaces and barges and even, some say, the Cross of Jesus. Since the end of World War II, the Lebanese government has been trying to restore the valuable forests by planting more than 200,000 cedars.

The mainstay of landscaping

Evergreens, their color and form constant through the seasons, formed the essential structure of the earliest gardens of which there is written record. A 3,000-year-old tablet records the boast of Assyrian King Tiglath-Pileser I: "Cedars and box I have carried off from the countries I conquered . . . and planted in my own country, in the parks of Assyria." The ancient Greeks and Romans delighted in strolling through shady groves of myrtle and cypress. The early Chinese learned to cultivate dwarfed evergreens, a skill later perfected by the Japanese. The elaborate gardens of Renaissance Europe featured exquisitely sculptured evergreens.

In America, the evergreen found new prominence. No colonial New England homestead was considered complete without a handsome stand of pines—which also served as a windscreen. The flowering evergreens of Charleston's Magnolia Gardens were listed in a 19th Century Baedeker, Europe's prestigious travel guidebook, as an American tourist attraction equal to Niagara Falls and the Grand Canyon.

Today the indispensable evergreens continue to play their role as the constant beauties of the garden in a variety of ways. They have few peers as border plantings, often in the form of hedges but also as graceful rows of majestic trees (right). A single full-grown spruce or live oak catches the eye as a garden centerpiece. Groupings of smaller evergreens—particularly yews and arborvitaes—provide harmonious accents for houses, lawns and patios. Ground-hugging junipers spread green blankets where grass is difficult to maintain.

Size and shape generally determine how an evergreen will be used. But from approximately 700 varieties commercially available, you can select shades and textures in any form that you may need or desire. All offer the permanence of color that has given evergreens their name and fascination, for it is when flowers fade and deciduous trees bare their limbs that evergreens provide what 19th Century landscaping pioneer A. J. Downing described as "an appearance of verdure and life . . . which cheats winter of half its dreariness."

Converging rows of Italian cypresses and a triangular bed of junipers set off the shape of a lot banked with ivy.

Trees tall or small for a showpiece

The evergreen family includes the world's tallest trees, and many a cute little "Christmas tree" planted in the backyard has matured into a house-dwarfing monster. It is a lesson every generation of gardeners relearns. During the 1876 Philadelphia Centennial Exposition, thousands of Norway spruce seedlings were sold as potted plants and later transplanted outdoors—there to reach heights of 100 feet or more.

Today small homes make such tall evergreens a liability unless they can be turned into spectacular showpieces, as shown below. But to grow a showpiece that will not overwhelm a small garden, choose a variety that will reach no more than 30 feet in height. Such trees, like the even shorter yew pictured at right, can also serve to camouflage awkward structures or, when set in a group, to form privacy-assuring hedges.

This California garden was built around a large live oak. The redwood-and-stone patio is bordered on the right by shade-tolerant camellias. At left of the steps, an ivy-covered wall edges evergreen azaleas and a small pear tree.

A fast-growing upright Japanese yew softens and partially conceals the geometric lines of a high porch in Massachusetts. Flanking the tree is a pair of hardy rhododendrons; at its base is a glossy carpet of bearberry.

Surprising shapes in small spaces

The evergreens nurserymen call medium-sized shrubs are so useful for all common purposes in the garden —borders, hedges, privacy screens, foundation plantings—that their adaptability to less ordinary needs is sometimes overlooked. An unusually shaped plant like the weeping hemlock, for example, whose drooping branches arch gracefully to the ground, makes a refreshing contrast when used against evergreens of the more familiar upright varieties *(top right)*. The holly osmanthus *(below, left)* is easily pruned to spread into a pleasantly textured low mound. And many medium-sized evergreens can be trained by pruning to assume unusual shapes—an art dating back to Roman times—so that they ornament small settings where a close-up view is the rule rather than the exception *(bottom right and overleaf)*.

A holly osmanthus, which is not a true holly but has spiny dark green hollylike leaves, flourishes under a long-needled loblolly pine tree in the warm shade of an Atlanta garden. Annual pruning maintains the low, rounded outline and size of this 30-year-old specimen.

A potted Texas privet, pruned from its normal bushy profile into an umbrella-shaped tree, provides an interesting contrast to the staked pair of slender podocarpus trees in front of this dignified California house. The shorter plants include Zabel cherry laurel and a ground cover of star jasmine; at the corner of the house is an olive tree.

A slow-growing weeping hemlock, its drooping branches counterpointed by the straight spread of the rhododendron behind it, is set among beach stones and lava rock in front of a Massachusetts home. The hemlock will not outgrow its space for many years; the rhododendron will be kept to size by regular pruning.

In an oval garden in Virginia, a flower-bedecked bank (right) is crowned with azaleas, providing a year-round edging of green. At the upper left are squared-off American boxwood and English boxwood sheared to billow.

Low shrubs to frame man-made forms

Many gardeners think of ornamental evergreens as a means of concealing a shed, a drying yard or trash barrels. Evergreens do a fine job of camouflaging eyesores, but those that grow relatively close to the ground are just as effective as frames for some of the more worthy works of man.

The owner of the contemporary home pictured below has used low-growing evergreens almost exclusively to display his outdoor living area in a setting of greenery, equally attractive at any season whether viewed from inside the house or looked at from beyond the terrace. For the driveway at lower right, yellow-foliaged evergreens add sunny glints to a border of green. And a 19th Century country home gains a note of unobtrusive dignity from a stately spreading English yew *(right)*.

Making a welcome splash of feathery green, a low-spreading English yew helps to soften the strong lines and rugged fieldstone surface of an 80-year-old home in New Jersey.

Enhancing a driveway border (and marking it clearly when caught by car lights at night) are plantings of a yellowish green juniper (foreground) and a golden thread false cypress (across the driveway). To the right of the false cypress are a cone-tipped Japanese black pine and hedges of Pfitzer juniper and taller arborvitae.

Groups of spreading evergreens, mostly tough, easy-to-grow Pfitzer junipers, soften the lines of this modern house in Massachusetts. The juniper border blends into Japanese black pines (right foreground and center of house) and a deciduous Japanese maple (far left).

41

Evergreens that creep and fall

At the opposite end of the height range from the monumental sequoias, spruces and firs of the forest are the trailing junipers, spruces and yews that never grow more than a foot above the ground—although one plant might spread across 15 feet. Because these ground covers are easy to grow and require less care than grass, they are frequently used as substitutes for grass. On sunny slopes or among rocks, they not only provide a perpetually green cover but also control erosion, for their foliage breaks the force of rain and their roots dig deep to hold the soil. Many gardeners have discovered that such evergreens, creeping over curbstones or cascading over retaining walls *(below),* break the harshness of flat, hard surfaces with a softening splash of green—sometimes dark and glossy, sometimes bluish, often tipped with red or gold.

A weeping Colorado blue spruce tumbles over a wall to contrast in color, height and texture with nearby evergreens—a low hedge of English yews (upper left) and spreading Wilton carpet junipers (upper right).

Looking like an egg-filled nest, a ringlet of ground-hugging Japanese garden junipers circles ocean-washed stones called popples in a Massachusetts garden. The dark rock is lava and the path edging is cedar-post sections.

Combinations for special problems

What do you plant around a circular driveway when you need a decorative border that will also give privacy and wind protection the year round? How do you create an illusion of depth in a swimming-pool screen that must be set in tight quarters? What is there to make wide steps fit smoothly into the surrounding garden? When you must solve practical problems like these, evergreens often provide the simplest and most effective answers. From their great variety of sizes, shapes and colors, it is possible to arrive at a combination that will fill almost any need. Plantings of evergreens can be tall or short, dense or airy, uniform or variegated—or all at once. The adaptable and undemanding evergreens provide all the materials necessary to create the kinds of plantings that your own requirements and taste dictate.

The screen shielding this California pool appears to be deeper than it really is because of evergreens arranged in varying sizes and colors. In the center, tall eucalyptus trees rise behind an acacia tree (bluish green) and a pine; the foreground shrubs are junipers.

Pairs of matched evergreens link an Atlanta terrace (below) with a garden at the foot of the stairs. Above the boxwood in the foreground are a bed of English ivy, a spreading blue-vase juniper and a potted lavender cotton.

A rounded Monterey pine and lacy deodar cedars alternate with eye-level shrubs (yellowish fire thorn, center, laurel sumac and brown-tinted cotoneaster at right) to screen this California driveway. A low border of Natal plum adds visual depth.

A miniature forest of evergreens fills the front yard of this California home, landscaped for maximum privacy and minimum maintenance. Flowering azaleas are set on either side of a path winding through a ground covering of junipers and light islands of pittosporum.

Caring for conifers 3

"It seems to me," a visitor once remarked as he watched me working on my narrow-leaved evergreens with pruning clippers, "that you spend more time keeping your plants from growing than helping them grow." Perhaps I do. Coniferous evergreens grow very well all by themselves. They rarely need fertilizer and are quite resistant to insects and diseases. Aside from some special precautions to protect them from damage by winter cold and snow, the principal part of their routine care is pruning.

By regular pruning I can limit an evergreen's size and keep it from hogging more space in the yard than I can afford to give it. Some species I can keep at a stable height and width indefinitely with clippers. Pruning also stimulates the growth of side branches and thus produces denser foliage, and it permits me to shape my shrubs if I want to use them as neatly clipped hedges—or even to try my hand at the topiary art and turn them into ornamental balls or fanciful figures. Finally, pruning is good for the trees. An aging or drooping specimen of a narrow-leaved evergreen can often be restored to vigor by pruning just as a broad-leaved evergreen can. (Pruning of broad-leaved evergreens is discussed in Chapter 4.) And of course pruning is essential to remove storm-broken or winterkilled branches that will weaken the tree if they are left to rot where they are.

Pruning is a simple art—if you know how. In late winter and early spring, before the ground can be worked but when my own gardening sap has begun to rise, pruning permits me to use up excess energy and make use of a few spare minutes—too few, say, for the drudgery of raking up the winter's debris, but too many to waste. Wandering around the garden, I snip at straggling Scotch pine branches here and cut back a Fraser fir there, enjoying the pale sunshine and the faint smell of resin. The task is made·easiest and most enjoyable if you use the right tools.

The simplest—and often the best—pruning tool is your fingers. Many young shoots, especially on pines, are tender enough to

Jewellike flowers of a Tanyosho pine nestle among sunburst clusters of needles. Fertilized, they become green cones (right), which as they mature turn brown and woody and open to disperse their seeds.

be snapped off cleanly by hand. With this method you run no danger of inadvertently cutting not only the new shoot but also the tips of some needles, which then become unsightly, stubby and brown. Let me pass on a piece of nonhorticultural advice on finger pruning: after your fingers get sticky from the resin in the shoots, do not try to get them clean by wiping them on a towel. It does not work. Use turpentine.

The next step up in complexity from fingers is a pruning knife, which I find very handy when I have only an errant branch or two to remove. This tool is a large pocketknife with a heavy blade that is hooked at the tip like an eagle's beak. It must be used cautiously to avoid cutting your fingers, but with practice you can learn to flick off stems up to ¼ inch thick with no effort at all.

Most pruning, however, is accomplished with the kind of clippers you operate with one hand. (This tool is confusingly called hand shears in many garden catalogues, although it is never used for shearing branch tips to shape a shrub.) There are two types of clippers. One has a cutting blade that strikes against a soft metal anvil. The other is made like scissors, with cutting blades that slide past each other. Either type is satisfactory for pruning evergreens. The anvil type is easier to use; the scissors type gives a closer cut, but the blades can get out of line if you twist the tool to get a tough

HOW TO SAW OFF A LARGE BRANCH

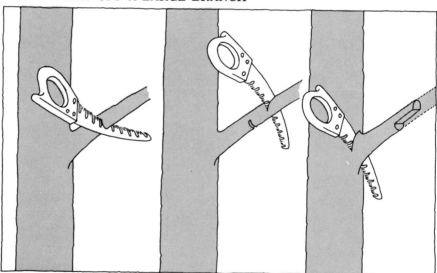

To remove a tree branch more than 2 inches thick, first saw up about a foot from the trunk with the pruning saw upside down (left), until the saw begins to bind. Then make a second cut downward a few inches *farther from the trunk (center). Cut until the branch's weight causes it to break off. The bottom cut prevents bark from ripping down the trunk. Finally, saw away the stub flush with the trunk (right).*

branch off. When choosing a tool of either design, try it a few times in the store to make sure the handles will not pinch the palm of your hand when you squeeze them together.

Hand clippers are effective only for branches less than ¾ inch thick. If you try to cut bigger branches with this tool, you may twist the blades and damage both clippers and the plant. Branches between ¾ inch and about 1¼ inches are easily cut with the two-handled tool called a lopper, which has long handles and short, scissors-type blades. For branches still larger, shift to a pruning saw *(drawings, left)*. A carpenter's saw will bind and stick, refusing either to cut further or to come free. A pruning saw has teeth set rather far apart so that they will not clog with sawdust and resin.

For shaping hedges you need shears. The electric ones, with their powered cutting blades, speed the work if you have a long hedge to trim. But a pair of hand-operated hedge shears—scissors with long blades and long handles—is useful for smaller jobs.

One other pruning tool you will find useful is, oddly enough, a spade —to trim the roots *(drawings, below)*. Although the obvious way to contain the growth of evergreens is to prune branches, a more lasting way is to restrict the root system, using the technique nurserymen employ automatically when they transplant seedlings. Do

ROOT-PRUNING

TRIMMING YOUNG EVERGREENS

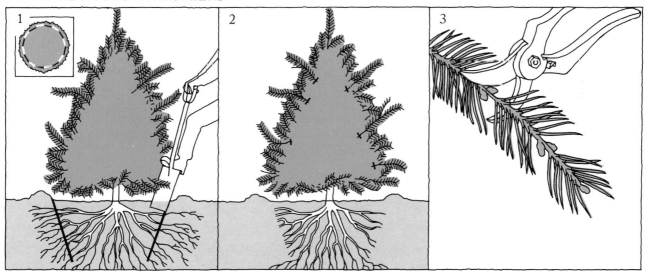

To trim young evergreens for compact growth, make alternate cuts into the roots below the outer limits of the foliage with a square-edged spade (inset); the next spring cut the rest of the roots.

Keep the tree's outline symmetrical by shortening the protruding branches of new growth each spring. Using hand clippers, reach inside the tree and cut where overlapping foliage will hide the cut ends.

If you are trimming back straggly branches of a stiff-needled tree such as a spruce or fir, watch for fat growth buds and make your cut just in front of them. These buds will start branches the following season.

not try to use an ordinary digging spade, for its curved bottom will slide past the heavy roots you want to cut. You need what is called a nurseryman's spade, which has a long blade with a square edge. Sharpen the edge with a file before you use it so it will cut cleanly.

The best time to root-prune, especially in regions of winter cold, is in the spring just as the buds begin to swell. This allows the plant full use of all its roots during the winter and gives it a chance to recuperate during the growing season. Sink the spade to its full depth through the tips of the roots. (The easiest place to do this is just below the perimeter of the widest branches.) If a root proves too tough to slice with the spade, snip it with a long-handled lopper slipped into the spade cut. Do not be afraid of hurting the tree. If it is in good health, it will quickly grow new roots while holding back on top growth, which is what you want. If the site is dry or windy, or the plant has been growing in one place for five years or more, make alternate spade cuts so you prune only half the roots at first. Prune the other roots the following spring. Cutting all the roots at once might strain the tree's recuperative powers.

ABOVEGROUND PRUNING   Just as root-pruning does, trimming branches aboveground controls the size of an evergreen. But, just as important, it also controls shape. You should not attempt to control one characteristic with-

PRUNING FINE-NEEDLED EVERGREENS

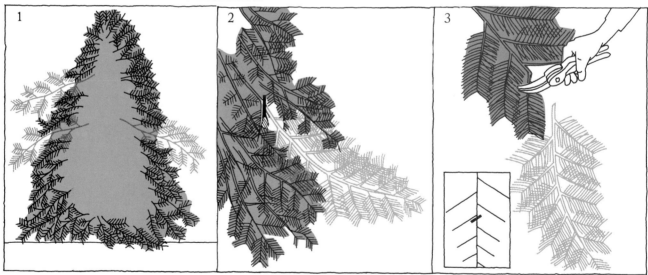

To preserve the natural shape of trees that have scalelike foliage and flexible drooping limbs—such as junipers, arborvitaes and hemlocks— prune branches (shown in gray) that grow beyond the silhouette.

Shorten the errant branches with cuts made far enough inside the outline of the tree so that other limbs cover the stubs. Spring pruning is preferred; at that season new growth develops quickly around the cuts.

Clip off each limb directly in front of one of its small branchlets; the latter will then send out new branchlets to camouflage the cut joint. An overlong stub (inset) will die and could let disease enter.

out considering the other. Nothing looks worse than an evergreen that is supposed to have a naturally shaggy conical shape but has been forced by shears into a smooth, tight ball. It does no good to try to correct by trimming a mistake you have made planting the wrong kind of shrub in the first place. You should know, before you start any pruning, what shape the plant would become if it were never pruned at all.

The drawings in the encyclopedia, Chapter 5, show the natural shapes of some 49 narrow-leaved evergreens; these illustrations can serve as a pruning guide to help you avoid trying to force a plant into an unnatural silhouette, and, more important, they will also help you choose the shape you want before planting. There is such a broad assortment of forms available that almost any desired one can be found. Among the conical plants, for instance, some, like the Siberian arborvitae, have wide bases and pointed tops. Others, like the Douglas arborvitae, are narrow at the bottom and taper upward only slightly. But some of the conifers, like Irish yew or Swedish juniper, are not conical in shape at all; instead they grow as straight-sided as columns.

You need one more bit of botanical information before you start clipping away: when does the plant sprout new shoots? The timing of growth determines the timing of pruning. Some ever-

HOW TO PRUNE A FORMAL HEDGE

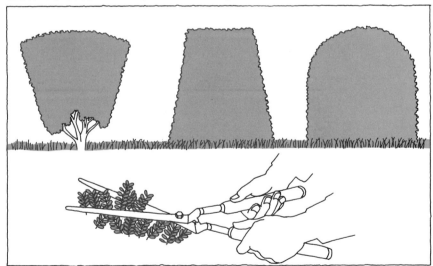

There are three ways to prune a formal hedge—one wrong, two right. If you trim it wider at the top than at the bottom (left), the shaded lower branches lose their foliage and die. But if you taper from the top outward (center) or cut the sides straight and round the top (right), you encourage compact growth and preserve the lower foliage. When pruning the top, tilt the shears upward (bottom) to avoid gouges.

greens produce their new shoots in a great spurt that starts early in spring and ends by the start of summer. Others begin growing in spring and continue slowly but steadily until the end of summer.

PRUNING IN THE SPRING The first group includes such narrow-leaved evergreens as pines, spruces and firs, which are generally pruned in the spring. If you look closely at one of these plants in fall you will see at the end of each branch a set of little buds, usually in a circle with a central bud larger than the others. These buds have formed during the spring and summer just past and, while the tree is dormant in winter, they become hard and brown. When spring comes around again, each bud swells and bursts out into a shoot covered with soft light needles. This needle-covered shoot is called a candle, and the central bud usually makes the biggest candle—the "leading shoot." It grows straight out or up, while the other candles, from the circle of buds around the leading shoot, grow off to the sides, developing into a whorl of branches. All the candles reach full size in just a few weeks and that is the end of that plant's growth for that season. If you want to restrict the plant's size, prune in spring when the candles are only partly grown and the needles not fully developed. Simply remove half or two thirds of each candle (drawings, below); do not snip off any needles sprouting from the rest of the candle. You

HOW TO PRUNE EVERGREEN CANDLES

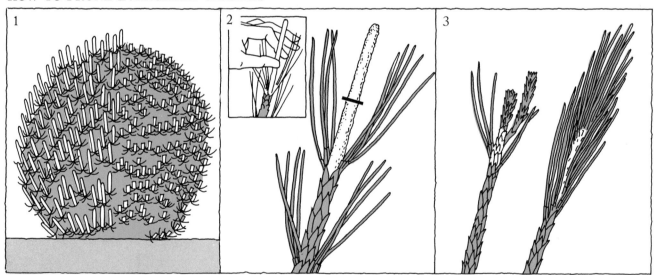

The light-colored shoots called candles that grow from buds on many evergreens (left half of this partly pruned mugo pine) should be trimmed (right half) in the spring to keep the plant compact.

For thicker foliage, pinch off half the candle (line); to maintain the tree's present size, snap it all off. Do this before needles form, while the candles are still soft enough to be snapped with two fingers (inset).

When a candle is shortened (left), buds form behind the stub and send out a thick spray of foliage. The tree's upward growth is slowed. An unpruned candle develops into a single thin, stiff plume (right).

can do the job with clippers, or just snap off part of the new growth with your fingers. In a few days or weeks, depending on the variety being pruned, the still-growing needles will have hidden all traces of the cut. New buds will form behind the cut, and the following year the foliage will be much denser and more compact than if the candle had grown to full length.

Snipping off candles during the spring is generally all the pruning that is needed to keep these types of evergreens to the size and shape you require. Occasionally, however, a whole branch—or a part of one—must be removed. Such mature growth can be trimmed at any time of the year if you make the cut at the right place (drawings, page 50). To remove the whole branch permanently, cut at the joint with the trunk; nothing will grow in its place. To remove part of the branch permanently, cut just above the point where a side branch is growing; the cut-off part will not come back, but the side branch will be unaffected and will continue to develop. To remove part of a branch and stimulate new growth in its place (for spruces and firs but not pines), cut just ahead of a bud; this bud will then sprout new shoots. But never cut a branch on a candle-growing tree part way back at a point where nothing else is growing. If you do, you will be left with a bare stub—no shoots will ever appear from its end. Your objective is to restrain growth, but not to prevent it altogether.

You need a different technique when pruning the conifers that grow continuously all through the summer rather than in one sudden burst in spring—the hemlocks, junipers, yews and podocarpuses are the most common examples. They do not have the end-of-branch buds that form candles, but send out new shoots from all over their branches—old branches as well as new. They can be pruned at any time during the growing season except during the last few weeks, when the new growth slows down and matures in anticipation of winter cold. Pruning done that late in the year will stimulate fresh new growth that will not have time to mature completely before cold weather arrives. Then winter may do some unwanted pruning for you, killing the still-tender twigs and perhaps weakening the whole plant.

The pruning of such long-growing plants is generally done lightly near the tips of branches, following the plant's natural shape. To save time you can use long-handled hedge shears, which cut across several inches of surfaces at a single snip. However, shearing gives the plant an unnatural, newly cut look that lasts several weeks, until new growth softens it. I do not usually recommend shearing except for shaping the geometric forms of formal hedges (page 53). There is a somewhat slower but better way. Reach in with pruning

SUMMER PRUNING

clippers beyond the natural silhouette of the tree, following the main stem of the branch to be trimmed until you find a place where side branches grow. Cut through here, just outside the side branches, so the foliage above and below will conceal the cut (drawings, page 52). This technique prunes without clipping any foliage, and the result is a soft look that seems natural right after the job is done. Branches can be cut back 6 to 12 inches without making the plant look as if it had just had a Marine Corps haircut. This kind of pruning provides an extra little dividend: use the cuttings as greens in your indoor bouquets. It is astonishing how much a few evergreen sprigs will improve many flower arrangements.

PRUNING HEDGES

Pruning evergreen hedges requires a special technique. If the hedge is a formal one kept to a smooth geometric shape, use hedge shears. With the electric type especially, you need a good eye and a steady grip. A slip of the hand or a glance at a passing blue jay can put a gouge in the surface that only months of growth will efface. A guide for shearing the top—a string stretched between stakes beside the hedge at the desired height—is always helpful; it is essential when you start a hedge and try to cut the tips of new, previously unpruned plants to precisely the same height.

Never trim an evergreen hedge so that the top is wider than the base. In fact, it should be a little bit the other way (drawings, page 53). Otherwise the lower branches will be shaded by the upper ones, and they will turn brown and die for lack of light. And an evergreen hedge achieves its beauty and utility by having living foliage all the way to the ground.

(continued on page 61)

Sculpture in evergreens

For many gardeners the most graceful evergreen is one shaped by nature, but others view a healthy shrub or tree as a sculptor does a block of marble. By trimming and training bushes and trees into fanciful images, gardeners have ornamented the palace grounds of the world's capitals ever since Roman times. Today, a private garden adorned with sculptured shrubs, called topiary, is a rare sight, but the art still flourishes on the Maryland estate of sculptor-gardener Harvey Ladew.

Ladew employs a short-order method that allows him to establish a fully formed figure in only two years. Once he has decided on the shape he wants to create, he makes a skeleton, or frame, for it out of wire. Next, he selects a bush with dense foliage and sturdy branches—usually a fast-growing Japanese yew, but sometimes a hemlock—that approximates the desired shape. He embeds the frame deep in the foliage, anchors it firmly to a metal pipe alongside the shrub's trunk, then uses the frame wires as a guide as he trims, sculpting the leafy figure he has imagined.

Surveying the garden from a 7-foot-high vantage point, a swan shaped from an upright yew floats atop a yew hedge.

A mounted hunter and his hounds, each carved from a single Japanese yew, bound past the natural cone shape of a dawn redwood tree. Ladew modeled this scene after a similar one he saw in England.

Some narrow-leaved evergreens—yew, arborvitae, podocarpus, false cypress, juniper or hemlock—grow steadily over the summer so that the foliage comes back quickly after trimming, especially if the work is done early in the growing season. They can be used for formal hedges. Pines or firs cannot be sheared without leaving stubs because these plants do not grow continuously; hence they cannot be clipped into the geometric shapes of formal hedges. But they make fine informal hedges. Prune them selectively with clippers, reaching in to cut out branches that are growing too long just as you would when trimming a single plant.

Most of the pruning of narrow-leaved evergreens aims merely to preserve their size and shape. Occasionally, however, surgery is needed to repair damage. If a branch breaks or dies, it should be cut away—at the trunk if necessary, otherwise at one of the intermediate points described previously. You may also have to prune branches around the damage to avoid a misshapen appearance.

REPAIRING DAMAGE

One kind of injury requires special treatment if the natural silhouette is not to be totally lost. This damage involves the loss of the uppermost vertical branch, called the leader, of an upright-growing conifer such as a pine, spruce or fir. Sometimes a leader is broken off by wind or heavy snow, but more often than not it is carelessly snipped off during pruning. When all of the leader is gone, several of the side shoots near the broken point will begin competing for the position of leader. The tree then loses its natural conical shape and may appear to have two or more little trees growing atop the original one.

What you must do in this emergency is create a new leader from a strong side shoot near the top. You force it to grow vertically with the aid of a wooden splint (drawings, page 62) so that it becomes the dominant branch at the top of the tree. Within a year or two, the new leader will have established itself, and the tree will look as if nothing had happened to it.

In addition to the pruning you should do to maintain narrow-leaved evergreens in their natural, healthy size and shape, there are other kinds of pruning that many gardeners undertake to achieve some special purpose. One of these techniques, called topiary, prunes evergreens so they look like what they are not, most often birds and animals; a simple method of achieving topiary effects in a short period of time is described on pages 56-60. Bonsai is the Oriental art of dwarfing normally large trees by pruning and other special handling so that they become miniatures for display in pots (one method is shown on pages 80-84). Espalier is still another technique; it is used to train trees to grow flat against a wall or trellis.

SPECIAL PRUNING

A frolicking sea horse in yew (far left) contrasts in mood with a solemn Buddha also carved from yew. The shaggy quality of the squirrel at left comes from its feathery hemlock foliage.

Upright yews and podocarpuses are suitable for this purpose, although broad-leaved evergreens are more commonly used (*drawings, page 77*). And it is also possible to use standard pruning techniques to convert an evergreen into a shade tree.

Gardeners do not ordinarily think of evergreens as shade trees —oaks, maples and lindens are more likely choices. Yet large needle-leaved evergreens with wide-spreading branches—particularly pines, Norway spruces and hemlocks—make wonderful shade trees if the lower branches are removed. When such a tree becomes so large that you are considering banishing it from your garden, decide first whether you would rather prune it so that you have room to sit or even to walk under it.

One of my neighbors planted five pines, cut off the lower branches as they grew and put his children's sandbox in the midst of his little grove. There the children make believe they are in the wilds of Maine. At the back of my garden are two lofty Scotch pines in whose shade we picnic, surrounded by our own small woodland full of wild flowers—hepatica, jack-in-the-pulpit, trillium, pipsissewa and partridgeberry.

When you prune off large branches for walking or sitting space, be sure to use the technique shown in the drawings on page 50 to avoid ripping the bark on the main trunk. And do the cutting

REPLACING A LOST LEADER

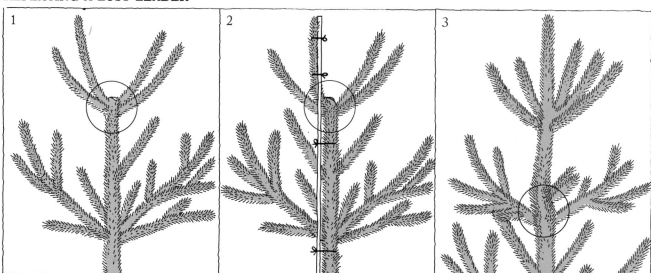

When an upright tree such as a pine loses its topmost tip, or leader, to ice, insects or wind, it also loses its symmetry. A side branch below the injury (*circle*) will twist to the center, but will not grow straight up.

To replace the lost leader, cut off the damaged stub, then bend up the longest nearby branch to parallel the trunk. Splint the branch to the trunk with a long, straight stick and stretchable plastic tree tape.

In a year or two, the new leader will take over the dominant position. When the tape and the splint are removed, the bend where the repair was made (*circle*) will be barely noticeable—and will become less so.

in the summer, when the resin flow diminishes, rather than in the spring when wounds exude large, sticky gobs.

Whenever you prune—for any purpose—there is always the danger that you will be carried away with enthusiasm and overdo. Don't. Once a branch has been clipped from a shrub or tree, there is nothing you can do to restore it. While pruning, step back from the plant frequently to evaluate your progress as you go along, and stop trimming too soon rather than too late.

Pruning is just about the only routine care that conifers require so long as they are healthy. Sickliness makes itself obvious in the appearance of the tree, particularly the needles. They should be dense and richly colored. Do not be alarmed if you notice that they fall off. Evergreens shed their needles on a regular schedule, sloughing off old ones as new ones sprout. The arborvitae and the white pine, for example, drop needles when the needles are two years old. They have a needle life, botanists say, of two years. Other trees have longer needle lives. That of the bristlecone pine is 8 to 15 years. But if needles fall so heavily that the tree looks bare and gangly, or if foliage seems discolored, the plant needs special attention. The cause might be disease, insects, drought, too little light, air pollution or a need for extra food.

CARE AND FEEDING

Ordinarily, fertilizing is not required by evergreens of this type (exceptions are noted in the encyclopedia). A deciduous tree, which drops its leaves in fall, needs enormous quantities of food and moisture when it grows a new set of leaves in the spring. But evergreens, since they retain their foliage from year to year, have no such need on this scale. If planted in properly prepared soil (page 24), most of them can go through a whole lifetime without needing any fertilizer at all. In fact, the addition of fertilizer might contribute to the kinds of excessive growth that you are trying to control by means of pruning.

But if a plant seems not to be doing well, supplementing its diet may help it. Sprinkle fertilizer lightly on the ground beneath, as far out from the trunk as the outer spread of its branches reaches. That is where the feeding roots are concentrated. Cottonseed meal, which is organic and very slow acting, is a good choice. Or you can use one of the special fertilizers sold for use on rhododendrons, camellias and azaleas.

Harm is sometimes caused to narrow-leaved evergreens by insects or fungi, although the plants are probably more resistant to such attacks than anything else growing in your garden. The most common insects to which they fall prey are illustrated in the chart on pages 150 and 151, which also describes symptoms of damage, prescribes treatment and lists the most susceptible plants. It is not necessary even to identify fungi that may harm these evergreens —experts have difficulty telling one type from another—for a readily available all-purpose fungicide, applied in early spring, will protect the plants from almost all of them.

Among the fungus diseases there is one oddity you should be aware of. If bright orange or yellow growths, looking like tropical flowers, suddenly appear on your red cedars (*Juniperus virginiana*), they have cedar-apple rust. It usually does the red cedars little harm (except to their appearance). But it will cause real damage to any susceptible apple trees in the neighborhood. The red cedar acts as a host to the fungus, which grows on its foliage, then sends out spores to infect the apple trees.

A hazard to narrow-leaved evergreens greater than any disease or insect is man-made—pollution in the air. Deciduous trees have a decided advantage here; the soot and grime that accumulate on their leaves drop away with the leaves every fall. They start each new growing season with a fresh, clean leaf crop. Evergreens suffer more since they do not change foliage so often. Chemicals in the air do some damage, but in most areas the main harm comes from the soot that settles on the evergreens and clings to the needles. This soot keeps sunshine from reaching the leaf cells so that the plant is, in effect, growing in the shade. Few evergreens can stand much shade. The remedy is plain water, applied forcefully to the foliage with a garden hose at least once a week, to help clean the soot off.

If you live in a metropolitan area where air pollution is a severe problem, keep in mind that some narrow-leaved evergreens are naturally more resistant to it than others. Perhaps the toughest of all under modern city conditions is the Japanese yew. Other good choices are the white fir, the Japanese black pine, the Colorado spruce and the Carolina hemlock. The Pfitzer juniper is very resistant to airborne chemicals, but it requires such an abundance of sunshine that it needs to be hosed frequently to keep its foliage washed clean of soot that settles on it.

WINTER PROTECTION   If evergreens are selected wisely, they will need no special protection against winter hazards. Yet an evergreen grown in a windswept spot near the northern edge of the areas for which it is recommended *(map, page 149)* may need to be shielded from the wind, which dehydrates foliage. If you have a tender evergreen, or if you want to experiment with a plant quite uncommon in your neighborhood, put up a wind screen of burlap tacked to stakes driven into the ground on the windward side of the plant. Where the wind is very strong, you may have to anchor the burlap and stakes with guy wires. If possible, set the stakes in a "V" heading into the wind. Green burlap is less obtrusive than the standard dun-colored stuff. Another effective windbreak is one that you can easily make of snow fencing—the wired wooden slats set along highways to control snowdrifts. This kind of fencing comes in several sizes—a 5-foot height is about right for most garden uses. Remember that you cannot keep all the wind out; your aim is simply to try to diminish its force or change its direction.

In areas where winters are long and bitterly cold, a 3- or 4-inch layer of mulch on the ground beneath the plant (drawings, page 29) will prevent deep freezing of the soil and permit the plant to draw up precious moisture all winter long. Snow also can be a problem, particularly a heavy, wet snowfall in late winter that makes your evergreen landscape look like something out of an old English print. It will bend the trees down mercilessly and may break off branches. Snow causes more harm in the garden than in the forest. Where there is light and space all around, evergreen branches spread wide so that snow at the ends weighs them down with extra force. The branches are flexible, but diligent pruning makes their foliage thicker and heavier and still more vulnerable, since the snow cannot slide through the tree.

To prevent snow damage, you can truss a tree up so its branches do not spread to catch a snow load; simply spiral heavy twine up around the plant, not too tightly. But you probably will not like the way this looks. The alternative is simply to go out and knock the snow off with a light stick or the flat side of a broom. Start at the lower levels and work your way up; if you begin at the top, the bottom branches get still more weight on them. Wear a coat with tight cuffs, otherwise you are likely to find you have snow up to your armpits.

Some trees stand up better under snow loads than others. The horizontal branches of spruces simply dip when the load gets too heavy, slough off the snow and spring back. Most pines are also resilient. But Douglas firs and many cedars have branches that are brittle and susceptible to breakage. And spreading yews offer such a thick platform for snow that boughs bend far over, exposing the unattractive browned centers of the plant.

Careful choice of plants will also eliminate the need for wind protection. The best burlap or fencing shelter is hardly likely to be an attractive addition to the yard, and it seems a shame to screen off evergreens at the very time of the year when they are most effective and appreciated—when the rest of the garden has lost its greenery. Far better to select plants that you know will go through the winter untended and undamaged. A hardy evergreen that goes into winter in good health and with plenty of moisture will make it through to spring in good shape.

KEEPING AWAY THE ANIMALS

The most effective means of protecting young evergreens from deer—which often devour choice plants even within 20 miles of New York City—is to scatter lion manure on the soil nearby. It makes even deer that have never seen or heard a lion sense that they are unwelcome. Of course, lion manure may be in short supply at your garden center. Alternatives are to enclose the trees in strong wire fences, or to try to bribe the deer by spreading hay on the ground around the evergreens.

Mice, rabbits, chipmunks and squirrels, however, are not intimidated by lion manure. But tobacco dust or camphor flakes scattered around young plants may keep these animals away. Camphor flakes serve better than camphor balls because the rodents deftly thread their way through the balls, presumably holding their breath. Neither tobacco dust nor camphor flakes are toxic to vegetation but the chemicals can be washed away and must be replenished after rainfall.

Where colorful evergreens thrive

Flowering broad-leaved evergreens, like the regal rhododendron at right, are the prima donnas of the garden. Doubly prized for their year-round foliage and their splendid blossoms or berries, they often require pampering, for these plants originated in climates as diverse as those of the jungles of Java and the snow line of the Alps. Today's refined garden varieties, though not quite so extreme in taste as their ancestors, still tend to be choosy about where they live.

Each of the flowering evergreens has its individual responses to temperature, soil, moisture (including humidity as well as rain and snow), sun and wind. The hot summer of Florida, for example, is as intolerable to the andromeda as the cold winter of Indiana is to the gardenia, and hibiscuses go so far as to demand an almost constant year-round temperature of 70°. Although most broad-leaved evergreens like fertile, well-drained acid soil, St.-John's-wort prefers rather poor, dry, sandy soil and is not fussy about its acidity or alkalinity. Where both climate and soil are ideal, the flowering evergreens thrive. Thus geography has made Sacramento, California, the camellia city and Connecticut the mountain laurel state.

In the cold and windswept plains and in the Rocky Mountain states, only a few broad-leaved evergreens are able to flourish—bearberries and holly grapes, for instance. In other areas, gardeners may take their pick from a generous spectrum, but they still need to be selective. On the following pages are 10 of the best-known flowering evergreens, each accompanied by a map that indicates—in deep blue—those parts of the country where the plant can be expected to bloom profusely and reach the maximum size described in its encyclopedic entry in Chapter 5. For the adventurous, the maps also show—in light blue—where each of these evergreens may be grown with the likelihood of some success if it is treated with special care. An evergreen magnolia, for example, can be planted in a sheltered place, mulched heavily and coaxed to grow as far north as New Jersey but it is unlikely ever to tower 90 feet high as it might in the climate of Mississippi.

Hybrid rhododendrons, like this Mrs.
Furnival, blaze with color each spring
as far north as the Great Lakes.

66

HYPERICUM

*St.-John's-wort (below), like all
hypericums, is bright with sunny flowers
most of the summer. Hypericums grow
as far north as New Haven, Connecticut, but
their strength diminishes in winter
cold. The plants often survive frosts that
kill branches to the ground, but they
never grow as large as they do in the South.*

Plants for any soil

The flowering evergreens that grow in any well-drained soil, acid or alkaline, are among the easiest to deal with—some do well anywhere winters are not bitter cold. Fire thorns *(below, left)* decorate gardens in parts of southern Canada. As the maps indicate, however, even tough broad-leaved evergreens are weather sensitive. Hypericums cannot tolerate cold inland climates but can withstand drought and are valuable in dry, sandy areas. Abelias endure temperatures as low as —10°; if frost kills branches, the roots often survive to spring back into life when the ground warms again. But others, like acacias, have tropical tastes and appear in North American gardens only in a strip of Southern California coastland.

FIRE THORN

ABELIA

Though laden with tiny white flowers in spring, fire thorns are most prized for their brilliantly colored berries in fall. The scarlet fire thorn above is hardy enough to survive winters in southeastern and southwestern Canada. But the hardiness of a fire thorn varies from one variety to another—making it essential to shop for plants that will grow well where you live.

The arching branches of the abelias cloak themselves with dainty blossoms from summer to fall. When the flowers fade, the purplish leaflike outer petals remain, adding weeks of color. These plants grow in much of the U.S., but they are dependably evergreen only along the Gulf and Pacific Coasts; in cooler or drier regions, they may lose foliage over winter.

CAMELLIA

*From midautumn until well into spring,
common camellias like this Pink
Perfection produce uncommonly lovely
blooms in southern gardens. The common
type is relatively hardy, growing as far
north as Long Island or Vancouver. More
fragile kinds, such as the sasanqua,
grow where temperatures stay above 10°.*

Classics for warm climates

Gardens near the Gulf of Mexico and in the coastal areas of Southern California enjoy the largest selection of blossoming evergreens because these regions provide not only the hot weather that most of these plants prefer but also the humidity and moist soil that they need. Moisture is more essential than high temperatures. Some varieties of these extravagantly blooming plants can be persuaded to grow in ocean-warmed areas farther north in the East if the site is chosen carefully. They must be shielded from winter wind, which quickly dehydrates broad-leaved evergreens in cold weather, and they need to be protected by a deep blanket of mulch against the ravages of alternate freezing and thawing.

SOUTHERN MAGNOLIA

Native to the U.S., the southern magnolia boasts giant flowers at least 8 inches across; they are so fragrant the Indians believed their scent could overpower a man. This spectacular evergreen grows up to 90 feet tall in the heat of Mississippi and Louisiana but can also grow—with extra care—in coastal areas where temperatures do not drop below −5°.

CHINESE HIBISCUS

In the constantly hot climate it needs, the Chinese hibiscus never stops blooming. But if winter temperatures fall below 50°, flowering is inhibited. The variety Brilliant (above), from Polynesia, is the most widely grown in the U.S. Though hypersensitive to chill, Chinese hibiscus does not mind the salt spray of the seashore or the airborne grime of cities.

GARDENIA

Prized for fragrance as well as form, gardenias blossom most profusely when days are warm and nights are cool. In the Deep South, they bloom from April through June; the variety Florida (above) flowers in May. But in parts of California—especially coastal areas where summer nights are 65° or lower— they bloom from May to November.

The wide-ranging forest plants

Along the Pacific Coast and in a broad swath of states from the Mississippi to the Atlantic, mild temperatures are coupled with moist, acid soil to provide the ideal setting for rhododendrons, mountain laurels and andromedas. These evergreens are forest plants, and to a great extent the areas where they now flourish were once wooded; even today the land tends to be rich in natural leaf compost. The mountain laurel grown in gardens still does best in its native territory—between Quebec and northern Florida. Andromedas, however, come in North American, Chinese and Japanese species that differ in their hardiness, and rhododendrons are available in varieties that withstand −25°, though others cannot survive below 32°.

RHODODENDRON

In spring rhododendrons, like Prodigal's Return (above), are engulfed by flowers. Each of the 10,000 or more hybrids available has its climate preferences: this Seattle-grown plant is hardy to 5°; the Ottawa, Canada, hybrid on page 67 is hardy to −5°. The related evergreen azaleas can tolerate intense heat and extend the range of this genus to the Gulf Coast.

ANDROMEDA

Clusters of bell-like flowers cloak the andromeda in spring; after they fade, the shrubs start new buds and seem to be in bloom most of the year. This Japanese variety, as well as the mountain andromeda native to the Alleghenies, thrives as far north as Boston; Chinese andromedas, more tender, do best in places like Atlanta or San Francisco.

MOUNTAIN LAUREL

Late in spring, porcelainlike blossoms almost hide the foliage of the mountain laurel. A slow-growing evergreen that rarely exceeds 8 feet in gardens, it can withstand winter temperatures as low as —20° in Maine or Michigan, and summer temperatures that soar as high as 95° in Louisiana and Georgia.

Growing the broad-leaved species 4

Although the many lovely broad-leaved evergreens that can be grown in home gardens generally demand little more of the gardener than their narrow-leaved cousins, their soil requirements are rather emphatic. Virtually all of them need a soil that is somewhat acid—and an important group of them demand soil that is very acid. In North America most soils naturally run between a pH reading of 4.5, which is very acid, and 8.5, which is highly alkaline. (A pH of 7, at the center of the scale, indicates a neutral soil.) Several factors go into determining the pH: the presence of limestone, which tends to make soil alkaline, an accumulation of decayed vegetation, which makes it acid, and the amount of rainfall in the region. Where rainfall is abundant, the water dissolves and washes away certain chemicals, largely calcium and magnesium, which make the soil alkaline, or sweet. With these chemicals washed away, the soil becomes acid, or sour—as it is in rainier parts of the United States —the Northeast, Northwest and Southeast. Where rainfall is sparser, these chemicals remain and the soil is alkaline—as it generally is in the Midwest and the arid areas of the West.

Most kinds of broad-leaved evergreens grow well in a soil with a pH of 5.5 to 6.5, somewhat on the acid side. These include such valuable plants as hollies, privets, live oaks, magnolias, fire thorns, camellias and gardenias. The few like cotoneaster and daphne that prefer a more alkaline soil are noted in the encyclopedia. But there are some broad-leaved evergreens that need an even more acid soil with a pH of 4.5 to 5.5—notably rhododendrons, azaleas, laurels, andromedas and heathers. These are members of the heath family, the *Ericaceae,* and are called ericaceous plants; they are prized for the beauty of their flowers.

Before you plant such acid-loving plants, test your soil with a kit that can be bought at almost any garden store, or send samples of the soil to your county or state agricultural extension service for testing. If the pH is too high, you can reduce it by applying sulfur or iron sulfate. To lower the pH ½ to 1 point, say from 6.5 to

Robust blossoms of a container-grown oleander, ordinarily a plant of the South and Southwest, give a dash of color to a New Jersey terrace. It winters in a warm garage and is moved outdoors in May.

6.0 or 5.5, add 3 pounds of iron sulfate or ½ pound of ground sulfur for every 100 square feet. In those rare cases where the pH is too low—say below 4.5—you can add ground limestone; 5 pounds per 100 square feet will raise the pH 1 point. If you do this at planting time, spade the powder into the planting bed; later you can simply spread it on the surface around the plants and water it in. Check every few years to make sure the pH stays at the desired level. If the leaves of your plants grow pale green with conspicuously dark veins, the pH of the soil may be getting too high again, or, in rare instances, too low. If the chemical balance is not right, the plant cannot absorb the iron it needs and, somewhat like people who lack iron, it begins to look anemic.

If you live in a region where the soil is quite alkaline, the job of maintaining a proper pH may seem too much for you. But it can be done and here I would like to tell you about a friend of mine who loves camellias and took on almost all the forces of nature in order to grow them.

She lives in Texas in a region where the pH is up around 8. Camellias will not do well in a pH higher than 6.5. At first, my friend simply tried the sulfur treatment. That worked, but only temporarily. Water, alkaline in that part of Texas, kept coming into the camellia bed from the surrounding soil and from below. She stuffed the bed with peat moss, which is quite acid, using 3 parts peat moss to 1 part soil. This helped, but still not enough. So she began all over again, from the bottom up.

She dug down a foot and a half and put a 12-inch layer of peat moss at the bottom to further neutralize the alkalinity in the ground water from the surrounding soil. For the rest of the bed, she made a mixture of ¼ soil and ¾ peat moss. Nor did she stop at ground level. She raised the surface of the bed 10 inches to keep alkaline water from seeping in from around the sides. She was about to put a little brick wall around the raised bed but her husband, who had been following this procedure with some interest, reminded her that mortar is almost pure lime and its alkalinity could defeat everything else she did. So she settled for railroad ties.

The raised bed required constant watering and this presented another problem. The house water was alkaline too. A couple of barrels to catch rain water, which is more nearly neutral, got past that obstacle. That took care of everything—except the earthworms. It came as a shock to her to find that they were not on her side. Normally earthworms are a gardener's best friend, aerating the soil in their travels and adding organic material to a flower bed as they ingest and excrete soil. But in doing this the worms that moved up into the bed made the soil slightly more alkaline. She could have discouraged them with a 2- to 4-inch layer of coarse gravel below the bed. But at this point my friend declared a truce with nature. Her camellias, with the help of regular applications of sulfur, would simply have to get along with the worms.

I am happy to say that this labor of love has paid off. My friend's camellias are doing very well indeed.

In preparing the bed, the lady in Texas was doing more than adjusting the pH. She was creating an efficient growing medium for her plants. The old saying that a rhododendron or a camellia will do well "in any soil so long as it's acid" is one of those miserable half-truths that mislead so many gardeners.

Along with the proper chemical balance, broad-leaved evergreens require soil with a lot of extra organic materials added; peat moss, ground redwood, partly decayed hardwood sawdust or oak leaves are all excellent soil conditioners. They make the soil more absorbent, able to hold water that the plants need, and they make it porous, giving the roots sufficient air. Broad-leaved plants, with few exceptions, cannot survive in soggy sites. Nonericaceous broad-leaved evergreens, however, do not require quite so much organic material. For them, a soil that is ⅓ peat moss, instead of ½ to ¾, will do. With properly prepared soil, the fertilizer needs of most broad-leaved evergreens, like most narrow-leaved ones, are

SOILS AND MULCHES

ESPALIER: MAKING A PLANT GROW FLAT

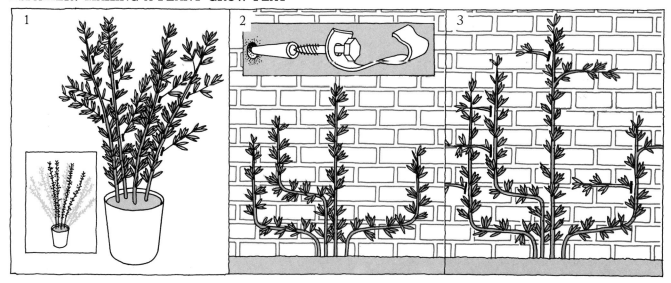

To train a fire thorn against a wall, using the espalier technique, select a plant with at least four strong, pliable shoots (inset). Remove the others below the soil level and cut off side branches flush (lines).

Plant the fire thorn close to the wall and bend and anchor its shoots. To make an anchor (inset), cut a small strip of lead and screw it into a lead wall plug set in a hole that has been drilled into a mortar joint.

As the plant grows, prune off the branches (lines) that spoil its shape. Train new growth with holders set inside corners where branches are to bend. Other evergreens to espalier are sweet bay magnolias and yews.

negligible; an annual light dusting of cottonseed meal, 5-10-5 or a rhododendron-azalea-camellia fertilizer under the plants will encourage healthy foliage and flowers in most species *(encyclopedia)*.

Mulching is particularly important with broad-leaved evergreens, since so many of them have shallow hairlike root systems that do not penetrate deeply into the soil. If the surface gets hot and dry, the roots and plant suffer. A mulch for broad-leaved evergreens should be thick and permanent. If you have an oak or beech tree, your problems are solved. Spread the leaves around the plants in the fall to provide winter protection. As the leaves decay, they will also provide organic food. Do not use maple, elm, linden, birch or poplar leaves: they become soggy and matted, cutting air off from the roots, and the first two tend to make soil alkaline.

Lacking this free source of mulch, you can buy many other good ones: wood chips, ground bark, pine needles, sawdust, cocoa beans or peanut shells, buckwheat hulls or other kinds of organic residue. Peat moss makes a good mulch provided you use the coarse or chunky kind sometimes called poultry grade or nursery grade. The fine variety used for potting-soil mixtures and for conditioning the garden soil itself is not appropriate; it cakes on top and water runs off rather than through it. The thickness of the mulch depends on the type of plant as well as the nature of mulching material.

PRUNING FLOWERING EVERGREENS

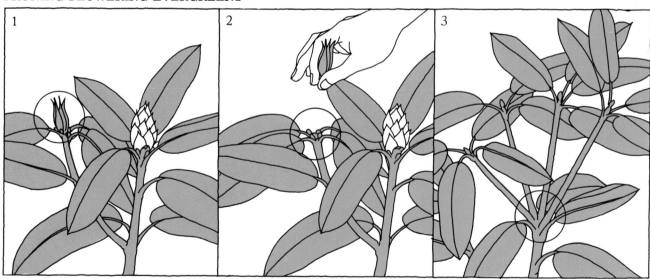

To prune large-flowered evergreens such as rhododendrons (above), azaleas and camellias, you must first distinguish between the slender terminal leaf buds (left) and the plumper flower buds (right).

Snap off only the terminal leaf buds to control growth of stems. Take care not to injure the tiny axillary buds beneath them, and be sure to leave the flower buds intact so that you do not sacrifice potential bloom.

After a terminal leaf bud is removed, each of its axillary buds develops into a leafy shoot, producing several branches where there would have been only one; the plant becomes bushier and bears more flowers.

Such plants as heather, which usually grow a foot or less in height, should have about 2 inches of a relatively compact material such as ground bark or wood chips around them. On the other hand, 6- to 8-foot rhododendrons thrive with up to 12 inches of fluffy oak leaves raked under the plants in the fall; these leaves will usually be compressed to less than half that thickness by spring.

Once you put the mulch on, leave it there; removing it can be disastrous. I know of people who, having bought a home with an established garden, cleaned up what they considered to be untidy azalea beds. They raked off all the old mulch and made the ground nice and neat—and bare. Then they wondered why their lovely shrubs suddenly began to lose leaves and refused to flower. The answer is, of course, that the shallow roots that had grown up into the mulch were broken off when the mulch was removed and the rest of the roots were left high and dry.

You can also plant a living mulch. Handsome, shade-tolerant ground covers like pachysandra and periwinkle set between shrubs insulate the ground, shade the roots and suppress weeds.

The beauty of their flowers, of course, is a main reason for planting many broad-leaved evergreens. There are a few things—besides making sure that your plants have good soil to grow in—that you

ENCOURAGING BLOOMS

REMOVING RHODODENDRON SEED HEADS

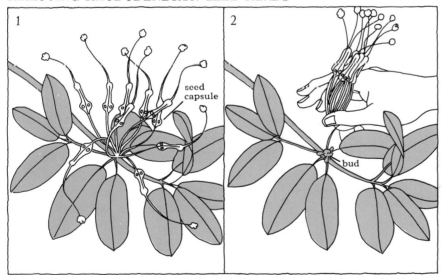

After its petals fade, a rhododendron flower starts producing unsightly clusters of seed capsules held on thin stems. Remove the seeds or they will sap the plant's energy away from forming buds for another year.

To snap off seed heads, first squeeze the capsules together. Holding the clump at its base, bend it back and forth until it snaps. Do not break the tender buds underneath— they will produce new branches.

can do to encourage flower production. One is to select the proper location. Too much hot sun will dry up the flower buds; complete shade will inhibit their formation. At the Brooklyn Botanic Garden an experiment was conducted with rhododendrons. One group was given full morning sun from the east but was cut off from the hot afternoon sun from south and west. Another group was deprived of morning sun but given full afternoon sun. Those that got only morning sun far outdid the others in profusion of bloom. If your rhododendrons seem to have everything they should have—including the right sun exposure—but bloom only sparsely, a small quantity of a fertilizer formulated for acid-loving plants, sprinkled around each bush in late winter or early spring, will help. But the most important thing you can do to assure good flowering is to pick off flowers once they start to fade. If you do not, the plants will devote their energies to producing seed instead of sprouting new growth that will flower the next year. In the case of rhododendrons and other plants with upright flower clusters, which usually come off easily, simply twist off faded flowers with your fingers; with andromedas and others that have hanging clusters tightly anchored to the branches hand clippers must be used. If you have been too busy to remove all fading flowers, remove as soon as possible the seed capsules that follow *(drawings, page 79)*.

(continued on page 85)

The small joys of bonsai

"The art of bonsai," writes one authority, "lies not in what the plant is, but in what it suggests." What it may suggest, a forest tree that looks old though it may be only 2 inches tall, is a gnarled juniper struggling against the elements or a stately pine in a clearing. Patiently pruned, potted, wired and repotted to restrict and shape its growth, the ideal bonsai tree evokes the loveliness of its full-sized counterpart. While the Japanese have taken centuries to bring bonsai to a peak of complexity and refinement, you can learn to produce a creditable specimen by following the instructions on these pages. The cost of materials should be less than $15. Among the narrow-leaved evergreens, mugo pine (shown in the drawings), Sargent juniper and Norway spruce lend themselves especially well to bonsai training; among the broad-leaved evergreens, fire thorn, cotoneaster and azalea are prime candidates. Bonsais are outdoor plants, but in harsh winters may need the shelter of a cold frame or an unheated (but not freezing) porch or garage. They require the same light that their fully grown counterparts do. Water them every morning and, on hot, dry days, again in the evening. Feed pines monthly with half-strength liquid house-plant fertilizer; all other evergreens should be fed every two months. To keep the plants small, sturdy and shapely like the classic bonsais shown in the photographs, groom them regularly: each spring, when the candles of pines become 1 to 1½ inches long, pinch them back halfway (page 54); the lighter-colored new growth on other narrow-leaved evergreens and all broad-leaved evergreens should be pinched off about halfway in spring and once or twice more during the year.

This Sargent juniper, stunted by a rigorous environment, was discovered in Japan and made into a bonsai. It is a century old and 17 inches tall. In the wild a Sargent juniper grows no taller than that, but may spread to 10 feet.

Branch pruning

The first step in creating a bonsai of mugo pine in the so-called "slanting" style is to prune the branches with hand clippers into approximately the desired shape. In early spring or late fall buy a 12- to 15-inch-tall container-grown plant with a tapering trunk and well-spaced branches whose form is conducive to the shape desired. At the nursery scrape away soil to make sure that there are two large side roots that meet the trunk at a 45° vertical angle when the tree is viewed from its finest profile—the "front" of the bonsai.

1. Remove the tallest, thickest vertical branch with hand clippers (dashed line); the new, thinner top limb should lean in the opposite direction from the tree's longest bottom branch.

2. Remove secondary branches with flower shears, making the cuts (dashed lines) flush with the trunk. Rub mud into the open cuts to darken them and make them look old.

3. Pruning will be finished when all but the following have been cut off: the long, low branch at the bottom, a second and third on opposite sides about midway and the new top structure.

Cut back from a 15-year-old nursery specimen, this fire thorn was 25 years old and only 11 inches high when it was photographed with its autumn decoration of ripe orange berries. In the garden, it would grow to a height of 6 feet or more.

Potting a bonsai

Pot the same day you prune, using a 5-by-7-inch pottery container, about 2 inches deep. To prepare the potting mixture, sift dry garden soil, sand, leaf mold and peat moss separately through a $\frac{1}{32}$-inch mesh screen, saving only what does not go through. Then sift each through $\frac{1}{16}$-inch mesh to provide ingredients for a coarse mixture and a finer one. Combine ingredients in a ratio of 8 parts soil, 4 parts sand, 1 part leaf mold and 1 part peat moss. Cover drainage holes in the container with $\frac{1}{16}$-inch mesh plastic screen.

4. Remove the tree from the nursery can and loosen the soil with a blunt fork, spreading out the roots. Cut off the central taproot about 1 inch below the bottom of the trunk (dashed line).

5. Insert an 18-inch length of 18-gauge copper wire through the pot's holes and screen (white). Put in ¼-inch layers of sand and coarse and fine potting mixture. Set the tree a bit off-center.

6. Twist the wire around the trunk's base over rubber patches. Fill the pot with fine mix; tamp with a stick. Soak in shallow water for half an hour; keep out of direct sun for three weeks.

This sinuous Japanese white pine bonsai was trained from one tree to give the look of a whole grove. It stands 27 inches high above its granite slab and is at least 75 years old. Such a pine normally might reach 90 feet.

Wiring and shaping

A few months after potting, the tree will be strong enough for the process of wiring, which shapes it and makes it look older. You will need about 20 inches of 12- or 14-gauge copper wire for the trunk and two lengths of 18- or 20-gauge wire about 15 inches long for the branches. To make the wire more flexible, heat it red hot over a gas flame and let it cool slowly. Leave the wires on for one growing season, loosening them if they cut into the bark. Remove the wire at the base of the trunk as soon as the plant stands steady.

7. Push heavy wire (white) into the soil against the container wall to anchor it (dotted line), then coil the wire upward around the trunk. Wind tightly to hold the trunk in any position.

8. Use one length of the lighter wire (thin white) for each pair of opposite branches. Wind the center section of the wire around the trunk, then wind the ends outward to the branch tips.

9. To shape the tree, bend it gently, if necessary, a little at a time each week over several months. Lower branches should drop with tips raised; the top one should lean slightly toward you.

More than 100 years old, this Japanese red pine was transplanted from the mountains around 1910. As a slanting bonsai it is 21 inches high; left to grow naturally, it might reach 100 feet.

Root-pruning and repotting

After three years, your bonsai will be ready for root-pruning and repotting. This step—like the original planting—should be done in spring or fall. Pruning the roots and repotting the plant will encourage the tree to grow more of the fine feeder roots it needs to stay healthy. The roots must not be allowed to dry out, however, not even briefly, so do your repotting in a sheltered, shady place, covering the roots with wet cloths if you are interrupted. After repotting, keep the tree out of direct sunlight for three weeks.

10. Remove the tree, earth and all, from the pot. Using a blunt fork, loosen the earth, taking care not to injure roots. Leave some earth intact near the trunk as you loosen and straighten out the roots.

11. Spread the roots out, holding the tree above the container. With clippers, snip off roots (dashed line) so that they approximate the container's shape but fall ½ inch short of its sides.

12. Prepare the pot with fresh mixture, sand, a wire anchor and drain-hole screens. Replace the tree, fasten the wire and rubber shields, add soil and water, and set out of direct sun for three weeks.

Flowers are not the only decorations that broad-leaved evergreens boast. Many have berries as handsome as any blooms—the bright red ones on hollies, the orange clusters on fire thorns, the rows of neat little red berries on cotoneasters. These are especially welcome because they come in fall when few shrubs bloom and they stay on into winter, pleasing both the gardener and the birds who feed on them. In some cases you must be careful about a plant's sex if you want to be sure it will bear berries. Some plants—among them fire thorn, bearberry and cotoneaster—are self-pollinating and therefore all plants will produce berries. In the case of others, such as most hollies, only female plants bear berries and a male plant must be somewhere in the neighborhood (best within 100 feet) to pollinate them. With still others, such as Japanese aucuba and Japanese skimmia, male and female plants must be planted next to each other for the female to produce berries. Nandinas produce male and female blossoms on the same plant but require pollination from another plant; if you want them to produce berries, plant groups of them. A few broad-leaved evergreens have poisonous berries, as specified in the encyclopedia. They should not be planted where children are apt to pick and eat them.

Pruning is much less of a task with broad-leaved evergreens than with the narrow-leaved kinds, and, as with broad-leaved evergreens, much of it can be avoided by choosing the right plant in the first place, getting one that will not quickly outgrow its allotted space. Some gardeners, however, still insist on making work for themselves. Just about the oddest boast I ever heard was made by a lady in Portland, Oregon, who said: "I'll bet I have the squarest azaleas in town." This was her wry way of complaining about her husband's pruning methods, which were conscientious but definitely self-defeating. An azalea that has been clipped into a square shape is a contradiction: it looks unnatural and produces fewer flowers.

HOW TO PRUNE

The only broad-leaved evergreens that should be sheared are those recommended in the encyclopedia for use as formal hedges —those that grow rapidly and continuously and have rather small leaves. These include Japanese holly, box and evergreen privet. On most broad-leaved evergreens, indiscriminate shearing cuts leaves in half and these cut surfaces turn brown and unsightly. The best procedure to keep such plants within bounds is to reach in beyond the outer fringe of foliage with your hand clippers and cut just above a place where side branches are growing *(drawings, page 86)*. Most broad-leaved evergreens will sprout new buds just below the cut. If a shrub has become impossibly overgrown, remove all of the tallest branches to within an inch or two of the ground. New canes will sprout, making a bushier and more compact plant. Such major surgery should be done only at the start of the growing season.

With some shrubs such as rhododendron, pruning can be done by removing leaf buds before they sprout. They grow in clusters, with a large bud in the center. This is the bud that will grow straight out, enlarging the plant. You can pluck it out with your fingers, leaving the smaller buds to become side branches. Be careful, however, not to pluck out flower buds; the drawings on page 78 tell you how to distinguish fat flower buds from thin leaf buds.

Except for removing leaf buds, flowering evergreens need little pruning. Unless otherwise specified in the encyclopedia, prune after flowers have bloomed so you do not deprive yourself of their beauty. Root-pruning, recommended in Chapter 3 for narrow-leaved evergreens, is not practical with most broad-leaved types because their roots are too fibrous and compact, but it is effective with a few such as holly and photinia, which have far-ranging root systems. Root-pruning should be done only in spring before the buds swell; to avoid too great a loss of moisture-supplying roots at one time, use only alternate cuts as shown on page 51.

NEW PLANTS FROM OLD   Propagating evergreens is something that most gardeners are quite willing to leave to the professionals in the field. Raising plants of useful size from seeds or from stem cuttings generally takes more

PRUNING BUSHY BROAD-LEAVED EVERGREENS

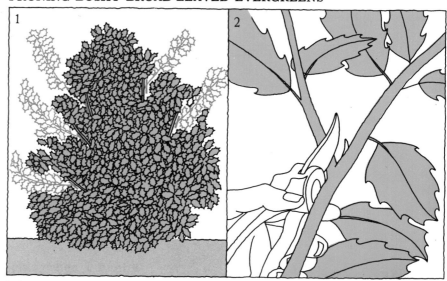

When evergreens such as thorny elaeagnus, andromeda or the English holly above send branches out beyond the silhouette of the plant, push the outer foliage aside to cut away these stragglers (lines).

With pruning clippers, cut off each straggler flush. New growth will soon fill any hole that is left. Although summer is the best pruning season, you can clip sprigs in December for holiday decorations.

time and attention than an amateur is willing or able to devote to the project. But there are a couple of easy and interesting methods of propagation that will give you fair-sized young evergreen plants within a matter of months.

One is known as ground layering and it is a natural way for many broad-leaved evergreens to reproduce themselves. A rhododendron, for example, has drooping branches that often touch the ground. Where they touch, roots often form and a new shrub starts. Laurels and andromedas, too, often reproduce this way. You can adapt the method for yourself. When new wood has begun to mature, find a strong branch growing low enough so that it can easily be bent to the ground. About 6 inches from the tip, on the underside of the branch, make a shallow cut. Dust the cut with rooting powder (which you can buy at any garden store), prop the cut open with a pebble or twig and bury the branch at this point about 2 to 4 inches in the ground. Anchor it with a stone or brick placed on top. After the branch has been in this position for about a year, roots will have formed. Sever the rooted branch from the mother plant and move it to a protected part of your garden until it has become large enough to warrant your planting it in a place where you want it to grow permanently.

Another method, suitable for plants that do not have long, flexible branches near the ground, is called air layering. Choose a healthy young branch. About 12 inches from the tip make several inch-long lengthwise slits around the branch with a knife, going through the bark but exercising care not to cut into the wood, which would open it to infection. Dust the cuts with rooting powder. Cut off the closed end of a clear plastic food bag and pull the bag over the branch down to where the bark is cut. Tie one end about 2 inches below the cut, then stuff the bag with well-moistened sphagnum moss (not peat moss) until it is about 4 inches in diameter. Tie the other end about 2 inches above the slits and wrap twine around the bag to lash it to the branch. Within a few weeks or months, depending upon the species, you will be able to discern roots growing in the damp moss. At this point cut the stem off, remove the plastic bag but not the moss and plant the rooted stem in your garden. Water it faithfully and within a reasonably short time you will find that the plant has taken hold.

These methods of propagation may seem like a lot of work to get a plant that can be bought inexpensively at a nursery. But they provide some deep satisfactions. One lies in watching a plant you have helped create take its place in your garden world. Another is having extra plants to give away as presents—and it is the giving and getting of plants between friends that, for me, provides one of the constant pleasures of gardening.

An illustrated encyclopedia of evergreens 5

Before you choose evergreens for your garden, you must decide what you want them to do. If you need an opaque screen for privacy, for example, look for fast-growing, densely branched types like upright hemlocks. If you need low plants to cover a rocky hill, the answer may be spreading evergreens like the bearberry. Evergreens are a long-term investment that must be made judiciously. Not only do the plants differ widely in their appearance, but they also vary in the climates and soils to which they will adapt.

The following encyclopedia chapter consists of two sections: one beginning on page 90 listing 29 genera of narrow-leaved evergreens (usually, but not always, needled and cone bearing) and, beginning on page 111, another listing 71 genera of broad-leaved evergreens (usually, but not always, notable for their flowers). The entries specify the characteristics and uses of each plant, the areas in which it can be grown (designated by letters keyed to the map on page 149) and the light, soil and care it requires.

Unless otherwise noted, plants that nurseries sell in containers may be set into the ground at any time, but any freshly dug plant whose ball of roots is wrapped in burlap should be planted in early spring or fall. Except where specified, no fertilizer or other additives are needed beyond the standard ones for soil preparation discussed in Chapters 2 and 4, and no pruning is required beyond minor shaping and the removal of dead branches. The entries for fruit-bearing plants indicate those whose fruit is edible and the few whose fruit is poisonous if eaten.

Each plant is listed alphabetically by its internationally recognized Latin botanical name. The compact strawberry tree, *Arbutus unedo compacta,* for instance, is listed under the genus name *Arbutus,* which is followed by the species name, *unedo,* and then by the variety name, *compacta.* Common names are cross-referenced to the Latin genus names.

For quick reference, a chart on pages 152-154 summarizes key characteristics of the plants illustrated in the encyclopedia.

The variety offered by evergreens is shown in this painting of a Colorado blue spruce surrounded by (counterclockwise from top right) a deodar cedar, abelia blossoms, a stem of upright Japanese yew, spring heath, the huge leaves of Japanese fatsia, a Swiss stone pine cone, a Schipka cherry laurel and the leaves of a variegated Japanese aucuba.

Narrow-leaved evergreens

A

ABIES

A. concolor (white fir, Colorado fir, concolor fir); *A. homolepis*, also called *A. brachyphylla* (Nikko fir); *A. nordmanniana* (Nordmann's fir); *A. pinsapo* (Spanish fir); *A. procera glauca*, also called *A. nobilis glauca* (blue-leaved noble fir); *A. veitchii* (Veitch fir)

Firs are so dense with branches they are almost perfectly conical when young, though their shape changes after about 30 years when they lose some of their lower branches. In forests, firs may tower more than 200 feet, but in gardens they rarely become more than one third that height. Even this size is too much for the average garden, but young firs make such striking focal points that they deserve to be more widely used with the understanding that the specimen planted may have to be removed when it outgrows its setting.

Fir needles are usually blunt-ended, flat in profile, soft to the touch and pleasantly aromatic. From 1 to 2 inches long, they vary in color from dark green to blue-green on the top and are usually silvery underneath. Because needles cling to the branches long after the trees are cut, firs are popular as Christmas trees.

Old fir trees bear their seeds in erect cones, mainly along the highest branches. The cones appear in early summer and mature in late fall; in time the scales fall away leaving sticklike cores atop the limbs.

White fir grows well in Areas B, C, F, G, H, I and J and is more tolerant of city conditions than any other species. The needles are bluish green. It becomes 50 to 60 feet tall after 30 to 60 years in the garden. Old trees bear 3- to 5-inch greenish purple or yellow cones. Nikko fir is suited to Areas B, C, H and I. Its thickly set dark green needles, silvery beneath, are arranged in a "V" shape along each branch. Trees become 40 to 50 feet tall in gardens in about 30 years and bear 3- to 4-inch deep purple cones that turn dark brown as they mature.

Nordmann's fir is recommended for Areas B, C, H, I and J. Its dark green shiny needles are silvery underneath and closely crowded all around the branches. It matures in 30 to 60 years, becoming 50 to 75 feet tall in the garden and bearing 4- to 6-inch reddish brown cones. Spanish fir grows well along the West Coast in Areas I and J. It has a very stiff symmetrical profile with sharply pointed bright green needles arranged all around the bushy branches. This species grows slowly in hot, dry climates and rarely exceeds 25 to 40 feet after about 30 years in a garden. It bears 6-inch grayish brown cones. Blue-leaved noble fir is adapted to Areas B, C, I and J. Its stiff branches are covered with grayish blue needles. Trees mature in 30 to 60 years, becoming 75 feet or more in height and bearing 4- to 6-inch light brown cones.

Like the Nikko species, Veitch fir grows well in Areas B, C, H and I, and is particularly easy to grow. It has dark green needles that are silvery underneath and attractive smooth gray bark. This species becomes 25 to 50 feet tall after 20 to 30 years, and bears 2-inch bluish purple cones.

Firs do not thrive where the air is polluted with dust and industrial impurities. Most species cannot stand hot, dry climates, for they require moist but well-drained acid soil. Young trees can tolerate light shade, but they do best in full sun. Firs need very little pruning; hand clippers may be used in early spring to remove the tip of an occasional errant branch. Each tree should have only one central top stem, called a leader; if more than one such leader develops, all but the strongest of them should be removed.

WHITE FIR
Abies concolor

NORFOLK ISLAND PINE
Araucaria heterophylla

90

ARAUCARIA

A. araucana, also called *A. imbricata* (monkey puzzle);
A. bidwillii (bunya-bunya); *A. heterophylla,* also called
A. excelsa (Norfolk Island pine)

Araucaria branches grow in layers as widely spaced
whorls that spiral into a symmetrical conical shape. The
trees are planted singly in lawns in Florida and California,
but are also commonly grown elsewhere in tubs for use indoors or on patios. They may become 30 to 80 feet tall
after 20 to 40 years in gardens; old trees bear erect cones
near the ends of their upper branches.

Hardiest of the araucaria species is the monkey puzzle,
which grows well along the coast in Areas D and I and in
all parts of Areas E and J. Its 2-inch dark green needles
—very stiff, wide and sharp-pointed—clothe the stems so
closely that the branches look like massive green ropes dip-
ping down from the trunk, then up at the tips. Because the
needles point upward, it is said that a monkey can climb up
this tree, but not down; hence the common name monkey
puzzle. Trees become 30 to 50 feet tall and bear 6- to 8-
inch oval cones containing edible seeds. The bunya-bunya
is suited to southern parts of Areas E and J. Young trees
have 1-inch narrow, sharp, dark green needles; older trees
have green needles ½ inch wide and 2 inches long. Trees
become 40 to 80 feet tall. They bear oval cones that grow
as large as 12 inches long and 9 inches in diameter and
that also have edible seeds. Norfolk Island pine, which has
closely spaced ½-inch dark green needles, also does well
in southern parts of Areas E and J. Norfolk Island pines
may become 50 or more feet tall in the garden and bear 3-
to 6-inch globe-shaped cones.

Araucarias do best in full sun in rich, moist, acid loam in
a climate with a relatively high humidity. Slow growing
when very young, they shoot up rapidly once they have attained a height of 3 to 4 feet, especially if fed annually in
early spring with any garden fertilizer. Plants are almost always sold in containers and can be set out at any time, although early spring planting is best in northern sections of
the recommended areas. Pruning is rarely necessary. The
pattern of growth is fixed within each branch—if a cutting
of a side branch is rooted it will always grow sideways and
never become a normal conical tree.

ARBORVITAE See *Thuja*

B

BEEFWOOD, HORSETAIL See *Casuarina*
BIG TREE See *Sequoiadendron*
BIOTA See *Thuja*
BUNYA-BUNYA See *Araucaria*

C

CALOCEDRUS See *Libocedrus*
CEDAR See *Cedrus*
CEDAR, INCENSE See *Libocedrus*
CEDAR, JAPANESE See *Cryptomeria*
CEDAR, OREGON See *Chamaecyparis*
CEDAR, PORT ORFORD See *Chamaecyparis*
CEDAR, RED See *Juniperus*
CEDAR, WESTERN RED See *Thuja*

CEDRUS

C. atlantica and varieties (Atlas cedar),
C. deodara and varieties (deodar cedar),
C. libani and varieties (cedar of Lebanon)

Many unrelated trees are called cedars, usually because
of their aromatic wood, but only five are true cedars and
only three grow in the United States. They are cone-shaped

BLUE ATLAS CEDAR
Cedrus atlantica glauca

DEODAR CEDAR
Cedrus deodara

when young, but become flat-topped when they reach the mature height of 60 to 80 feet after 40 or 50 years. The branches may spread 40 feet or more.

Cedars have 1- to 2-inch needles borne in clusters of 7 to 12 needles along the branches. These trees have separate male and female flowers, but only the males are noticeable—they are yellow, cone-shaped and 1 inch across, and they dispense great clouds of golden pollen. The 2- to 5-inch brown cones stand erect on upper branches; they ripen during the second year and then drop their scales to leave upright sticklike cones.

The Atlas cedar grows well along the coast in Area C and in all parts of Areas D, E, G, I and J. It bears unusual branches that point upward rather than weighing down as do those of most conifers. Rather straggly until it becomes 8 to 10 feet tall at about six years of age, it may reach 40 to 60 feet in gardens in 30 to 40 years. The variety *C. atlantica glauca*, blue Atlas cedar, whose needles are almost electric-arc blue, is more popular than the dark green common type. *C. atlantica glauca pendula*, the weeping blue Atlas cedar, has blue-needled branches that cascade gracefully like a waterfall.

The deodar cedar is suited to Areas D, E, I and J. Native to the Himalayas, its fragrant wood is burned as incense by the Hindus. This species is one of the most graceful evergreens, bearing soft bluish green needles on horizontal branches that bend down at the tips. Even the tip of the central trunk is delicately pendant. The deodar cedar may become 40 to 60 or more feet in height in 30 to 40 years, growing 2 feet or more a year when young. There are also golden-tipped and weeping varieties; the latter must be supported by a stake until they are strong enough to stand alone.

The cedar of Lebanon grows well along the coast in Area C and in Areas D, E, I and J. Native to Asia Minor, its durable wood was used for the timbers of King Solomon's Temple. Its green needles are borne on stiffly horizontal branches. These trees grow slowly, becoming 40 to 60 or more feet tall after 40 to 70 years, and they bear cones only when they are very old. The variety *C. libani stenocoma* is recommended for its cold resistance. There are also dwarf and weeping varieties.

Cedars thrive in full sun in almost any well-drained soil. They are notoriously difficult to transplant except when bought in containers. If you have to purchase balled-and-burlaped trees, plant them in early or late summer. In northernmost sections of their growth areas, cedars are more likely to survive winters if planted on hillsides, which are generally warmer than the lowlands. To shape young trees, cut off branch tips with hand clippers. Regular pruning will thicken the foliage but is seldom necessary.

CEPHALOTAXUS
C. harringtonia, also called *C. drupacea*
(Japanese plum yew, cow's-tail pine)

The Japanese plum yew is a shrubby multistemmed evergreen with dark green 1½-inch needles that are striped with silver underneath and soft to the touch. Although the plum yew may become 30 feet tall in its native Japan, it rarely exceeds 5 to 10 feet in this country after 15 to 20 years in the garden.

The common variety is a round-topped bush with many stems that is excellent for use in a hedge or privacy screen, since its dense leaves grow down to the ground and it is not damaged by regular shearing to control its shape. One variety, *C. harringtonia fastigiata,* grows upright into a column while its needles spiral around the branches; it grows 10 feet tall after 15 to 20 years. The name plum yew is an

CEDAR OF LEBANON
Cedrus libani

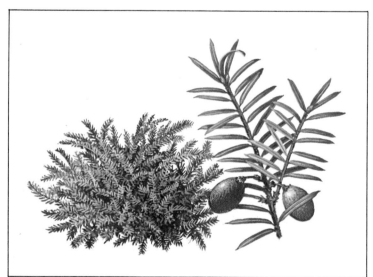

JAPANESE PLUM YEW
Cephalotaxus harringtonia

allusion to the 1-inch plum-shaped purplish to greenish fruit, which requires two years to mature.

Plum yews grow well in areas that have cool, moist summers, such as the coastal sections of Areas C and D, the northern parts of Area E, all of Area I and the coastal sections of Area J. They do best in moist acid soil and partial shade and cannot tolerate hot dry winds. Feed the shrubs once a year in early spring with an organic fertilizer such as cottonseed meal. Pruning should be restricted to trimming occasional branch tips with hand clippers.

CHAMAECYPARIS

C. lawsoniana varieties (Lawson's false cypress, Port Orford cedar, Oregon cedar); *C. obtusa* varieties (hinoki false cypress); *C. pisifera* varieties, also called *Retinispora pisifera* (sawara false cypress)

The wild forms of the three species of false cypress important to gardeners grow so tall they are rarely sold, but each has dozens of varieties of such diverse size and shape that one can be found for nearly any landscaping purpose. Those with bright-colored foliage catch the eye when set alone in the lawn; miniature ones are excellent in rock gardens; others make good screens around a foundation or along a boundary.

Most false cypresses have tiny, soft wedge-shaped leaves that look like scales. Color ranges from rich dark green to bright blue-green and yellow, with many intermediate shades. The cones are tiny and inconspicuous.

The Lawson's false cypress varieties grow well in eastern sections of Areas C and D, as well as in all parts of Areas I and J. *C. lawsoniana allumii*, scarab false cypress, is often used to form a narrow dense hedge. Its vertical sprays of rich blue-green foliage make a compact and narrow conical form. Unpruned plants may become 20 to 30 feet tall after about 40 to 50 years, but close shearing keeps them smaller. *C. lawsoniana ellwoodii*, Ellwood false cypress, has thick soft blue-green foliage. It grows only 6 to 8 feet tall and 2 to 3 feet in diameter after about 10 years. *C. lawsoniana nestoides*, bird's-nest false cypress, has dark green foliage; its spreading branches may become 6 to 8 feet in diameter on a flat-topped plant only 3 to 4 feet tall after 10 years. The foliage of *C. lawsoniana stewartii*, Stewart golden false cypress, has yellow tips in spring, turning dark green later in the year; this color change is especially noticeable on the lower branches. This variety may become a 20- to 30-foot broad cone-shaped tree after 25 to 30 years and should be placed with care because its color demands attention.

Hinoki false cypress varieties grow well in eastern sections of Areas B, C and D, as well as in all parts of Areas I and J. The foliage of the varieties listed here is arranged in cupped twisted sprays. *C. obtusa crippsii*, Cripps golden false cypress, has foliage that is yellow when new, turning dark green later in the year. It is narrow and becomes 20 to 30 feet tall after about 25 years if unpruned. *C. obtusa gracilis*, slender hinoki false cypress, is one of the most ornamental evergreens. Its dense, dark green foliage is set on slender stems that droop at the ends. The narrow, conical plants rarely exceed 6 feet in height in gardens and may be kept smaller by pruning the ends of branches. *C. obtusa nana gracilis*, dwarf hinoki false cypress, is often mislabeled *C. obtusa nana*, the name for a similar but exceptionally slow-growing variety. The dwarf hinoki false cypress has thick dark green foliage. It grows slowly, reaching a height of about 4 feet with a spread of 3 feet after about eight years; it is often used as a bonsai specimen *(page 80)*. Sawara false cypress varieties grow well in eastern sections of Areas B, C and D, as well as in all parts of

SLENDER HINOKI FALSE CYPRESS
Chamaecyparis obtusa gracilis

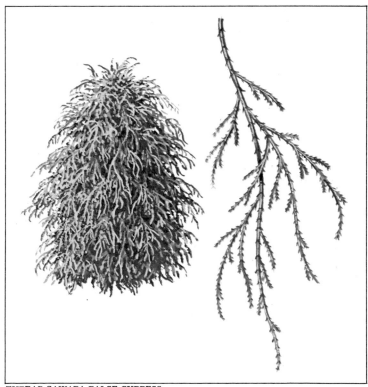

THREAD SAWARA FALSE CYPRESS
Chamaecyparis pisifera filifera

For growing areas, see map on page 149.

MOSS SAWARA FALSE CYPRESS
Chamaecyparis pisifera squarrosa

JAPANESE CEDAR
Cryptomeria japonica

CHINA FIR
Cunninghamia lanceolata

Areas I and J. *C. pisifera* 'Boulevard,' Boulevard sawara false cypress, sometimes labeled *C. pisifera cyanoviridis*, has soft mossy foliage that is silvery green in summer and grayish blue in winter. It becomes 8 feet tall and up to 4 feet wide in 20 years. *C. pisifera filifera*, thread sawara false cypress, has drooping stringy twigs and forms a dense green mound, usually no more than 6 to 8 feet tall after 10 years. A similar variety with golden twigs is *C. pisifera filifera aurea*, golden thread sawara false cypress. *C. pisifera plumosa*, plume sawara false cypress, has bright green foliage in soft feathery sprays. This variety, as well as *C. pisifera plumosa aurea*, golden plume sawara false cypress, may grow 20 to 50 feet tall. As they get old, these latter two varieties may lose some of their lower branches, revealing the shaggy brown bark on the trunks. *C. pisifera squarrosa*, moss sawara false cypress, is broad and conical with soft gray-green foliage. It becomes 20 to 40 feet tall in 20 to 40 years.

False cypresses do best in full sun in rich moist well-drained soil. They thrive in a cool moist atmosphere where they are protected from drying winds. If fast growth is desired, make a single application of an organic fertilizer such as cottonseed meal in the early spring. For compact growth, shape the varieties that have soft foliage with hedge shears in early spring. Prune away long branches on any type of false cypress with clippers at any time.

CRYPTOMERIA
C. japonica (Japanese cedar, cryptomeria),
C. japonica lobbii (Lobb cryptomeria),
C. japonica nana (dwarf Japanese cedar)

A narrow cone in shape, the Japanese cedar has tiny blue-green or bright green needles that hug the branches closely. During the winter the needles take on a bronzy hue, then become green again in the spring. This tree, which is widely used in the temple gardens of Japan and lines some of its stateliest avenues, makes a stunning centerpiece for the lawn, growing to 50 or 60 feet in height after 30 years. Old trees have great charm because the branches are far enough apart to allow the shaggy reddish brown bark on the trunks to be seen (the bark is of practical value, too—when trees are cut down in Japan, the attractive bark is carefully stripped and used for roofing houses and other buildings). Old trees bear globe-shaped cones, about 1 inch in diameter, that cling to the ends of branches for several years. Although Japanese cedars grow 2 to 4 feet a year when young, they are so graceful in shape that they rarely need pruning. The variety *C. japonica lobbii* is a bit hardier and more compact than *C. japonica*. *C. japonica nana*, dwarf Japanese cedar, is mound-shaped and seldom becomes more than 3 feet tall. It is an excellent choice when a low planting is needed; in mild climates, it can be grown for years as a patio tub plant. Its crowded foliage is a rich dark green.

Japanese cedars grow well in the coastal sections of Areas C and D and throughout Areas E, I and J. They do best in deep, moist but well-drained acid soil and should be planted in a sunny location out of the wind.

CUNNINGHAMIA
C. lanceolata, also called *C. sinensis* (China fir)

The China fir is wide and conical with horizontal branches that dip slightly at the tips. Trees may grow 2 to 3 feet a year when young, and will become 20 to 30 feet high after about 15 years. The dense, sharp-pointed 2-inch bladelike needles are shiny green on top with white lines underneath. During cold winters the needles take on a bronze hue. Old trees bear round 2-inch cones, usually in clusters, near the ends of the upper limbs. As a tree ages, the shaggy brown bark peels off the trunk to expose a reddish inner bark.

The China fir grows well in Area D, Area E except from mid-Florida south, Area I and the northern part of Area J. It does best in full sun or light shade and prefers a place sheltered from the wind. Any well-drained acid soil is suitable. Near the northern edge of the areas where the China fir will grow, a severe winter may kill all growth aboveground. Such damage would destroy most other conifers, but the roots of this unique tree will stay alive and send out a number of new shoots when spring arrives. In cases of less drastic damage, when only the tips of branches are killed by an early frost, new cells develop at the edges of the injured areas; these cells throw off the dead tips, and later the same season new shoots appear.

CUPRESSOCYPARIS
C. leylandii (cupressocyparis)

One of the fastest growing of all evergreens, the cupressocyparis often averages 5 feet a year when young. It is narrow and conical with branches thickly covered by blue-green foliage so small it looks scalelike. Cupressocyparis is a good plant for a screen, and is also excellent as a hedge because it tolerates the heavy pruning necessary to maintain a formal shape. Unless pruned, the trees become 50 to 60 feet or more tall after about 30 years; old trees bear round 1-inch cones.

The cupressocyparis is a natural hybrid of *Cupressus macrocarpa*, Monterey cypress, and *Chamaecyparis nootkatensis*, Nootka false cypress or Alaska cedar, plants native to separate parts of the Pacific Coast. The first trees were found in Welshpool, Wales, in 1888 by C. J. Leyland, who had the parent trees growing at Leighton Hall; the Nootka false cypress in this first instance was the female plant bearing the seeds. In 1911 a nephew of Leyland's, Captain J. M. Naylor, raised an identical tree at Leighton Hall, but in this case the cross was reversed and the Monterey cypress was the female. The cupressocyparis grows faster than either of its parents, demonstrating the vigor that is characteristic of hybrid plants.

The cupressocyparis grows well in Areas C, D, E, I and J. It does best in full sun and average soil.

CUPRESSUS
C. arizonica and varieties (Arizona cypress),
C. sempervirens varieties (Italian cypress)

The tiny scalelike aromatic foliage of the cypress grows so close that its twigs resemble heavy braided twine. Cypresses bear round brown cones about 1 inch in diameter even when the trees are young.

Arizona cypress, which withstands drought remarkably well, thrives in Areas G and J and is often used for screens and windbreaks. It has bluish green foliage and becomes a conical tree 35 to 40 feet tall after about 20 years. Three particularly fine varieties are *C. arizonica bonita*, also called *C. glabra*, smooth Arizona cypress, with grayish blue-green foliage; *C. arizonica gareei*, Garee Arizona cypress, with silvery blue-green foliage; and *C. arizonica watersi*, Waters' Arizona cypress, with silvery green foliage.

The famous Italian cypress, native to the Mediterranean region, grows well in coastal sections of Area D, Area E (though not in southern Florida), the southern part of Area G and all of Area J. It is best known in the variety *C. sempervirens stricta*, also called *C. sempervirens fastigiata*, the narrow column of a tree that becomes 20 to 60 feet tall but only 2 or 3 feet wide after 20 to 30 years. It is used alone as an accent plant but also makes a good screen

CUPRESSOCYPARIS
Cupressocyparis leylandii

GAREE ARIZONA CYPRESS
Cupressus arizonica gareei

For growing areas, see map on page 149.

ITALIAN CYPRESS
Cupressus sempervirens stricta

GOLD COAST JUNIPER
Juniperus chinensis aurea 'Gold Coast'

without using up much space. It has somber dark green foliage. Two other excellent varieties, differing mainly in color, are *C. sempervirens glauca*, blue Italian cypress, with bluish green foliage and a very compact habit of growth, and *C. sempervirens indica roylei (C. roylei)*, Royle's Italian cypress, which has bright green foliage.

Cypresses require full sun and a well-drained soil without added fertilizer. They must not be overwatered. They are at their finest where long, hot, dry summers restrict growth, for then the foliage becomes very dense. Cypresses grow 2 feet or more a year when young, sometimes shooting up too fast for the roots so that they must be staked to stay upright in windy locations. Prune only the very young spring growth of Arizona cypresses because old branches do not send out new buds readily after cutting. It is best to use hand shears and cut back to where a side branch is already growing. Italian cypresses rarely need pruning.

CYPRESS See *Cupressus*
CYPRESS, BALD See *Taxodium*
CYPRESS, DECIDUOUS See *Taxodium*
CYPRESS, FALSE See *Chamaecyparis*

D

DEODAR See *Cedrus*

F

FIR See *Abies*
FIR, CHINA See *Cunninghamia*
FIR, DOUGLAS See *Pseudotsuga*
FIR, RED See *Pseudotsuga*

H

HEMLOCK See *Tsuga*

J

JUNIPER See *Juniperus*

JUNIPERUS

J. chinensis varieties (Chinese juniper); *J. communis* varieties (common juniper); *J. conferta*, also called *J. litoralis* (shore juniper); *J. horizontalis* and varieties (creeping juniper); *J. procumbens* and varieties (Japanese garden juniper); *J. sabina* and varieties (savin juniper); *J. scopulorum* and varieties (Rocky Mountain juniper); *J. squamata meyeri* (Meyer juniper); *J. virginiana* and varieties (eastern red cedar)

There are junipers for all parts of the United States and Canada, hot or cold, wet or dry. Creeping forms make carefree ground covers; broad spreading ones are the backbone of most permanent plantings close to the house. Dwarf varieties thrive in rock gardens or in containers on a patio. Tall varieties are handsome as isolated points of interest and are so wind resistant they are among the most satisfactory trees for windbreaks. Some types of junipers grow slowly, only an inch or so a year; others shoot up rapidly, growing a foot or more each season. All varieties respond to pruning so well that it is easy to keep juniper hedges at a desired size for many years.

Junipers bear two kinds of needles, and both may appear on a plant simultaneously. The juvenile foliage is composed of tiny sharp-pointed needles; mature foliage is made up of tiny scalelike needles that cling so closely to twigs that they often seem like twisted twine. In color, the needles vary from the darkest green to light shades of blue and gray. Some varieties become purple during cold weather; others have gold- or white-tipped branches when new growth appears. Junipers are unusual among conifers in being single-sexed plants. A tree is either male or female; the female bears pea-sized bluish gray or green cones with scales so tightly compressed they look like berries. These cones cling for a season or two, according to species.

J. chinensis, the original form of the Chinese juniper, is rarely found in this country, but its many descendants include varieties that are very popular in Areas B, C, D, E, F, G, H, I and J. *J. chinensis aurea* 'Gold Coast,' Gold Coast juniper, is a compact spreading type with gold foliage that deepens in color during cold weather. It grows slowly, and pruning will keep it 12 to 18 inches tall and no more than 4 or 5 feet across indefinitely. *J. chinensis columnaris,* blue column juniper, is a narrow cone with dense blue-green foliage. Unpruned plants may become 15 to 20 feet tall in about 20 years, but they can be kept much smaller by pruning. *J. chinensis hetzii,* Hetz blue juniper, is a rapidly growing, spreading variety with bluish foliage that becomes 6 or more feet tall and 10 feet or more across at age 10 if not pruned. Regular pruning with hand shears is needed to keep this variety under control. *J. chinensis keteleeri,* Keteleer juniper, grows fast into a broad conical tree with bright green foliage and blue berrylike cones. This variety, which may become 20 feet or more tall in 30 years, has an attractively open and graceful habit of growth if not pruned severely; it is best used alone on a lawn or in a screen. *J. chinensis pfitzeriana,* Pfitzer juniper, is one of the fastest growing and most widely used of the spreading varieties. It is one of the few junipers that will tolerate light shade as well as full sun. It has sharp-pointed, feathery gray-green foliage, and if unpruned will become 6 feet tall and 15 feet across in only 10 years. If you use it in a foundation planting, be prepared to prune often with hand clippers to hold it within bounds. *J. chinensis pfitzeriana compacta,* Nick's compact Pfitzer juniper, has denser foliage. It grows slowly, reaching a height of only about 12 inches and a spread of 6 feet in 10 years. *J. chinensis pyramidalis,* pyramidal Chinese juniper, is often sold under the name spiny Greek juniper *(J. excelsa stricta),* which is a different species somewhat similar in appearance but more susceptible to cold. It has sharp blue-gray needles and grows rather slowly, becoming 15 feet or more tall in 15 to 25 years. It forms a graceful broad cone without pruning, but may be shaped lightly with hedge shears. *J. chinensis sargentii,* Sargent juniper, makes a good ground cover. Its branches, covered with steel-blue foliage, rarely grow more than 12 to 15 inches tall but may spread to a diameter of 10 feet in about 10 years. *J. chinensis* 'Kaizuka,' Hollywood juniper, also called *J. chinensis torulosa,* grows into a broad cone shape. Although the main body of its foliage becomes as thick as if it had been sheared, delicately twisted branchlets emerge gracefully all around the plant. It may grow 15 feet tall in 25 years, often leaning to one side in a picturesque manner, and should not be pruned. An attractive type of this variety, *J. chinensis* 'Kaizuka Variegated,' variegated Hollywood juniper, has needles accented with creamy white markings.

The common juniper, *J. communis,* is rarely found in gardens in its basic form, but its varieties grow well in Areas A, B, C, D, E, F, G, H, I and J. *J. communis depressa,* prostrate juniper, has prickly grayish green foliage; it grows 3 to 4 feet tall and may spread to 15 to 20 feet or more in 10 to 15 years. In full size it serves well as a cover for banks, but it can be kept smaller if necessary by removing long branches with hand clippers. *J. communis hibernica (J. communis stricta),* Irish juniper, has dark green needles; *J. communis suecica,* Swedish juniper, has blue-green needles. Both become columns 10 feet or more tall in 15 to 20 years. They can be pruned to 5 or 6 feet by light

BLUE COLUMN JUNIPER
Juniperus chinensis columnaris

HOLLYWOOD JUNIPER
Juniperus chinensis 'Kaizuka'

For growing areas, see map on page 149.

97

shearing with hedge shears, which also encourages dense foliage. Where wind or heavy snow may pull branches away from their normally tight, erect pattern of growth, the inner branches can be tied in place unobtrusively with green plastic-covered wire.

Shore juniper rarely exceeds 1 foot in height, but spreads a blanket of soft, bright green foliage to a diameter of 6 to 8 feet in 15 to 20 years. It is ideal for seaside planting as a ground cover, growing well in Areas C, D, E, G, I and J. Remove unwanted branches with hand clippers.

Creeping juniper and its varieties grow well in Areas A, B, C, D, F, G, H, I and J. They are effective as ground covers and may grow to a diameter of 10 feet in about 10 years if unpruned. They are sometimes pruned to a low tree shape so the trailing stems cascade from the top of a short upright trunk. All should be pruned with hand clippers only. *J. horizontalis* 'Bar Harbor,' 1 foot tall, has steel-blue foliage that becomes plum-purple in the winter. *J. horizontalis douglasii,* Waukegan juniper, 1 foot tall, has blue-green summer foliage that turns purplish in the winter. *J. horizontalis plumosa,* Andorra juniper, 15 to 18 inches tall, has feathery gray-green foliage that becomes pinkish purple in cold weather. *J. horizontalis wiltonii,* Wilton carpet juniper, also called blue rug, 4 inches tall, has silvery blue foliage all year.

The Japanese garden juniper grows well in Areas C, D, F, G, H, I and J. It has blue-green needles and becomes about 2 feet tall and up to 10 feet or more across in 10 years. Remove unwanted branches with hand clippers. The compact dwarf variety, *J. procumbens nana,* has rich blue-green needles that turn purplish in cold weather; mature plants rarely exceed 1 foot in height and may become 4 to 5 feet across in 10 to 20 years. Both forms are excellent ground covers; the dwarf variety is especially suited for rock gardens and the front of foundation plantings.

Savin juniper grows well in Areas B, C, D, E, F, G, H, I and J, and will stand alkaline soil as well as the poor growing conditions of city gardens better than most evergreens. It has rich dark green needles and is low and bushy with gracefully arching branch tips. It becomes about 4 feet tall and up to 10 feet across in about 10 years. Pruning should be done by removing long branches with hand clippers. Two low, spreading varieties make excellent ground covers: *J. sabina* 'Buffalo' has bright green needles and grows 12 inches tall and about 8 feet across in about 10 years; *J. sabina tamariscifolia,* tamarix juniper, has thick feathery blue-green foliage and grows about 18 inches tall and 10 to 15 feet across in 15 to 20 years.

Rocky Mountain juniper and its varieties grow well in Areas C, D, F, G, H, I and J. Prune with hand clippers to remove long branches; it can also be pruned to a desired shape with hedge shears. Outstanding varieties include Blue Heaven, also called Blue Haven, a cone with very dense deep blue-green foliage that becomes about 20 feet tall in 15 to 20 years. Gray Gleam has gray-green foliage and grows slowly into a column 15 to 20 feet tall in 30 to 40 years. Lakewood Globe has blue-green foliage and becomes a globe 4 to 6 feet in diameter in about 10 years. Pathfinder has dense blue-gray foliage and grows into a narrow cone about 20 feet tall in 15 to 20 years. Table Top Blue is a flat-topped variety with silvery blue foliage; it becomes 5 to 6 feet tall and 8 feet across in about 10 years.

Meyer juniper grows well in Areas B, C, D, F, G, H, I and J. Its old foliage is a rich blue-green color, but is often accentuated by the pinkish tones of new growth. The Meyer juniper sends out gracefully ascending branch tips in such a way that the plant often has an unbalanced, aged effect. Because this unique branching is one of their greatest

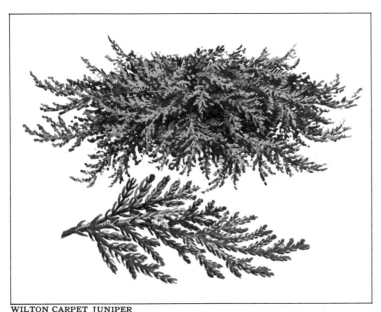

WILTON CARPET JUNIPER
Juniperus horizontalis wiltonii

TAMARIX JUNIPER
Juniperus sabina tamariscifolia

charms, the plants should be left unpruned if possible. They become 6 to 8 feet tall and 2 to 3 feet in diameter after about 15 years.

Eastern red cedar grows well in Areas A, B, C, D, E, F, G, H, I and J. Its naturally compact habit can be accentuated by light shearing with hedge shears. For a more informal outline, remove erratically long branches with hand clippers. *J. virginiana canaertii,* Canaert red cedar, bears rich dark green tufted foliage set off by heavy crops of pale blue berries. It becomes a cone about 20 feet tall in about 15 years. Unlike most eastern red cedars, which turn brownish in cold weather, this species holds its rich green color all winter. The variety Hillspire is narrow and has dense bright green foliage throughout the year. It grows to about 15 to 20 feet in about 10 years. Manhattan Blue has blue-green foliage and is very compact; it rarely exceeds 10 to 15 feet after 15 years. Silver Spreader is a spreading form of *J. virginiana* with silvery green foliage; it becomes about 18 inches tall and 6 to 8 feet across in about 15 years. *J. virginiana pyramidalis hillii,* Dundee juniper, narrowly conical and slow growing, becomes 8 to 12 feet tall in about 10 years. Its compact foliage is grayish green in summer and becomes purple in cold weather.

All junipers do best in full sun with well-drained soil. They tolerate both acid and alkaline soil conditions and are tough enough to grow in dry rocky soil.

L

LARCH See *Larix*
LARCH, GOLDEN See *Pseudolarix*

LARIX

L. decidua and varieties (European larch); *L. laricina* (eastern larch or tamarack); *L. leptolepis,* also called *L. kaempferi* (Japanese larch)

Larches are not real evergreens—they lose their foliage during the winter—and in strict terms they are classed as deciduous trees. But they are more closely related botanically and in garden usage to evergreens than they are to other deciduous trees. They are narrowly conical in shape when young, becoming broad with age, with horizontal or slightly ascending branches. Even in winter, when bare of foliage, they provide an interesting pattern against a background of evergreen conifers. Their soft 1-inch needles are bright green from early spring through summer; in the fall they turn a glowing golden yellow on branches more than one year old. The needles are arranged in tufts on short spurs that line the branches; on new branches the needles are arranged spirally down the stems. When young, larches often grow 2 to 3 feet a year. After trees become about 20 years old, they bear 1-inch brown cones that stand upright on the branches for several years and add to the winter interest of the trees. The cones are preceded in early spring by showy reddish purple female flowers about ½ inch tall that sit atop the branches (the male blossoms are separate and inconspicuous).

The European larch grows well in Areas A, B, C, F, H and I. It becomes 30 to 60 feet tall after 15 to 40 years in the garden. The variety *L. decidua pendula,* weeping European larch, has gracefully hanging branches. The eastern larch or tamarack grows well in Areas A, B, C, F, H and I. It becomes 40 to 60 feet tall after about 30 years in the garden. The Japanese larch grows well in Areas B, C, F, H and I. It becomes 60 or more feet tall in the garden after about 40 years. The branches and trunk of the Japanese larch present an interesting two-toned appearance. Bark on young branches is reddish, as is the inner bark of older wood; the reddish color shows through as the outer brown

CANAERT RED CEDAR
Juniperus virginiana canaertii

JAPANESE LARCH
Larix leptolepis

For growing areas, see map on page 149.

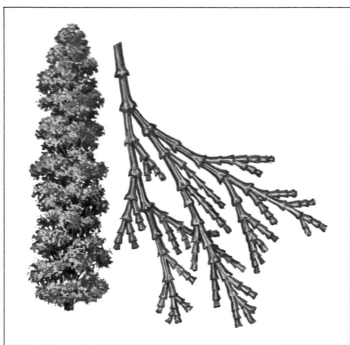

CALIFORNIA INCENSE CEDAR
Libocedrus decurrens

DAWN REDWOOD
Metasequoia glyptostroboides

bark splits to accommodate the tree's increasing girth.

In forests larches often grow in wet or even boggy locations, but they thrive in almost any moist garden soil. They grow best in full sun, but survive shade a few hours of the day. The less pruning the better, but no harm is done if long branches are removed with hand clippers to make trees symmetrical, or if lower branches are cut off to provide walking space beneath old trees. All pruning should be done in midsummer when trees heal most quickly.

LIBOCEDRUS
L. decurrens, also called *Calocedrus decurrens*
(California incense cedar)

The California incense cedar, which may grow 2 feet a year when young, may become a narrow cone shape 50 to 70 feet tall after 30 to 50 years in the garden. It is best used in a tall thin screen or set singly or in a small group as a lawn centerpiece. The aromatic needles, shiny dark green and scalelike, cling closely to small vertical branches. The branches do not drop off and even on old trees reach to the ground if not shaded by other trees. Old trees have cinnamon-red furrowed bark and bear ¾-inch brownish cones hanging near the ends of their branches. This species grows well in Areas C, D, E, I and J. It thrives in either full sun or light shade if given moist soil, but will not do well in smoggy or windswept locations. Pruning is rarely necessary because of the naturally compact growth.

M
METASEQUOIA
M. glyptostroboides (dawn redwood)

Until 1945 the dawn redwood was known only in the form of fossils collected by paleobotanists and was thought to have been extinct for perhaps a million years. After it was discovered alive and well in the remote village of Mo-tao-chi in the Chinese province of Szechwan, the Arnold Arboretum of Boston sent a special expedition to the area. The seeds collected were shared with other botanical gardens around the world, and this deciduous conifer is now widely available from nurserymen. Mature trees in China are broadly conical and grow about 100 feet tall from thick buttressed roots. Presumably they will eventually attain a similar size in this country—young plants grow 3 feet or more a year—making them too tall for the average garden. On a large lawn, however, they can attract attention not only for their history but for their foliage. Soft, bright green needles, about ¾ inch long, appear in early spring, then turn pinkish brown before falling in the autumn. Brown cones ¾ inch long ripen each year.

Dawn redwood grows well in Areas B, C, D, E, I and J. It thrives in full sun in almost any moist soil. Because it tends to continue growing until late in the summer, it should be planted in a location not subject to early frosts —such as on a hillside rather than in a valley. Growth is symmetrical and pruning is not necessary.

MONKEY PUZZLE See *Araucaria*

P
PICEA
P. abies and varieties (Norway spruce), *P. engelmanni* (Engelmann's spruce), *P. glauca* and varieties (white spruce), *P. omorika* (Serbian or Servian spruce), *P. orientalis* (Oriental spruce), *P. pungens* and varieties (Colorado spruce)

Spruces are forest trees common through much of the Northern Hemisphere. Naturally symmetrical, they have the typical cone shape associated with Christmas trees.

Though they may grow 1 to 2 feet a year when young and become 75 feet or more tall after 60 to 75 years, spruces are useful in small gardens if you are aware that they might have to be removed later. Often this decision is not difficult because the trees begin to lose lower limbs after 20 years or so if they are shaded by other trees.

Spruces are at their finest grown free-standing in an open space where their natural beauty will increase as the years pass. They also make superb windbreaks and privacy screens where there is space enough for such large spreading trees. In areas such as the plains of the north central states and central Canada, spruces tolerate constant wind and become living barriers behind which farmsteads nestle. They can also serve as hedges in smaller yards if pruned regularly. For use near a house, in rock gardens and in other locations where space is restricted, there are many slow-growing dwarf varieties that never grow more than 3 to 5 feet tall.

Spruces have a dense appearance because their needles cling for many years and accumulate to thicken the foliage. The needles are square in cross section, stiff, sharp-pointed and variable in size, ranging from ½ to 1½ inches in length. Their color ranges from bright green through bluish green to bright blue and dark green. Cones, usually brown, are 2 to 6 inches long; they hang down from the branches and fall in one piece late in the year, after the scales open and let the seeds drift away in the wind.

The Norway spruce grows well in Areas A, B, C, D, F, H and I. It is a fast-growing, inexpensive cone-shaped tree with very dark green needles. It may become 75 feet or more tall after 50 years in the garden. *P. abies pendula,* weeping Norway spruce, has extremely pendulous branches as well as a drooping central stem, or leader, growing from the top of the trunk. It grows 50 feet tall in about 70 years. Over the hundreds of years that *P. abies* has been cultivated, a number of dwarf forms have appeared spontaneously; most attain a height of only 2½ to 4 feet, with a spread of 12 to 15 feet, after 30 to 40 years. Sometimes a normal shoot appears from amid the dwarf growth and must be removed before it takes over and attains treelike proportions. Three excellent dwarf varieties are *P. abies clanbrassiliana,* Barry spruce, *P. abies maxwellii,* Maxwell spruce, and *P. abies nidiformis,* bird's-nest spruce.

Engelmann's spruce grows well in Areas A, B, C, F, H and I, becoming 50 or more feet tall after 40 to 60 years in the garden. It has a narrowly conical outline and ascending branches that start at ground level. They are densely covered with blue-green needles.

The white spruce grows well in Areas A, B, C, F, H and I. The wild species is sometimes used in windbreaks and privacy screens, but two of its varieties are more common as garden ornaments. *P. glauca conica,* the dwarf Alberta spruce, was discovered in 1904 at Lake Laggan, Alberta, by professors J. G. Jack and Alfred Rehder of Boston's Arnold Arboretum. This species is a natural dwarf that becomes broadly conical and about 7 feet tall in 15 to 20 years. The tightly set, light green needles are about ½ inch long. The plant grows slowly, only 1 to 4 inches a year. *P. glauca densata,* Black Hills spruce, is a slow-growing conical variety, which becomes 20 to 40 feet tall after 40 to 80 years. It is widely used for screens, windbreaks and hedges in the plains states because it withstands wind, heat, cold, drought and crowding.

The Serbian spruce grows well in Areas B, C, F, H and I, becoming a narrow, conical tree 50 to 60 feet tall after about 60 years. Its lower branches dip deeply near the trunk, then rise toward the tips in a graceful curve.

The Oriental spruce grows well in Areas B, C, H and I,

DWARF ALBERTA SPRUCE
Picea glauca conica

SERBIAN SPRUCE
Picea omorika

MOERHEIM COLORADO SPRUCE
Picea pungens moerheimii

For growing areas, see map on page 149.

SWISS STONE PINE
Pinus cembra

TANYOSHO PINE
Pinus densiflora umbraculifera

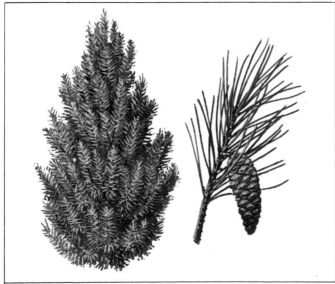

ALEPPO PINE
Pinus halepensis

becoming 50 to 60 feet tall after about 80 years. It is one of the most beautiful of spruces, with glistening dark green needles and an open, graceful conical profile.

The Colorado spruce, of a broader conical shape, grows well in Areas A, B, C, F, H and I, becoming 50 or more feet tall after 35 to 50 years in the garden. Seedlings vary in color from dark green to steel blue. Nurserymen usually charge more for the blue-foliaged seedlings, known botanically as *P. pungens glauca,* Colorado blue spruce; among those with the most distinctive blue color are Moerheim, Koster and Hoops blue spruces. A weeping blue variety is *P. pungens pendens (P. pungens kosteriana),* Koster weeping blue spruce.

Spruces do best in full sun. They grow well in moist ground, yet are able to survive in light dry soil if they are watered frequently for the first few years while their roots become established. Pruning of individual trees is rarely necessary because of their natural symmetry. An occasional wayward branch can be removed with hand clippers; if more than one central stem, or leader, develops, it should be removed with hand clippers also. Spruce hedges can be controlled by pruning them in either of two ways. The easy method is to shape them with hedge shears in early spring so that the stiff stubs of the branches will be quickly covered by new growth. The second way is to reach into the tree and remove selected branches with hand clippers; stubs will be concealed by other branches so the outline is always soft and natural rather than stiff and formal.

PINE See *Pinus*
PINE, AUSTRALIAN See *Casuarina*
PINE, NORFOLK ISLAND See *Araucaria*
PINE, UMBRELLA See *Sciadopitys*

PINUS
P. aristata (bristlecone pine, hickory pine); *P. canariensis* (Canary Island pine); *P. caribaea* (slash pine); *P. cembra* (Swiss stone pine); *P. densiflora umbraculifera* (Tanyosho pine, table pine); *P. halepensis* (Aleppo pine); *P. mugo mugo,* also called *P. montana mugo* (mugo pine, Swiss mountain pine); *P. nigra,* also called *P. austriaca* (Austrian pine, black pine); *P. ponderosa scopulorum* (ponderosa pine, Rocky Mountain yellow pine); *P. resinosa* (red pine, Norway pine); *P. strobus* (eastern white pine, Weymouth pine); *P. sylvestris* (Scots pine, Scotch pine); *P. thunbergii* (Japanese black pine)

Pines are the predominant conifers of the Northern Hemisphere; 40 species are native to North America alone, and some of them are bound to thrive wherever you live. Most are broad conical shapes when young, but their tops round with age. Although most pines become 40 to 80 feet tall in 20 to 50 years, there are slow growing and dwarf types suitable for the smallest garden. Branches grow down to the ground when the trees are in the open, but the lower branches can be cut off if you wish to provide a shady sitting or walking space. Often the shade beneath pines is so dense that grass will not grow, but grass is not needed: the fallen needles make a superbly resilient brown mulch that serves as a practical ground cover, sturdy enough for normal use. The graceful symmetry of pines makes them beautiful ornamental trees when planted in open lawns where there is room for them to develop. They are also excellent for use in tall screens and windbreaks. Low-growing types such as the mugo pine and dwarf varieties of the white pine are often set in front of foundations. Even the white pines that grow very tall in the forest can be kept to hedge size for years if their new shoots, called candles, are cut back part way in the spring *(page 54).*

The distinctive needles of pines are usually borne in clusters of two to five, called bundles, each wrapped around at the base with a papery sheath. The individual needles vary in length from the 1 inch of the bristlecone pine to the 9 to 12 inches of the Canary Island pine. Pine flowers are not conspicuous. They are followed by brown cones, most of which take two or three years to ripen and may cling to the branches for several years after ripening.

The bristlecone pine grows in Areas A, B, C, F, H, I and J. Specimens of this species still alive after more than 7,000 years—thought to be the oldest living plants on earth, even older than the giant sequoias—have been discovered growing in the White Mountains of California. The bristlecone grows very slowly and rarely becomes more than 8 to 20 feet tall after 10 years in the garden. It has dense dark blue-green needles and is often miniaturized for a bonsai planting or grown in a container on a patio.

The Canary Island pine grows in Areas E and J. It is fast growing (3 or more feet a year when young), eventually reaching 70 to 80 feet after 30 to 40 years in the garden. It has hanging grass-green needles 9 to 12 inches long.

The slash pine is suited to Area E and will tolerate both moist and dry soils. Fast growing (3 feet or more a year), this species will eventually reach 70 to 100 feet. Its shiny dark green needles become 8 to 12 inches long.

The Swiss stone pine grows in Areas A, B, C, H and I. Its dense dark blue-green needles, compact conical growth, and slow rate of growth (a foot or less a year) make it suitable for small gardens; it rarely becomes taller than 25 feet even after 25 or 30 years.

The Tanyosho pine, which has blue-green needles, is recommended for Areas B, C, H and I. Its shape is unusual —a flat toadstoollike form noticeable even when the tree is very small. Trees 3 feet tall have an equal spread; after many years the plants may reach a height and breadth of 10 or 12 feet. They are useful in rock gardens because they can be kept quite small indefinitely with pruning.

The Aleppo pine grows well in Areas E and J and will tolerate heat, drought and windy seaside conditions. Its needles are light green. Fast growing (3 to 5 feet a year), this species becomes 30 to 50 feet tall after about 8 to 15 years in the garden.

The mugo pine grows well in Areas A, B, C, F, H and I and is one of the few pines that will tolerate light shade. Some plants in this species never become more than 2 to 3 feet tall but spread 8 to 10 feet across; others may become 8- to 10-foot-tall mounds of bristly bright green needles.

The Austrian pine does well in Areas B, C, D, F, H and I. Notable for its stiff black-green needles, this species is unusually resistant to harm from the polluted air of cities, as well as from drought, heat, cold, alkaline soil and seaside conditions. It grows fast when young (about 2 feet a year), becoming 35 to 50 feet tall after 20 to 30 years.

The ponderosa pine, which has dark green needles, grows well in Areas F, G, H, I and J and will tolerate alkaline soils and drought. Fast growing when young if given ample moisture, this species becomes 75 feet or more tall after 40 to 50 years in garden.

The red pine thrives in Areas A, B, C, H and I and will tolerate both wet and dry soils. Despite its name, it has long, flexible, dark green needles. Fast growing when young (2 feet a year), the red pine becomes about 50 feet tall after 25 to 30 years in the garden. (The often-used name for this species, Norway pine, can also be misleading; it was given these trees because so many of them grow wild in the vicinity of Norway, Maine.)

The eastern white pine is suited to Areas B, C, D, H and I and is another that will tolerate light shade. It has soft

MUGO PINE
Pinus mugo mugo

RED PINE
Pinus resinosa

For growing areas, see map on page 149.

103

EASTERN WHITE PINE
Pinus strobus

JAPANESE BLACK PINE
Pinus thunbergii

blue-green 3-inch needles. It grows fast when young (2 feet a year), becoming 50 to 75 feet or more tall in gardens in 25 to 40 years. There are two varieties of special merit: *P. strobus fastigiata,* pyramidal eastern white pine, which is really columnar and not pyramidal and becomes 20 feet tall after 12 to 15 years, and *P. strobus nana,* dwarf eastern white pine, which grows very slowly to form a soft tight mound 1 to 2 feet tall and 2 to 4 feet across.

The Scotch pine grows well in Areas A, B, C, D, F, H and I and tolerates wet or dry soil. It has stiff blue-green needles and flaking orange-brown bark on upper limbs. Fast growing when young (2 feet a year), this species eventually becomes 40 to 70 feet tall in gardens and often takes on a picturesquely crooked shape. *P. sylvestris fastigiata,* pyramidal Scotch pine, is again not pyramidal but narrowly columnar, and *P. sylvestris nana,* dwarf Scotch pine, is a low-growing mound-shaped variety.

The Japanese black pine is recommended for Areas B, C, D, G, I and J. Especially useful for windy seaside locations, this species also tolerates drought and is often grown in containers or miniaturized for bonsai plantings. Its foliage is deep rich green and the bark is black. It grows fast when young (1 to 2 feet a year), attaining an irregular, graceful outline that often makes it seem to be older than it is. Trees vary from 20 to 80 feet in height after 10 to 40 years in the garden.

Pines must have abundant sunlight and do best when planted in well-drained soil that is not especially rich in nutrients. Rocky, sandy, problem soils unsuited for most other plants will often serve pines because in such a location they grow slowly and become compact, densely needled specimens. Pines do not need fertilizer, nor is it necessary to add more than a small amount (¼ by bulk) of peat moss when initially preparing the soil for planting. Pruning will restrict the growth of pines and make them bushy. The easiest and most successful way to prune them is to pinch off part of the central candles of new growth in the spring after they have attained up to one third of their normal growth *(page 54).* More severe pruning may be done by clipping off the ends of branches to a point where side branches originate *(page 50).* It is possible to shear pines to create a formal outline, but shearing leaves stiff stubs unless it is done as new spring growth is just getting underway.

PLATYCLADUS See *Thuja*

PODOCARPUS
P. elongatus, P. gracilior (both called fern podocarpus); *P. macrophyllus* (yew podocarpus)

Podocarpuses are to mild-climate gardens what yews are to colder areas. They are related plants and much alike in appearance; both have soft needles and are superior evergreens for most home uses. Podocarpuses generally grow erect, with ascending branches and a broad columnar shape. They are widely grown as tub plants for patios in warm climates and as indoor foliage plants elsewhere. The new needles are always several shades lighter green than mature ones, resulting in an interesting color variation during the growing season. The ½-inch purplish fruit is practically unnoticeable among the foliage.

The two species of fern podocarpus grow well in Areas E and J. They are so similar that their names are often interchanged by nurserymen. They have 1- to 2-inch, ⅛-inch-wide dark green or gray-green needles thickly set on drooping branches, and become 25 to 60 feet tall after 20 to 50 years in the garden.

The yew podocarpus is suited to Areas D, E, I and J. Its

¼ to ½ inch wide, are dark ~~~~~~~~~ height of 20 to 30 feet
in ~~~~~~~~~~~~ *us maki,* shrubby or
Chinese ~~~~~~~~~~~~~ parts than other
plants of the ~~~~~~~~~~~~ o 12 feet tall,
it is useful where s~

Podocarpuses grow b~~~~~~~~~~~~~ il. They
thrive in full sun or light sh~~~~~~~~~~~ refer-
able where summers are hot. The~~~~~~~~~~ inst
a sunny wall because they suffer from~~~~~~~~ Fertilizer is usually not required, but if the~~~~~ become
pale, scatter a light dusting of cottonsee~~~~~ l on the
ground beneath the plants in the spring. Podc rpuses can
be pruned with hedge shears, but it is preferable to remove unwanted branches selectively from inside the plant
with hand clippers to avoid a shorn appearance.

PSEUDOLARIX
P. ambilis, also called *P. kaempferi, Chrysolarix amabilis*
(golden larch)

The golden larch, found growing in a tub in a Chinese
garden in 1850, is an anomaly—a needled conifer that is
not truly evergreen but drops its needles every year (it is
nonetheless treated as an evergreen by gardeners). It grows
so slowly that the oldest tree in the United States is, after
100 years, only 45 feet tall and of equal spread. It bears
feathery, bright green 2-inch needles in clusters along horizontal branches that are more than one year old; on new
branches the needles are arranged spirally. The needles appear in early spring and yellow just before falling in
autumn. The 3-inch cones stand erect on the branches.

The golden larch grows well in Areas B, C and I. It
thrives in moist, well-drained acid soil in full sun but needs
protection from wind. It can live for many years in a container, and is easily miniaturized for a bonsai planting. In
the garden the golden larch looks most dramatic when
planted where its handsome autumn foliage will be seen
against a background of dark green conifers.

PSEUDOTSUGA
P. menziesii, also called *P. douglasii, P. mucronata,*
P. taxifolia (Douglas fir, Douglas spruce, red fir)

As the variety of names for this tree indicates, its proper botanical classification has long been a matter of dispute.
Not a true fir of the genus *Abies,* although once considered
one, the Douglas fir has finally been classed as *Pseudotsuga,* false hemlock, adding still more confusion, for it is
not a hemlock. Regardless of its scientific name, the Douglas fir is one of the most useful of narrow-leaved evergreens.
It has densely set 1-inch aromatic blue-green needles, which
are soft and pleasant to the touch. Broadly conical in shape,
it grows 40 to 100 feet tall after 50 to 75 years in the garden, shooting up 1 to 2 feet a year when young. It is
valuable in tall screens or hedges for it tolerates shearing
well, and alone it makes a handsome lawn ornament. Old
trees bear 4-inch hanging brown cones. Because the Douglas fir's needles cling to the branches long after the tree
has been cut, it is often grown for use as a Christmas tree.

Douglas firs vary in cold resistance, depending on the
source of the seeds, which are gathered from wild trees.
Those from coastal sections of the Northwest grow well
only as far north as Area C. Seeds from trees native to the
high Rockies yield plants hardy in Areas A and B as well,
and most nursery-grown plants are started from seeds from
this area. Such hardy trees are sometimes known as *P. menziesii glauca* because they have a deeper blue color than
trees from other areas.

Douglas firs do best in full sun with moist but well-

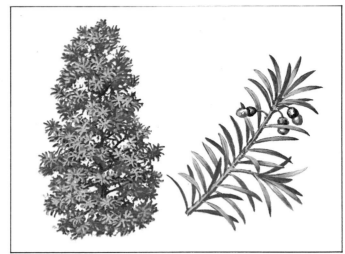
YEW PODOCARPUS
Podocarpus macrophyllus

GOLDEN LARCH
Pseudolarix amabilis

DOUGLAS FIR
Pseudotsuga taxifolia

For growing areas, see map on page 149.

UMBRELLA PINE
Sciadopitys verticillata

GIANT SEQUOIA
Sequoiadendron giganteum

drained soil. If the trees are used in a hedge, prune them with hedge shears in early spring before growth begins.

R

REDWOOD, DAWN See *Metasequoia*
RETINOSPORA See *Chamaecyparis*

S

SCIADOPITYS

S. verticillata (umbrella pine)

The umbrella pine is thought to be the last remaining survivor of a group of similar plants long extinct. It grows exceedingly slowly, about 6 inches a year. Trees 50 years old are only 25 to 30 feet tall with a symmetrical, narrowly conical profile. The common name is an allusion to the soft dark green needles, 5 to 6 inches long, which are arranged on twigs in whorls like the ribs of an umbrella. Old trees bear erect 3- to 5-inch cones that take two years to ripen. This is a collector's tree, a choice lawn specimen.

The umbrella pine is suited to Areas C, D, I and J. It grows best in moist, neutral-to-acid soil in full sun and does not prosper in dry sandy places. Late afternoon shade is advantageous in hot areas; wind protection is desirable. If the foliage becomes yellow-green, scatter a light application of cottonseed meal under the tree in early spring. Pruning is rarely necessary, but if a tree sprouts two top vertical branches, prune off one.

SEQUOIA See *Sequoiadendron*

SEQUOIADENDRON

S. giganteum, also called *Sequoia gigantea*
(giant sequoia, big tree)

The giant sequoia is famous for its immense size—some old trees are more than 300 feet tall and 35 feet in trunk diameter at the base. It makes a striking lawn ornament for many years but you may have to remove it when it outgrows your garden. When young, the giant sequoia forms a symmetrical conical tree with handsome blue-green needles, ½ inch long, that cling closely to the branches. Given good care, it grows 2 to 3 feet a year. Old trees bear 1-inch hanging cones that remain on the trees for several years after seeds have fallen from them.

The giant sequoia grows well in Areas I and J and, if it is given painstaking care, it will survive in coastal sections of Areas C and D. Despite the fact that it is native to the Sierra Nevada of California, where the snow may be over 20 feet deep, and that fine specimens grow near the eastern coast as far north as Massachusetts, the giant sequoia is not able to cope successfully with the vagaries of winter in most of the northern states. It does best in full sun in any moist soil. Pruning is not necessary.

SPRUCE See *Picea*
SPRUCE, DOUGLAS See *Pseudotsuga*

T

TAMARACK See *Larix*

TAXODIUM

T. distichum (bald cypress)

The bald cypress, a deciduous tree that, like the larch, is generally treated as an evergreen, is among the few conifers that will thrive in very wet or swampy areas. It is native to the East Coast from Delaware to Florida, west to Texas and north in the Mississippi Valley to southern Illinois. Round-topped and more than 100 feet tall in forests, it usually becomes 50 to 70 feet tall in gardens in about 30 to 50 years. Its shape is broadly conical while young, becoming flat-topped at maturity. The needles are about ½ inch long, light green and feathery from spring until autumn, when they become orange yellow and fall from the tree. Old trees bear round 1-inch cones.

Bald cypress grows well in Areas B, C, D, E, G, I and J. It is especially vigorous in wet soil beside a pond or stream, but will do well in well-drained garden soil if the soil is acid. Full sun is necessary. Pruning is not required.

TAXUS
T. baccata and varieties (English yew), *T. canadensis stricta* (upright Canada yew), *T. cuspidata* and varieties (Japanese yew), *T. media* varieties (intermediate yew, Anglo-Japanese yew)

Yews are grown by the millions throughout most of the northern two thirds of the country, for they are among the most versatile and satisfactory of all narrow-leaved evergreens for general use on home grounds, large or small. Yews grow in every conceivable shape; some creep only inches above the ground while others achieve upright forms that are nearly treelike. Between these extremes there are globular, columnar, conical and bushy yews—more than 100 different kinds are available nationwide. Yews grow very slowly when young—five-year-old plants of good varieties are usually only 10 to 12 inches tall—and they may seem expensive, but they are gilt-edged investments because they will last indefinitely with proper maintenance. (Some yew hedges in England are over 300 years old.)

The yews' most compelling feature is their rich green shiny needles, soft, slender, flat and about ¾ inch long, arranged featherlike along the branches. Some varieties have golden-tipped twigs, but such a spectacular plant should ordinarily be reserved for use where a single accent is needed. Yews bear male and female flowers on separate plants. Both males and females are necessary if berries are to appear, and then only the female plants of some varieties bear the fruit—½ inch in diameter, red and pulpy around a central seed. (The seeds are poisonous, as are the bark and the foliage.)

The English yew grows well in the eastern parts of Areas C and D and throughout Areas I and J. Among the varieties commonly grown is *T. baccata adpressa,* shortleaf English yew, a bushy slow-growing type that has needles about ½ inch long and bears fruit. Although it may become 5 to 6 feet tall after many years, it can be kept smaller by pruning. *T. baccata stricta,* Irish yew, is one of the most impressive of all yews. Tightly covered with dark green needles, it is narrowly columnar when young, becoming oval in profile with age. After about 20 years in the garden it becomes 10 to 12 feet tall, retaining an erect shape. *T. baccata stricta aurea,* golden Irish yew, is similar, but newly sprouted tips are golden yellow. Both bear berries. *T. baccata repandens,* spreading English yew, grows well as far north as the southern part of Area B. Plants 3 to 5 feet wide grow 12 to 18 inches tall; old plants may reach a diameter of 8 to 10 feet if left unpruned and become 4 to 5 feet tall. They, too, bear fruit.

The upright Canada yew is suited to Areas A, B, C, H and I. It becomes 2 to 4 feet tall with a similar spread and is extremely resistant to cold. It is useful only in shade, however, and even there turns brownish in the winter. Fruit production is sparse and undependable.

The Japanese yew grows well throughout Areas B, C, F, H, I and in the northern part of Area D. The type sold as *T. cuspidata* or *T. cuspidata expansa* is a relatively fast-growing (12 to 18 inches a year) spreading shrub; it becomes 15 to 20 feet across with a height of 10 to 15 feet

BALD CYPRESS
Taxodium distichum

SPREADING ENGLISH YEW
Taxus baccata repandens

IRISH YEW
Taxus baccata stricta

For growing areas, see map on page 149.

UPRIGHT JAPANESE YEW
Taxus cuspidata capitata

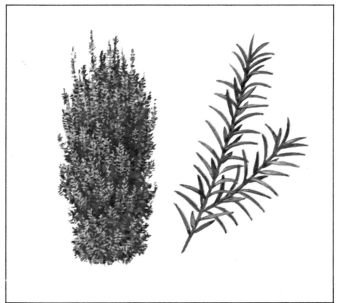

HICKS YEW
Taxus media hicksii

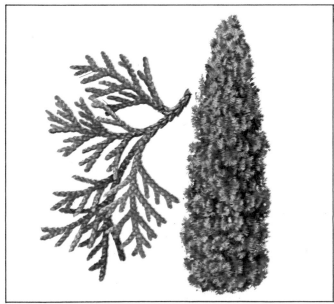

DOUGLAS ARBORVITAE
Thuja occidentalis douglasii pyramidalis

in about 12 to 15 years if unpruned. Both fruiting and non-fruiting plants are available. The more useful *T. cuspidata nana,* dwarf Japanese yew, has a growth rate, needle length and ultimate size about half that of other Japanese yews. It bears berries prolifically. *T. cuspidata capitata,* upright Japanese yew, available in both fruiting and nonfruiting plants, is a relatively fast-growing type whose shape is broadly conical. If unpruned it may become 20 feet or more tall after 16 to 20 years in the garden. Like the spreading Japanese yew, this variety requires considerable regular pruning to keep it small enough for most gardens. *T. cuspidata densa,* dense spreading Japanese yew, a slow-growing variety with abundant fruit, becomes 8 feet across and about 4 feet tall in 12 to 15 years if unpruned.

Intermediate yew is the name given to a number of hybrids between English and Japanese yews that grow well throughout Areas B, C, F, H, I and in the northern part of Area D. Their deep green color and definite, dependable shape make them extremely useful. They require little care, and many varieties are exceptionally resistant to cold. *T. media brownii,* Brown's yew, which bears no fruit, is globular in outline and has a moderate growth rate, becoming 9 feet tall and 12 feet across in about 15 to 20 years if unpruned. *T. media hatfieldii,* Hatfield's yew, a nonfruiting variety, is broadly conical in shape, becoming 12 feet tall and 10 feet across after about 20 years if unpruned. *T. media hicksii,* Hicks yew, which bears fruit, is column-shaped with many ascending branches and exceptionally dark green foliage. It becomes 20 feet tall after 15 to 20 years in the garden. *T. media kelseyi,* Kelsey's yew, famous for the great quantities of its fruit, is erect and bushy, becoming 12 feet tall and 9 feet across in 12 to 15 years.

Yews flourish in any light from full sun to fairly deep shade and do best in well-drained slightly acid fertile soil with an even supply of moisture. They cannot tolerate locations where water stands for any length of time, and even soggy subsoil will limit their growth. To maintain their rich color it is usually necessary to fertilize yews. A single annual application of 5-10-5 garden fertilizer or cottonseed meal, scattered lightly on the soil surface in the spring, will suffice. Water thoroughly after fertilizing.

Yews may be sheared early in the growing season to produce the formal clipped appearance often desired for hedges. But by pruning yews with hand clippers, taking out long branches from within the plants so that no stubs show, the plants can be kept to the desired size almost indefinitely, yet look as if they had never been pruned.

THUJA, also called THUYA
T. occidentalis and varieties (American arborvitae); *T. orientalis,* also called *Biota orientalis, Platycladus orientalis,* and varieties (Oriental arborvitae); *T. plicata* and varieties (giant arborvitae, western red cedar)

Arborvitaes are sometimes looked down on because they are so common—speculative builders use them in housing developments because they grow so fast they produce a quick effect. But there are numerous fine slow-growing ones very well suited for low, informal and easy-to-care-for hedges or for planting around house foundations. Fast-growing erect types are quite inexpensive and are good choices for tall hedges and screens. Arborvitaes have flat sprays of green, or in some varieties golden-tipped, pleasantly aromatic foliage composed of tiny scalelike needles that cling closely to the twigs. The needle sprays of Oriental arborvitae are held in a characteristic vertical plane; the new growth on other species takes the same angle but sprays on older branches are likely to be nearly horizontal. The slender oblong brown cones, about ½ inch long, are usually hidden by the needles. Arborvitaes usually retain all of their branches, even old ones close to the ground. This attribute is of immense value in hedgemaking, since the lower sections do not become thin and straggly. Some arborvitaes turn brownish in the winter.

American arborvitae grows well in Areas A, B, C, D, F, H and I. Forest trees become 40 feet or more tall, but a number of varieties are smaller and suited to garden use. *T. occidentalis douglasii pyramidalis*, Douglas arborvitae, grows in a slender conical shape and becomes 18 to 20 feet tall in about 15 to 20 years. It has exquisitely twisted sprays of dark green fernlike needles that hold their color over winter. *T. occidentalis lutea*, George Peabody arborvitae, is one of the finest golden-leaved varieties, forming a broad conical shape up to 20 feet tall in 15 to 20 years if unpruned. *T. occidentalis nigra*, dark American arborvitae, forms a broadly conical tree 20 feet tall in 15 to 20 years if unpruned; it holds its rich green color over the winter. *T. occidentalis pyramidalis*, pyramidal American arborvitae, forms a narrow cone that may reach 20 to 30 feet in height in 20 to 25 years. *T. occidentalis wareana*, Ware or Siberian arborvitae, is broadly conical and becomes 5 to 6 feet tall after 10 to 15 years. It holds its dark green color over winter. *T. occidentalis woodwardii*, Woodward globe arborvitae, forms a dependable globular shape, only rarely exceeds 3 feet in height and stays green long into winter.

Oriental arborvitae grows well in Areas D, E, G, I and J. It can also be grown in the southern part of Area C, but needles may discolor and branches may die in winter cold. Vertically held sprays of bright dark green foliage and many low branches are hallmarks of most of the varieties of the Oriental arborvitae. *T. orientalis aurea nana*, Berckman's golden arborvitae, is a nearly oval or globular compact form that becomes about 5 feet tall in 8 to 10 years if unpruned. Its foliage changes from golden in the spring to green in the summer to bronze in the winter. *T. orientalis* 'Baker' has bright green foliage, dense needles and a broadly conical shape. It thrives in hot dry places and becomes 5 to 8 feet tall in 8 to 10 years. *T. orientalis sieboldii*, Siebold's arborvitae, has very bright green tightly compressed foliage on a broadly conical plant that rarely exceeds 3 feet in height. *T. orientalis* 'Westmont' is a compact globe-shaped slow-growing variety, whose rich dark green foliage is brightly tipped with yellow from spring through fall. After 10 to 15 years the plants become about 3 feet tall.

Giant arborvitae, also called western red cedar, grows well in Areas C, D, H, I and J; trees grown from seeds collected in the cold inland area of the Northwest are more resistant to cold damage. An immense tree in the forest, this species becomes 50 or more feet tall in gardens after 40 to 60 years; it is used mainly as a lawn ornament or to create tall screens. Its foliage stays green all winter. A particularly fine variety with a straight slender shape is *T. plicata fastigiata*, columnar giant arborvitae.

Arborvitaes do best in moist soil and most flourish where the air is humid, but there are varieties such as Baker and Westmont suitable for hot and dry parts of the country. While full sun is best, arborvitaes will tolerate some shade, although growth will become thin over a period of years. If the needles become pale in color, a light dusting of 5-10-5 garden fertilizer around the plants in the spring will restore the green color of the foliage that season. Pruning is best done by shearing plants lightly early in spring just before new growth begins. Several vertical top branches are desirable, for they contribute to the bushy appearance of plants. Arborvitaes can be shortened by removing any or all of the top vertical branches to the desired height. New foliage soon covers the stubs. Many arborvitaes, especially

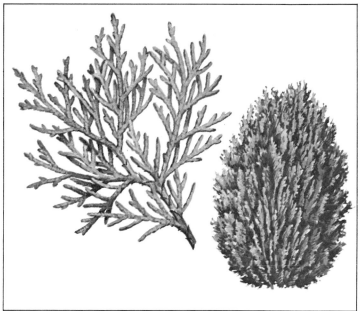

BERCKMAN'S GOLDEN ORIENTAL ARBORVITAE
Thuja orientalis aurea nana

GIANT ARBORVITAE
Thuja plicata

For growing areas, see map on page 149.

CANADA HEMLOCK
Tsuga canadensis

SARGENT'S WEEPING HEMLOCK
Tsuga canadensis pendula

CAROLINA HEMLOCK
Tsuga caroliniana

Oriental varieties, send up numerous ascending stems that tend to break off in high winds or under snow loads as the plants get old. To prevent such damage, loosely truss the main stems with heavy plastic-coated wire to give them support; the dense foliage of the plants will hide the wire.

THUYA See *Thuja*

TSUGA
T. canadensis and varieties (Canada hemlock),
T. caroliniana (Carolina hemlock),
T. diversifolia (Japanese hemlock)

Hemlocks rank among the most graceful and adaptable of all conifers. The narrowly conical trees, usually 25 to 50 feet tall in gardens if unpruned, have slender main branches that dip away from the trunks to rise again at the tips. Hanging branchlets and twigs are featherlike with soft, flat, dark green needles, usually about ½ inch long. Hemlocks make good single-tree ornaments as well as screens and foundation plantings. They are especially suitable for hedges because they may be easily sheared to shape.

Canada hemlock is suited to all of Areas B and C, the northern part of Area D and all of Areas H and I. Unpruned, this species grows 25 to 50 feet tall in 15 to 30 years. Over the years, many mutations have occurred. The shape may be a slender column or a flat globe, the needles gold-colored or unusually small; there are even dwarf weeping types that grow less than 1 inch a year. Few of these types are available in average nurseries because of the labor and cost of propagating them, but many are sold by nurseries specializing in dwarf evergreens. The original Canada hemlock is difficult to improve upon but an elegant exception is *T. canadensis pendula,* Sargent's weeping hemlock. After 25 or 50 years, this hemlock can become 15 or more feet tall and 40 or more feet across, forming a living fountain of soft hanging branches. Even as a young plant it is worthy of a conspicuous spot in the garden; it also serves well in a tub on a patio.

Carolina hemlock thrives in all of Area B, the eastern part of Area C, the northern part of Area D and all of Areas H and I. It becomes 15 to 40 feet tall after 15 to 20 years. The needles, grass-green on top and streaked with white below, wind in spirals around slender twigs.

Japanese hemlock grows well in the southern part of Area B, all of Area C, the northern part of Area D and all parts of Areas H and I. This species has very dense foliage and is compact and slow growing; it rarely exceeds 20 feet after 20 years in gardens in this country and often becomes a low, many-trunked bush rather than a tree.

Hemlocks do best in cool, moist, acid soil in full sun or light shade; however, they require light shade in the southern sections of the recommended areas. Except for the Carolina hemlock, this genus does not tolerate city conditions or dry windswept situations, but will thrive on the north side of a house, where many other plants do not do well. Fertilizing is rarely necessary, but if the foliage becomes sparse or pale, apply a light dusting of cottonseed meal beneath the plants in early spring. Hemlocks may be sheared very closely for a formally shaped hedge because the foliage is fine and soft, the branches are flexible and new shoots sprout readily even from the stubs of heavily pruned branches. For an informal or natural shape, use hand clippers to cut off unwanted branches inside the plant outline.

Y

YEW See *Taxus*
YEW, PLUM See *Cephalotaxus*
YEW PODOCARPUS See *Podocarpus*

Broad-leaved evergreens

A

ABELIA

A. 'Edward Goucher' (Edward Goucher abelia, also called pink abelia), *A. grandiflora* (glossy abelia), *A. grandiflora prostrata* (prostrate white abelia)

Abelias are considered by many gardeners to be indispensable broad-leaved evergreens because they bloom so much later than most flowering shrubs. The varieties recommended here bear clusters of 1-inch-long flowers from June or July until late fall. Even after the flowers fade, star-shaped reddish outer petals, the sepals, remain colorful for weeks. The inch-long shiny leaves, reddish bronze in spring, turn dark green in summer, then bronzy again in the fall.

The Edward Goucher abelia, with pinkish lavender flowers, and the glossy abelia, with pale pink flowers, grow in mounds 3 to 5 feet tall with equal spread in four or five years. They are useful near a house foundation where both summer color and winter foliage are desirable, and make graceful shrub borders next to a walk. The prostrate white abelia grows only 1½ to 2 feet tall and is often used as a grass substitute. Abelias grow well in full sun or partial shade in Areas C, D, E, G, I and J. They may drop their leaves in severe winters in Areas C, D and G. When the temperature falls to zero, all the plant aboveground may be killed but usually will blossom again by midsummer.

Since abelias produce flowers on the current season's growth, prune only before new growth appears. If the plants become too tall or lose their lower branches with age, rejuvenate them by cutting them off at ground level just before new growth starts. Remove wayward branches any time. Abelias are sometimes sheared to formal outlines, but their grace is better preserved by cutting back long stems with hand clippers.

ACACIA

A. baileyana (Cootamundra wattle, Bailey acacia, fern-leaved acacia), *A. baileyana purpurea* (purple-leaved acacia), *A. longifolia floribunda* (everblooming acacia, Sydney golden wattle, Sydney acacia)

These plants from Australia, only a sampling of the many handsome acacias available, may be pruned to grow as small single-trunked trees or large multistemmed shrubs. They may reach a height of 20 to 30 feet in five years and are widely grown in the southern parts of California and Arizona for their fragrant yellow flowers. The tiny blossoms appear in clusters on the Cootamundra wattle and the purple-leaved acacia, nearly hiding the foliage from January to March. The fernlike leaves of the Cootamundra wattle are steel blue; those of the purple-leaved acacia are—as its name implies—purplish. On the everblooming acacia, the flowers appear in 2-inch spikes; they are most colorful in February and March but bloom intermittently throughout the rest of the year.

Acacias grow well only in Area J. They are excellent seaside plants and once established will withstand considerable drought. In fact, omitting watering during a dry summer is helpful, slowing a young plants' fast growth (4 to 6 feet a year) and making the wood stronger. Acacia wood is brittle and subject to wind breakage. Prune broken branches flush with the larger limbs from which they originate. Shape young plants by pruning with hand clippers at any time. Acacias mature quickly but live only about 20 years. They are notably free of pests and diseases.

ANDROMEDA See *Pieris*
ARALIA See *Fatsia*

For growing areas, see map on page 149.

GLOSSY ABELIA
Abelia grandiflora

COOTAMUNDRA WATTLE
Acacia baileyana

COMPACT STRAWBERRY TREE
Arbutus unedo compacta

BEARBERRY
Arctostaphylos uva-ursi

ARBUTUS

A. unedo (strawberry tree),
A. unedo compacta (compact strawberry tree)

The strawberry tree is most often seen as an 8- to 15-foot multistemmed shrub, but it can grow as tall as 25 feet in about 10 years and be pruned to a single trunk. The compact strawberry tree, identical in other respects, grows to about half that size. Shiny dark green pointed leaves about 3 inches long surround the tiny flowers, which hang in 2-inch clusters from October to January. These flowers often appear while the brilliantly colored fruit from the previous year is still clinging to the branches. The edible fruit is strawberrylike in size and shape, with a warty skin that changes from yellow to red as it matures in the fall.

The strawberry tree grows well in full sun or light shade in Areas E, I and J. It will tolerate seaside conditions and does best in well-drained acid soil that is not moist, and is therefore more satisfactory on the West Coast than in the Southeast or around the Gulf. Train to bush or tree shape by pruning in summer with hand clipper or lopping shears.

ARCTOSTAPHYLOS

A. uva-ursi (bearberry, kinnikinnick)

A low-growing evergreen shrub, the bearberry makes an easy-to-care-for ground cover for dry, sandy or rocky banks. It forms a mat only 6 to 12 inches high and spreads slowly (6 to 18 inches a year) to a diameter of more than 15 feet; its stems often root wherever they touch the ground. Its 1-inch oval leaves, reddish when young in the spring, become an extremely glossy dark green in midsummer, then turn bronze in the fall. In the spring, usually from April to June, the plants bear tiny pale pink flowers, which are followed by shiny, bright red berries ¼ inch in diameter that persist through the fall and winter.

Bearberries grow well in Areas A, B, C, F, H, I and J. They do best in infertile sandy acid soil with abundant sunshine but will also grow—with fewer berries—in light shade. They thrive in seaside locations. They are extremely difficult to transplant from the wild because of their wide-spreading root system, but container-grown nursery plants are easy to start. Prune only to remove creeping stems that grow beyond their allotted space.

ASH See *Fraxinus*

AUCUBA

A. japonica and varieties (Japanees aucuba)

A shade-tolerant bush that bears huge green-and-yellow leaves and bright red berries—that is the spectacular Japanese aucuba, an evergreen shrub that grows 6 to 15 feet tall in about 10 years. Aucubas are thickly covered with shiny leaves half a foot long that are often boldly marked with yellow. Tiny purple flowers bloom in February and March. In October 2- to 3-inch clusters of bright red oval berries appear on the ends of the branches of female plants and last until February. To assure the production of fruit, plant both male and female plants together, using one male to every 10 female plants. Many varieties are sold at nurseries. *A. japonica variegata* is called the gold-dust tree because of the yellow speckles on its leaves. *A. japonica picturata* has leaves with bright yellow centers and deep green edges. The leaves of *A. japonica* 'Sulphur' show a reverse coloration—green centers and yellow edges.

Aucubas grow well in Areas D and E, the southern part of Area G and Areas I and J. They flourish most luxuriantly in light to deep shade in moist soil, but aucubas tolerate almost any soil, and established plants withstand drought. They are easy to grow in containers on the patio or indoors. A light application of cottonseed-meal fertilizer in early spring spurs growth. Pruning is rarely required; it may be done at any time, although very early spring is best. Use hand clippers and cut just above any leaf joint; a new branch will then grow from the bud at the base.

AZALEA See *Rhododendron*

B

BAMBOO, HEAVENLY See *Nandina*
BAMBOO, SACRED See *Nandina*
BARBERRY See *Berberis*

BAUHINIA
B. blakeana (Hong Kong orchid tree)

Many gardeners in southern Florida and California consider the Hong Kong orchid tree to be the most spectacular of all flowering trees. It grows up to 25 feet tall in about 10 years and from late fall until spring bears orchidlike flowers up to 6 inches across. The colors range from pink to deep wine and purple, often in the same blossom. The foliage is unique too; each rounded leaf is so deeply cleft that it seems like twin leaves joined in the middle—a structure that accounts for the tree's Latin name, which honors twin Swiss botanists, Jean and Gaspard Bauhin.

Honk Kong orchid trees grow well in the warm parts of Areas E and J, where they decorate lawns and shade patios. They do best in full sun but will tolerate light shade and can grow in almost any slightly acid soil. Temperatures below 30° damage but may not kill them; new plants often sprout from frostbitten trees. Prune early in the spring after the flowering season has ended, and trim only enough to shape the trees.

BAY, BULL See *Magnolia*
BAY, SWEET See *Laurus*
BEARBERRY See *Arctostaphylos*
BEECH, AUSTRALIAN See *Eucalyptus*
BEEFWOOD, HORSETAIL See *Casuarina*

BERBERIS
B. buxifolia nana (dwarf Magellan barberry), *B. chenaultii* (Chenault barberry), *B. darwinii* (Darwin barberry), *B. gagnepainii* (black barberry), *B. julianae* (wintergreen barberry), *B. mentorensis* (Mentor barberry), *B. triacanthophora* (three-spined barberry), *B. verruculosa* (warty barberry)

The evergreen barberries are decorative plants with glossy dark green spiny leaves, usually about an inch long, which on many species turn bronzy in the winter. Most bear clusters of tiny yellow-to-orange flowers in the spring, followed by oval purplish black berries, about ½ inch long, that last into winter. Barberries are superb hedge plants—the spiny branches discourage both dogs and humans from taking shortcuts. They are at their best when their branches are left unpruned or at most, are pruned very lightly with hand clippers to maintain size.

The dwarf Magellan barberry rarely exceeds 18 inches in height and is suited for use in rock gardens and low hedges; it seldom bears friut. The Chenault barberry grows 3 to 4 feet tall in about five years. The Darwin barberry grows 4 to 8 feet tall in 5 to 10 years and bears spectacular masses of orange flowers. The black barberry grows 4 to 6 feet tall in about five years and has narrow 4-inch-long leaves. The wintergreen barberry grows 5 to 6 feet tall in 8 to 10 years and has 2- to 3-inch leathery leaves. The Mentor barberry, which loses its leaves where winters are cold, grows 5 to 7 feet tall in three to five years; it bears dull red ber-

VARIEGATED JAPANESE AUCUBA
Aucuba japonica picturata

HONG KONG ORCHID TREE
Bauhinia blakeana

WINTERGREEN BARBERRY
Berberis julianae

For growing areas, see map on page 149.

ries and tolerates both cold and dryness. The three-spined barberry grows 3 to 5 feet tall in about five years and has narrow, bright green 2-inch leaves. The warty barberry, so-called because of bumpy growths on its stems, grows 2½ to 4 feet tall in three to five years; its leaves are dark green on top but nearly white beneath.

These species grow well in the southern part of Area C, the northern part of Area E and all parts of Areas D, G, I and J—except the Darwin barberry, which does not do well in Areas C and G. All thrive in full sun or light shade and prefer moist soil. Feed plants each spring by scattering a 5-10-5 fertilizer around them and watering.

BLUE BLOSSOM See *Ceanothus*
BOTTLE BRUSH See *Callistemon*
BOX See *Buxus*
BOX, FALSE See *Pachistima*
BOXWOOD See *Buxus*
BOXWOOD, MOUNTAIN See *Pachistima*
BOXWOOD, OREGON See *Pachistima*

BRUNFELSIA

B. calycina floribunda
(yesterday, today and tomorrow; chameleon plant)

This unusual shrub gets its common names from the fact that its sweetly scented 2-inch blossoms begin as deep purple with white centers, then fade to lavender on their second day and to white on the third day. The flowers bloom profusely in spring and intermittently the rest of the year. The plants usually grow about 3 feet tall and equally broad, but can become 10 feet tall in four to five years in warm climates. Their 3-inch dark green leaves are likely to fall if temperatures drop below 40°. Because of this susceptibility to cold, and because the plants blossom best when their roots are crowded, they are often grown in containers and moved under cover in cold weather.

Yesterday, today and tomorrow grows well only in the southern parts of Areas E and J. It does best in light shade and fertile, moist, acid soil. Scatter a 5-10-5 fertilizer on the ground under plants in the garden once each spring and water it in. For potted plants grown indoors, use commercial potting soil and feed with house-plant fertilizer every two weeks while the plants are actively growing; use no fertilizer when they are resting. Prune in spring with hand clippers after the first flush of bloom.

BUXUS

B. microphylla and varieties (littleleaf box or boxwood),
B. sempervirens and varieties (common box)

Since the earliest days of gardening, box has been esteemed for hedges because it can be sheared into precise shapes. It is densely covered with small (1¼- to 1⅓-inch) leaves, oval or tongue-shaped. Though the plants respond well to shearing, they can also be allowed to grow naturally, forming low irregular billowy mounds of dense foliage. Some of the finest box in America grow at Mount Vernon and in Williamsburg; many of these plants were brought from England more than 150 years ago.

One of the best varieties of littleleaf box is *B. microphylla koreana* 'Wintergreen,' which grows 2 feet tall, spreading about 4 feet, in 8 to 10 years, and retains its bright green leaf color through the winter; other varieties may turn brownish in cold weather. Common box, whose blue-green foliage is delicately fragrant, especially in warm humid weather, includes among its varieties *B. sempervirens suffruticosa,* the edging box, which seldom grows more than 3 feet tall in 25 years. Two other varieties, both cold resistant, are Vardar Valley, which grows about 2 feet

YESTERDAY, TODAY AND TOMORROW
Brunfelsia calycina floribunda

EDGING BOX
Buxus sempervirens suffruticosa

tall and spreads to 4 to 5 feet in 15 years, and Northern Find, which forms a 3-foot rounded bush in about 10 years.

Box does best in warm moist climates that do not have extremes of summer heat or winter cold. Littleleaf box grows well in Areas C, D, E, I and J. Common box grows well in the coastal regions of Area C from Rhode Island south, the northern part of Area E and all parts of Areas D and I. Both thrive in full sun or light shade in almost any moist soil. Plants do best when transplanted in the spring. After planting, apply a 1-inch mulch of chunky peat moss, wood chips or peanut shells. The first season, mist the foliage with water in warm weather. If the leaves become pale, scatter cottonseed meal or lawn fertilizer under the plants in early spring. Near the northern limits of the recommended areas, give the plants extra winter protection as described on page 24. Geometrical shapes can be maintained with hedge shears; otherwise prune with clippers only to remove dead branches.

C

CALICO BUSH See *Kalmia*

CALLIANDRA
C. haematocephala (red powder puff); *C. inaequilatera* (pink powder puff); *C. tweedii*, also called *C. guildingii* (Trinidad flame bush)

The pride of hot-climate gardens, powder puffs and flame bushes are well named. Their rounded mounds, generally 4 to 8 feet in diameter, are covered with feathery foliage —bronze-tinted when young, dark green when mature— and bear 2- to 3-inch flower heads composed of hundreds of fluffy pink or red stamens. Powder puffs bloom from autumn until spring; Trinidad flame bushes bloom in late spring and summer. They make good screens as well as single-plant lawn decoration.

Powder puffs and flame bushes grow well in gardens in the southern parts of Areas E and J; elsewhere they may be grown as large house plants. In the garden, they do best in full sun in moist but well-drained soil. Prune with hand clippers after the bushes have flowered.

CALLISTEMON
C. citrinus, also called *C. lanceolatus* (lemon bottle brush); *C. viminalis* 'McCaskill' (McCaskill weeping bottle brush)

Shrubs or small trees that often grow 2 or 3 feet a year when young, bottle brushes are aptly named because their red flowers, composed of hundreds of silky 1-inch stamens, appear along stems like the bristles on a bottle brush. The willowlike leaves are copper-colored when young, bright green when mature. Drooping, graceful branches move in the slightest breeze. These evergreens make handsome single-plant displays and practical screens or informal hedges. They also may be trained by the espalier technique (*page 77*) to grow flat against a wall or fence.

The lemon bottle brush, usually an 8- to 10-foot-tall shrub, can reach 20 feet or more in 5 to 10 years if most side branches are pruned away to leave a single main stem. The 3-inch leaves have a citrus fragrance when crushed. The flowers are most abundant in spring and summer but appear intermittently throughout the year. The McCaskill weeping bottle brush is usually grown as a small tree, becoming 20 to 25 feet tall in 10 to 12 years. Its branches are covered with leaves 6 inches long, and it blooms in summer and frequently in other seasons as well.

Bottle brushes grow well in Areas E, I and J. They need full sun and well-drained soil, and can tolerate alkaline soil. Prune only to thin out top-heavy growth, using hand clippers after the major flowering season has passed.

PINK POWDER PUFF
Calliandra inaequilatera

LEMON BOTTLE BRUSH
Callistemon citrinus

For growing areas, see map on page 149.

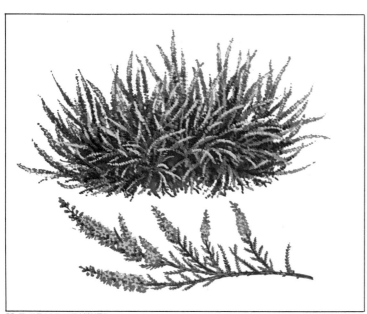

H. E. BEALE HEATHER
Calluna vulgaris 'H. E. Beale'

COMMON CAMELLIA
Camellia japonica

CALLUNA
C. vulgaris and varieties (Scotch heather)

The beauty of Scottish moorlands carpeted with lavender heather has inspired poets for so long that it is surprising these plants are not grown more often in gardens. Heather comes in many varieties suitable as ground covers or to add color in rock gardens or shrub borders. All varieties bear spikes of tiny flowers that blossom heavily, usually from late summer into autumn. The minute scale-like leaves are usually dark green but occasionally golden.

Among the particularly good varieties are Alba Plena, 8 to 12 inches tall, with white flowers; Aurea, 10 to 18 inches tall, with purple flowers and golden foliage; County Wicklow, 10 to 18 inches tall, with pink flowers; H. E. Beale, 18 to 24 inches tall, with pink flowers; and Nana Compacta, 4 to 6 inches tall, with pinkish purple flowers.

Heathers grow well in Areas C, D, and I and the northern part of Area J. They thrive in poor sandy soil and full sun; they also tolerate light shade but bear fewer flowers in it. Heathers are best planted in early spring in cold climates, but may be set out in spring or fall where winter temperatures rarely drop below zero. Do not cultivate the soil around plants—their roots are shallow and easily damaged; instead, mulch heathers with 1 to 2 inches of wood chips, sawdust, buckwheat hulls or similar material, and water during dry periods. To keep plants bushy and stimulate blossoming, shear them back halfway with hedge shears in early spring just before new growth begins. Do not prune at any other time. If the leaves are pale and growth is not satisfactory, apply a small amount of cottonseed meal or an acid fertilizer, of the kind sold for rhododendrons or camellias, in early spring.

CAMELLIA
C. japonica and varieties (common camellia), *C. reticulata* and varieties (netvein camellia), *C. sasanqua* and varieties (sasanqua camellia), *C.* hybrids

Camellias are among the most spectacular of the broad-leaved evergreens. They are native to China and Japan, where trees sometimes become 40 feet tall; in this country camellias rarely exceed 15 feet even after 20 to 25 years. Their flowers, 2 to as much as 9 inches across, make them the pride of Southern and Western gardeners. The blossoms may be pink, red, white or combinations of these colors; they vary from those with a single row of petals to double forms, including the so-called anemone and peony camellias. Varieties listed here are multipetaled.

The common camellia grows well in Areas D, E, I and J. Early varieties blossom in midfall and the late ones extend the season until midspring. Common camellias have wide glossy leaves 2½ to 4 inches long and become 6 to 10 feet tall in 10 to 15 years. Some choice varieties are Alba Plena, early flowering, pure white; Betty Sheffield Supreme, midseason flowering, white petals edged in pink; Chandleri Elegans, midseason flowering, rose pink, mottled white; Daikagura, early flowering, rose red splashed with white; and Kramer's Supreme, midseason flowering, deep red.

Netvein camellia grows well in Areas E and J only. Most varieties blossom from early to late spring. The plant is a rangy shrub with large dull green leaves veined in a net pattern; it becomes 8 to 12 feet tall in about 10 years. Excellent varieties are Buddha, rose pink; Butterfly Wings, rose pink; and Pagoda, deep scarlet.

Sasanqua camellia grows well in Areas D, E, I and J, although fall rains sometimes damage flowers in Areas D and I. Plants blossom from early fall to early winter. They have slender shiny leaves about 2 inches long. Sasanqua camellias usually grow 5 to 6 feet tall in 8 to 10 years and are widely used for informal hedges. Three fine varieties are Cleopatra, rose pink; Sparkling Burgundy, ruby rose; and White Doves (also called Mine-No-Yuki), pure white.

Many fine hybrid camellias have been developed, including China Lady, early flowering, orchid pink; Forty-Niner, midseason flowering, brilliant red; and Howard Asper, mid- to late-season flowering, salmon pink.

Camellias generally do best in light shade, but in places like the Gulf Coast, where both soil and air are moist, they can be grown in full sun. Toward the northern limit of their growing area, where their roots are in frozen ground during the winter, they must be sheltered from the drying effects of the sun. The best soil mixture for camellias is ½ peat moss and ½ sandy loam. It should be acid *(page 75)* and kept evenly moist, not wet or dry. Drying out during flowering often causes unopened buds to drop. Hosing the leaves with a stream of water in hot, dry weather moistens the plants and washes off insects.

Camellias are shallow-rooted. When planting, set them so that the soil line, indicating the level at which they had been growing, is 1 inch above the new soil level. Deeper planting may smother the roots. For balled-and-burlaped plants, spring planting is best in the northern part of Area D, but fall through spring is suitable in Areas E, I and J. Container-grown plants can be set out at any time. Do not cultivate around camellias or the shallow roots may be damaged; instead, apply a 2- to 4-inch mulch of a light material such as pine needles, wood chips or ground bark. Feed camellias just as new growth begins in the spring, scattering a small amount of cottonseed meal or special rhododendron-azalea-camellia fertilizer beneath the plants. Repeat at eight-week intervals until early fall. Limit pruning to shaping bushes in early spring with hand clippers.

Many gardeners try to grow camellias somewhat north of the areas in which they do best. To experiment, select a late-flowering variety, shelter it from wind and mulch the soil heavily to keep the soil from freezing *(page 29).*

CAMPHOR TREE See *Cinnamomum*

CARISSA
C. grandiflora, also called *C. macrocarpa,* and varieties (Natal plum)

A thorny evergreen shrub from South Africa, the Natal plum grows well only in southern parts of Areas E and J. The many varieties include spreading forms about 1 foot tall, such as *C. grandiflora* 'Green Carpet,' and upright bushes that become 6 to 8 feet tall after about five years. Because of their thorns Natal plums are valuable barrier plants in hedges. A variety such as *C. grandiflora* 'Tuttle,' which forms a dense mound, looks good in front of a house foundation; low-growing varieties are used as ground covers. Natal plums have smooth oval light green leaves and bear fragrant pinwheel-shaped white flowers about 2 inches across, followed by edible, 2-inch plum-shaped fruit. Flowers and fruit appear all year.

Natal plums do best in full sun but will endure even deep shade. Any well-drained soil is suitable and all varieties tolerate seaside conditions. Prune with hand clippers to restrict size or adjust shape at any time.

CARROTWOOD See *Cupaniopsis*

CASUARINA
C. equisetifolia
(horsetail beefwood, also called Australian pine, she-oak)

At first glance the horsetail beefwood tree might be mistaken for a pine. Its tiny scalelike leaves cover jointed

Illustration by Eduardo Salgado

GREEN CARPET NATAL PLUM
Carissa grandiflora 'Green Carpet'

HORSETAIL BEEFWOOD
Casuarina equisetifolia

CALIFORNIA LILAC
Ceanothus thyrsiflorus

CAMPHOR TREE
Cinnamomum camphora

twigs, which look like needles. Moreover, its ½-inch brown fruit is cone-shaped. But this genus is not even remotely related to pines or to any other conifer.

The beefwood is an Australian tree that, in North American gardens, becomes 50 to 60 feet tall in 20 to 25 years and grows well in southern parts of Areas E and J. It flourishes in full sun or partial shade in almost any soil, wet or dry; it thrives near the sea and will grow in desert areas. Unpruned trees grow very fast (2 feet or more a year when young) and can be used to gain light shade quickly. Their branches droop and move gracefully in the lightest breeze. When pruned regularly to force growth of many branches, beefwoods make a fine privacy screen or windbreak. They can be sheared closely into a formal hedge or the fanciful figures of topiary. Prune any time.

CEANOTHUS
C. griseus horizontalis (Carmel creeper),
C. impressus 'Mountain Haze' (Mountain Haze ceanothus), *C. thyrsiflorus* (blue blossom)
(all also called wild lilac, California lilac)

All the evergreen species of ceanothus bear a great many flower clusters, resembling those of lilac, from March to May. Carmel creeper grows 18 to 30 inches tall and spreads widely, sometimes to a diameter of 10 to 15 feet in five years, making it useful as a ground cover. It has 2-inch clusters of bright blue flowers. Mountain Haze ceanothus spreads about as much as Carmel creeper but grows taller, reaching 4 to 8 feet in three to five years. It has many 1-inch clusters of dark blue flowers. Blue blossom usually grows 4 to 8 feet tall in about three to five years and has 1- to 3-inch clusters of blossoms in varying shades of blue.

Ceanothus grows in Areas I and J only; even there it does best close to the ocean. It is excellent for windy seaside places. The plants need full sun and very well-drained soil. Care must be taken not to overwater them. Set out container-grown plants in the fall for best results, mulching the soil with leaf mold, wood chips or similar organic material. Prune only to remove deadwood or lanky branches.

CHAMELEON PLANT See *Brunfelsia*

CINNAMOMUM
C. camphora, also called *Camphora officinarum*
(camphor tree)

The camphor tree becomes 30 to 50 feet tall in gardens after 25 to 50 years if unpruned and has a broad spreading crown of dense foliage that casts deep shade. Its aromatic 2- to 4-inch leaves are the source of camphor and have that scent when crushed. They are pink, rose or bronze when they unfold in spring, becoming shiny light green during the summer and yellow-green in cool weather. In the spring camphor trees bear tiny yellow flowers followed by ⅜-inch shiny black berries, which can be a nuisance on a driveway or patio, but are not objectionable on a lawn. Though the bark and leaves are used in medicine, the berries are poisonous. When grown as hedges or windbreaks, camphor trees can be kept at any height by regular shearing.

Camphor trees grow in Areas E and J. They do well in full sun or light shade in nearly any soil. They are very difficult to transplant successfully except as small container-grown plants, but in this form they can be set out at any time. Water young trees thoroughly and regularly to encourage deep roots. Camphor trees should be pruned in the fall. Remove the lower branches of young trees so there will be walking space beneath them when the trees mature. Thin out branches every few years to permit sufficient light to get through so grass can grow below.

CITRUS

Many varieties of orange, lemon, lime, limequat, grapefruit, tangelo and tangerine

Many gardeners in Areas E and J, where these evergreen trees and shrubs can be grown outdoors, have not taken full advantage of their usefulness in landscaping. Standard-sized trees may become 20 to 30 feet tall, with an equal spread, after 15 to 20 years, and if you prune the lower limbs the trees provide both shade and fruit. Dwarf varieties, 5 to 10 feet tall, serve as garden ornaments and produce fruit as well. A number of citruses such as calamondin orange and kumquat form thick bushes 6 to 10 feet tall suitable for hedges or screens. Citruses are famous for the fragrance of their white blossoms, about 1 inch across, which usually appear in late winter and early spring. The leaves are dark green and shiny. (Kumquat, though not strictly a citrus—it is of the related genus *Fortunella*—is often lumped with them and used similarly.)

Citruses such as calamondin orange and bergamot or bouquet orange can grow even where winter temperatures drop to 20°, but others such as the lime tolerate only three or four degrees of frost. The main kinds in order of increasing cold sensitivity are calamondin orange, bergamot orange, Satsuma or Owari orange, Meyer lemon, tangerine or mandarin orange, sweet orange, tangelo, lemon, grapefruit, limequat and lime.

Citruses need full sun and a soil that is moist but never wet; excellent drainage is imperative. Trees need to be fed three times a year: in late winter, early summer and late summer. Use fertilizer sold especially for citruses and spread a light dusting on the ground starting 2 feet from the trunk and extending 2 to 3 feet beyond the spread of the branches. To keep the roots cool and moist, cultivate the soil around the plants but dig no deeper than 1 to 2 inches; alternatively, mulch with 2 to 3 inches of wood chips, sawdust or ground bark. Prune the trees and bushes at any time to shape them. Only named varieties of citruses are worth growing because they produce the largest, sweetest fruit. When grown indoors, citruses need four hours of direct sunlight a day, night temperatures of 50° to 55° and day temperatures of 68° to 72°. Soil in the pots should dry slightly between waterings.

CLUSTERBERRY See *Cotoneaster*

CODIAEUM

C. variegatum and varieties (croton)

No plant exhibits such a wide range of leaf color as croton, which combines yellow, green and red on the same leaf, and sometimes orange, brown, ivory and pink as well. The leaves are leathery and of many shapes—broad, narrow, scalloped, lobed or twisted. Specialists list over 100 named varieties. Flowers and fruit are inconspicuous.

Crotons grow 3 to 10 feet tall in about five years and thrive in moist soil in full sun or shade. They survive winter outdoors only in frost-free locations in the southern part of Area E, where they are useful as hedge plants, in shrub borders and as color accents. Elsewhere they are grown indoors or planted in the garden after danger of frost has passed in spring and moved indoors before frost in fall.

COTONEASTER

C. dammeri, also called *C. humifusa* (bearberry cotoneaster); *C. horizontalis* (rock spray, rock cotoneaster); *C. parneyi* (Parney's cotoneaster, red clusterberry)

The evergreen cotoneasters are easy-to-care-for shrubs whose small pink or white flowers, appearing in early spring, are followed by tiny red berries that often cling to

SWEET ORANGE
Citrus sinensis

CROTON
Codiaeum variegatum

BEARBERRY COTONEASTER
Cotoneaster dammeri

For growing areas, see map on page 149.

119

CARROTWOOD
Cupaniopsis anacardioides

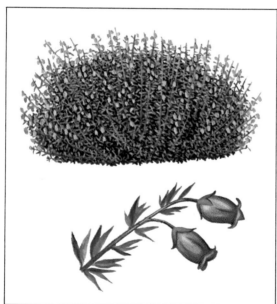

IRISH HEATH
Daboëcia cantabrica

the branches well into the winter months. Bearberry cotoneaster grows well in Areas C, D, E, G, I and J. Though 1 foot or less in height, one plant may spread to a diameter of 10 feet in 8 to 10 years, its horizontal stems rooting as they go. This species has 1-inch leaves and small white flowers followed by bright red berries. It is particularly useful as a ground cover or rock garden plant in sun or light shade. Rock spray grows well in Areas C, D, E, G, I and J. It becomes 4 to 5 feet tall in five to eight years and may spread to 10 to 15 feet across. Its ½-inch leaves, flat like an opened fan, are evergreen in mild areas, but they turn red or orange in the fall in cool regions, then fall off. It has small pinkish white flowers and tiny glossy red berries. This species makes a good plant to set in front of a shrub border or a house foundation, and it also serves well as a fairly tall ground cover. Parney's cotoneaster grows well in Areas D, E, I and J. A mound-shaped shrub with arching branches, it becomes 5 to 8 feet tall in three to five years and has 2-inch dark green leaves that are pale underneath. Its small clusters of white flowers are followed by 2- to 3-inch clusters of red berries. Readily shaped, it is a good choice for espaliering *(page 77)* or for screens or hedges.

The cotoneasters are among the few evergreens that prefer slightly alkaline, rather dry soil. They do best in full sun and will tolerate wind. Except for the specialized espalier training that can be applied to Parney's cotoneaster, pruning should be kept to a minimum. Deadwood can be removed at any time, but other light pruning to control shape should be undertaken in late winter or early spring just before new growth begins. Keep cotoneasters far enough away from drives and walks so the ends of the graceful branches do not have to be clipped. Cotoneasters are exceedingly difficult to transplant except when grown in containers.

CREEPER, CARMEL See *Ceanothus*
CREEPER, WINTER See *Euonymus*
CROTON See *Codiaeum*

CUPANIOPSIS

C. anacardioides, also called *Cupania anacardioides* (carrotwood, tuckeroo)

Carrotwood is becoming increasingly popular as a shade tree in Southern California despite its slow growth (1 to 2 feet a year when young), for it is a sturdy, pest-free evergreen in Areas E and J and becomes 25 to 30 feet tall after 15 to 20 years, developing a dense rounded crown up to 40 feet across. Its leaves are divided into stiff, leathery dark green leaflets, each about 4 inches long. Carrotwood thrives in almost any soil, moist or dry, and flourishes by the sea or in hot inland areas. Prune in winter.

D

DABOËCIA

D. cantabrica, also called *D. polifolia*, and varieties (Irish heath, Irish bell heather)

Irish heath is neither a heath *(Erica)* nor a heather *(Calluna)*, but a compact bushy plant well suited for use in a rock garden or in front of a bed of rhododendrons or azaleas. It grows 1 to 2 feet tall in three to four years, with an equal spread, and has thin green leaves only ½ inch long. From late spring until midfall it produces erect 3- to 6-inch clusters of small bell-shaped flowers of purple, white, pink or purple and white. In the Pacific Northwest, it may bear occasional flowers all year if the winter is mild.

Irish heath grows well in the eastern part of Area C, and throughout Areas D, I and J. It needs full sun in the cooler parts of these areas, light shade in the warmer sections. It requires a moist acid soil that has been mixed with an equal amount of peat moss. In early spring scatter a small amount of rhododendron-azalea-camellia fertilizer or cottonseed meal under the plants as far as the branches spread. Since roots are shallow and easily damaged by cultivation of the ground around the plants, use a permanent mulch of chunky peat moss, wood chips, sawdust or ground bark to keep the soil cool and moist. Water the plants frequently enough the first season to keep the soil always moist until the roots become well established. Prune just before new growth starts, cutting off about one third of each plant. Snip off faded flowers at any time. In the northern parts of Areas C and I, give the plants a 6-inch winter mulch of salt-marsh hay to shade the plants from winter sun, which would dehydrate them.

DAHOON See *Ilex*

DAPHNE
D. burkwoodii 'Somerset' (Somerset daphne), *D. cneorum* (rose daphne), *D. odora* (winter daphne)

All daphnes have delicate four-petaled blossoms with a roselike fragrance. Somerset daphne grows 3 to 5 feet tall in about five years, thriving in Areas C, D, I and J. In late spring the final 6 to 8 inches of each stem is enveloped in dozens of small pale pink flowers that darken as they age. In early summer tiny red berries appear. The narrow dull gray-green leaves are about 2 inches long. This variety is useful for borders and for planting in front of a house or a foundation; it is doubly appreciated if it is set near a window so that its fragrance can permeate indoors. Rose daphne rarely grows more than 6 to 12 inches tall, forming a circular mound of gray-green foliage about 2 feet across in three to five years. It does well in Areas C, D, I and J. One-inch clusters of tiny pink flowers cover it in spring and dot it sparingly in autumn. The narrow leaves are only about ¾ inch long and are borne all around the stems somewhat like bristles. It is very useful along the edges of borders and beds and is handsome in rock gardens. A recommended variety with dark pink flowers is Ruby Glow. Winter daphne, a 3- to 5-foot shrub maturing in about five years, grows well in Areas D, I and J, and has the sweetest and strongest fragrance of all. Its small rosy purple flowers cloak the ends of its branches in late winter and early spring. Leaves are 2 to 3 inches long. The leaves, bark and berries of all daphnes are poisonous to eat.

Daphnes do best in well-drained but moist soil near neutral on the pH scale. Mix 1 part peat moss or leaf mold to 2 parts soil to hold moisture. A permanent mulch of chunky peat moss, wood chips, sawdust or ground bark helps keep the soil cool and moist. Feed early each spring with a light application of cottonseed meal or a rhododendron-azalea-camellia fertilizer. It may be necessary to add a small amount of ground limestone to counteract the acidity of peat moss or fertilizer. Daphnes prefer light shade but will tolerate sun close to the coast and in the cooler parts of the recommended areas. If pruning is necessary, cut back to a side branch. Daphnes are difficult to transplant except as small container-grown plants. In Areas C and D set them out from early spring to early fall; in Areas I and J plant them at any time.

E

ELAEAGNUS
E. pungens and varieties (thorny elaeagnus)

The thorny elaeagnus is valued for its usefulness in screens, hedges and borders. If unpruned, it becomes a sprawling spiny-branched impenetrable shrub 8 to 15 feet tall in 8 to 10 years, densely covered with wavy-edged 2-

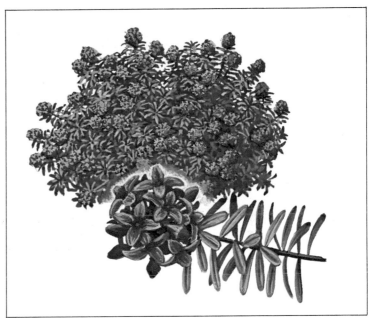

ROSE DAPHNE
Daphne cneorum

THORNY ELAEAGNUS
Elaeagnus pungens

For growing areas, see map on page 149.

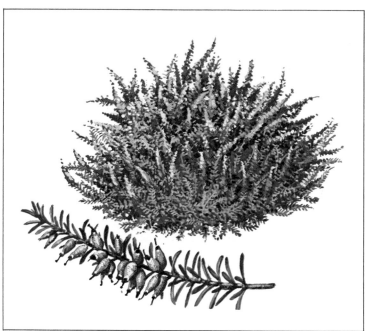

SPRING HEATH
Erica herbacea

to 4-inch leaves. Thorny elaeagnus may be pruned at any time and can be kept at any height, either sheared geometrically into a formal hedge or pruned with hand clippers to retain its normal arching outline. Thorny elaeagnus bears small but fragrant ivory-white blossoms in late fall; by spring these mature into ½-inch red berries.

Thorny elaeagnus grows well in Areas D, E, G, I and J. The Fruitland variety is a compact shrub with silvery wavy-edged leaves; *E. pungens maculatus* has leaves prominently marked with a gold-colored blotch in the center; *E. pungens marginatus* has silvery white leaf edgings; and *E. pungens variegatus* has ivory-white leaf edgings. All varieties thrive in almost any soil, moist or dry, in direct sun or light shade. They tolerate heat and wind, are not attacked by pests and can be transplanted easily.

ELM See *Ulmus*

ERICA
E. canaliculata, also called *E. melanthera* (Christmas heath, incorrectly called Christmas heather); *E. cinerea* and varieties (twisted heath); *E. herbacea,* also called *E. carnea,* and varieties (spring heath); *E. purpurescens darleyensis,* also called *E. darleyensis, E. mediterranea hybrida* (Darley heath); *E. tetralix* and varieties (cross-leaved heath); *E. vagans* and varieties (Cornish heath)

These plants are closely related to the heathers, which belong to a separate genus, *Calluna*. Except for Christmas heath, they are small, bushy plants grown chiefly for their tiny, bell-shaped flowers. The leaves are short and narrow, but so thick the plants give a green carpet effect when not in bloom. Some varieties withstand cold well.

Christmas heath grows well in Areas E and J. The tallest of the heaths, it becomes 4 to 6 feet high and bears clouds of rosy purple flowers in fall and winter. Twisted heath grows well in Areas C, D and I and the northern part of Area J. It becomes 12 to 18 inches tall and bears white, pink, red or purple flowers from early summer to early fall. Spring heath grows well in Areas C, D, I and J. It becomes 6 to 12 inches tall and produces spikes of white, pink, red or purple flowers from late fall to early spring in mild climates; in the North flowering starts in very early spring and continues for about three months. Darley heath grows well in the southern part of Area C and all parts of Areas D, I and J. It becomes 1 to 2 feet tall and has pale rosy flowers from November until May. The very hardy cross-leaved heath grows well in Areas A, B, C, D and I and the northern part of Area J. It becomes 1 to 2 feet tall and bears white, rosy pink or red flowers from midsummer until late fall. Cornish heath grows well in Areas C, D, I and J. It becomes 8 to 12 inches tall and bears white, pinkish purple or deep red flowers from midsummer until fall.

All species of heath do best with direct sun in a moist but well-drained mixture composed of 1 part peat moss, 1 part coarse sand and 1 part soil. Most require an acid soil, although twisted heath and Darley heath will tolerate alkaline conditions. Feed in early spring with a light dusting of cottonseed meal or rhododendron-azalea-camellia fertilizer scattered on the ground as far as the branches spread. Do not cultivate the soil around heaths because their shallow roots are easily damaged; instead maintain a 2- to 3-inch mulch of chunky peat moss, wood chips, sawdust or ground bark. Do not prune Christmas heath and Darley heath; simply snip off faded flowers. Shear spring heath back one half to two thirds of its height after flowering to encourage new growth. Prune other low-growing types just as new growth begins. Heaths can be transplanted easily at almost any season.

LOQUAT
Eriobotrya japonica

ERIOBOTRYA

E. deflexa (bronze loquat),
E. japonica and varieties (loquat)

Loquats are small trees or large shrubs that grow about 20 feet tall in 8 to 10 years under favorable circumstances. Trained to a single trunk, a loquat makes a fine small shade tree; a line of them, grown as multistemmed shrubs, makes a thick screen or informal hedge. Loquats can be espaliered to grow flat against a trellis, open fence or north-facing wall, but they cannot tolerate the reflected heat from a sunny wall. Their 6- to 12-inch sawtooth-edged leaves are dark green on top; the undersides are coated with tan fuzz, which adds a color accent as the wind moves the foliage. The bronze loquat is further accented in spring by the coppery bronze color of new leaves. The standard loquat, *E. japonica,* bears 6- to 8-inch clusters of small, fragrant, creamy white flowers in late fall and early winter, and produces tartly sweet, aromatic 1½-inch golden-yellow to orange fruit in mid- to late spring in frost-free locations, with more limited production in cooler areas; the variety Golden Nugget is particularly recommended. The bronze loquat usually does not bear flowers or fruit.

Both species thrive in Areas E and J. *E. japonica* also does well in Areas D and I and the southern part of G. Both will grow in direct sun or partial shade in almost any moist soil, and they are well suited to seaside gardens. If fast growth is desired, feed once in early spring with a dusting of cottonseed meal or rhododendron-azalea-camellia fertilizer applied beneath the plants. Prune in early spring.

ESCALLONIA

E. 'Fradesi' (pink princess escallonia), *E. 'Jubilee'* (Jubilee escallonia), *E. montevidensis* (Montevideo or white escallonia), *E. organensis* (Organ Mountain escallonia)

Evergreen escallonias are widely grown in Southern California for their rich glossy foliage and for the 2-inch clusters of flowers borne on the ends of branches intermittently throughout the year. Among the hybrids, two 4- to 6-foot shrubs that are recommended for planting near foundations or in borders and informal hedges are the pink princess escallonia, which is easily kept small by pruning and bears abundant rose-pink flowers in spring and summer, and the Jubilee escallonia, noted for its compact bushy growth and its rich pink flowers, which bloom abundantly in summer. Two other species can be pruned to grow into 15- to 25-foot trees with several trunks supporting wide crowns of foliage and flowers, in about 10 to 15 years. The two are Montevideo escallonia, whose white flowers bloom primarily in late summer and fall, and Organ Mountain escallonia, a densely branched plant that has coppery green leaves and in early summer produces pink buds opening to white or blush pink blossoms.

Escallonias grow well in Areas E and J. They thrive in seaside areas, enduring heat and wind in direct sun or light shade in almost any well-drained soil. Prune after the flowers fade to shape plants and to encourage the development of new flower-bearing branches.

EUCALYPTUS

E. camaldulensis, also called *E. rostrata* (red gum, river red gum); *E. citriodora,* also called *E. maculata citriodora* (lemon-scented gum); *E. erythrocorys* (red cap gum); *E. ficifolia* (red or scarlet flowering gum); *E. leucoxylon* (white ironbark); *E. polyanthemos* (red box gum, silver dollar gum, Australian beech); *E. pulverulenta* (silver mountain gum); *E. rudis* (desert gum); *E. sideroxylon rosea* (red or pink ironbark); *E. torquata* (coral or goldfield gum)

For growing areas, see map on page 149.

PINK PRINCESS ESCALLONIA
Escallonia fradesi

RED FLOWERING GUM
Eucalyptus ficifolia

123

EMERALD 'N GOLD WINTER CREEPER
Euonymus fortunei 'Emerald 'n Gold'

POINSETTIA
Euphorbia pulcherrima

Australian trees, commonly called gums because of their thick sap, eucalyptuses grow from 10 feet to more than 100 feet tall. They are noted for their attractively shaggy bark, fragrant blue-green foliage and extremely fast growth (3 to 6 feet a year). They make highly decorative shade trees—some species are grown for their conspicuous flowers as well—and they are also often used as windbreaks and screens in Southern California and Arizona.

The red gum, which grows 80 to 120 feet tall, makes a particularly fine shade tree for a large garden. The lemon-scented gum, 50 to 75 feet tall, is distinguished by its pinkish or greenish white bark and—as its name indicates—lemony foliage. A smaller species, the red cap gum, grows only 10 to 30 feet tall but often produces several trunks, making it a good windbreak; it displays bright yellow flowers in winter. The red flowering gum, a 20- to 40-foot-tall tree, bears clusters of brilliant red or pink fuzzy flowers in January and February and again from July to October. The white ironbark grows 40 to 80 feet tall and has white flowers in winter. The red box gum, another fine windbreak, grows 30 to 70 feet tall and bears small clusters of white flowers in winter and spring. The silver mountain gum, 15 to 30 feet tall, is excellent in both windbreaks and screens; it has interesting silvery blue leaves that clasp around the stems, and it bears tiny white flowers in midwinter. The desert gum—so called because it endures very hot and dry locations—grows 30 to 50 feet tall and bears small fuzzy white flowers in late summer and fall. The red or pink ironbark, 30 to 50 feet tall, has clusters of pink flowers in midwinter and early spring. The coral gum grows 15 to 20 feet tall, often developing several trunks, and bears pink or red flowers all through the year.

Because they are native to arid lands, eucalyptuses grow well only in Area J. There they thrive from oceanside to desert in sun and almost any soil. When planting container-grown plants, spread out the roots carefully after removing the container. Water heavily. Prune in midsummer, cutting back to just above a side branch if possible.

EUONYMUS
E. fortunei, also called *E. radicans,* and varieties (winter creeper); *E. japonicus* and varieties (evergreen euonymus); *E. kiautschovicus,* also called *E. patens,* and varieties (spreading euonymus)

Euonymuses are among the most valuable of ornamental plants in much of the United States because of their ability to thrive in many climates and their all-round usefulness in landscape plantings. The fast-growing evergreen types listed here have shiny leathery bright green leaves, mostly oval and 1 to 2 inches long, and bear inconspicuous flowers followed by small but showy pink-to-orange berries in the fall. Several varieties with yellow or white markings on their foliage are used as accent plants. Low-growing varieties are valued as ground covers. Upright bushy types are useful near foundations and as hedges.

Many varieties of winter creeper hold their foliage through the year under all but the most severe of winter conditions; even if leaves drop, plants send out new leaves early in the spring. *E. fortunei vegetus,* the bigleaf winter creeper, usually grows about 4 feet tall with an equal spread in 8 to 10 years. Its Emerald strains, outstanding both in beauty and in resistance to frost, smog and dog urine, include Emerald Charm, a columnar type that grows 6 to 7 feet tall; Emerald Cushion, a 3-foot mound-shaped dwarf; Emerald Gaiety, 4 to 5 feet tall with distinct white edges on its leaves; Emerald 'n Gold, 4 feet tall with yellow-edged leaves; and Emerald Pride, 4 to 5 feet tall and upright growing. The species commonly called evergreen euonymus may become 6 to 15 feet tall in 8 to 10 years but can easily be kept pruned to any smaller size. Among its fine varieties are *E. japonicus albo-marginatus,* with white-edged leaves; *E. japonicus aureo-marginatus,* with yellow-edged leaves; *E. japonicus aureo-variegatus,* whose leaves are green at the edges and yellow at the center; and *E. japonicus microphyllus,* a dwarf variety so compact that it rarely needs pruning. Spreading euonymus grows about 4 to 6 feet tall with an equal spread in five to six years; excellent varieties are Dupont and Manhattan.

All three species grow well in Areas D, E, G, I and J; in addition, winter creepers do well in Areas B and C, spreading euonymuses in Area C. They thrive in direct sun or partial shade in almost any soil, wet or dry. Prune at any time; they respond well to shaping with shears for hedges.

EUPHORBIA
E. pulcherrima (poinsettia)

Poinsettia, the Christmas pot plant, grows rapidly outdoors as a garden shrub in warm climates. It becomes 4 to 10 feet tall in a single season, and has coarse leaves 4 to 8 inches long. It owes its great popularity not to its true flowers, which are tiny chartreuse nubs at the tips of mature stems, but to brightly colored petallike upper leaves, the bracts, which grow as much as 12 inches across; most poinsettias have red bracts, but there are also pink, white and pink-and-white varieties.

Poinsettias grow well in Areas E and J. They thrive in direct sun with rich moist soil that is slightly acid. They are susceptible to frost and are therefore best planted among hardier evergreens so that if the poinsettias are killed by cold, their loss will not create a noticeable gap in the planting. Feed them in early spring, early summer and early fall with a light dusting of any 5-10-5 garden fertilizer spread around the plants. If many medium-sized bracts are desired, encourage branching by pinching off the tips of the stems every two months until mid-August. If fewer but larger bracts are preferred, limit the number of canes allowed to grow from each plant by clipping out all but a few. Cut plants back to within 6 inches of the ground in the spring to create entirely new top growth each year. Potted plants that have blossomed indoors, as well as container-grown plants purchased from a nursery, can be set out in the spring.

F

FATSIA
F. japonica, also called *Aralia japonica, A. sieboldii* (Japanese fatsia, Japanese aralia)

The Japanese fatsia is a bold-leaved shrub with the exotic look of a jungle plant. It usually grows 4 to 8 feet tall in three to five years. Luxuriant fan-shaped leaves, up to 16 inches across and deeply cut into seven to nine lobes, are held out horizontally from the stems. Candelabralike stalks bearing golf-ball-shaped heads of small creamy flowers bloom in winter; small inedible blue berries follow in spring. *F. japonica variegata,* variegated Japanese fatsia, has creamy or yellow markings at the ends of its leaves.

Fatsias grow well in the southern part of Area D and in all parts of Areas E, I and J. They are grown as house plants elsewhere. In the garden, they thrive in moist soil, in partial to deep shade, but will grow in sun near the coast and near the northern edges of the recommended areas. Feed every month or two with a light dusting of 5-10-5 fertilizer scattered beneath the plants. Prune straggly plants back low in early spring to force lush new growth. If only foliage is sought, remove the flower stalks as they appear; the leaves will grow even larger.

JAPANESE FATSIA
Fatsia japonica

For growing areas, see map on page 149.

PINEAPPLE GUAVA
Feijoa sellowiana

WEEPING FIG
Ficus benjamina

MAJESTIC BEAUTY SHAMEL ASH
Fraxinus uhdei 'Majestic Beauty'

FEIJOA
F. sellowiana (pineapple guava)

A broad, fast-growing shrub or small tree of many uses, the pineapple guava usually grows 6 to 8 feet in five years, but old, unpruned plants may reach a height of 15 to 20 feet. Its many branches bear 2- to 3-inch oval leaves—green on top, chalk-white beneath but with an overall bluish cast when seen from a distance. This color effect makes the plants seem farther away than they really are, and helps create an illusion of space when they are placed at the back of a garden. The 1½-inch blossoms with bristly crimson stamens appear in spring and early summer, and are followed by dull reddish green 1- to 4-inch edible fruit that has a distinct pineapple flavor. To bear fruit, most pineapple guavas require cross-pollination from another plant, but among the recommended varieties that do not are Coolidge and Pineapple Gem.

Pineapple guavas grow well in Areas E and J. They thrive in full sun or partial shade, in almost any soil so long as it is moist. Feed in early spring and early summer with a small amount of 5-10-5 fertilizer scattered beneath the plants. Size can easily be limited by spring pruning.

FICUS
F. benjamina (weeping fig, Benjamin fig),
F. retusa nitida (Indian laurel)

Unlike their deciduous relatives, evergreen figs bear inedible fruit and serve only as ornaments prized for their glossy dark green leaves. The weeping fig reaches 50 feet in height in about 30 years in the warm moist climate of Florida and about 30 feet in the drier climate of Southern California. It has pointed leaves, 3 to 6 inches long, that hang from gracefully drooping branches, and makes an excellent small tree for patios or lawns; it is also eye catching when trained to grow flat against a wall as an espalier. The upright Indian laurel grows at the same rate and to the same height as the weeping fig; it has 2- to 4-inch blunt-ended leaves and serves as a shade tree and, because of its adaptability to shaping, is widely used for formal hedges and the fanciful figures of topiary. Aerial roots often descend from its trunk or branches.

Evergreen figs grow well only in the frost-free parts of Areas E and J. They grow in full sun or partial shade and need a moist soil. Feed by scattering a small amount of 5-10-5 fertilizer beneath the trees in early spring.

FIG See *Ficus*
FIRE THORN See *Pyracantha*
FLAME BUSH See *Calliandra*
FLAME-OF-THE-WOODS See *Ixora*
FORTUNELLA See *Citrus*

FRAXINUS
F. uhdei (shamel ash, evergreen ash)

The shamel ash grows 3 feet a year when young, eventually forming a broad-crowned tree up to 70 feet tall by the time it is 30 to 40 years old. Virtually pest free, it is fine for shade and is often planted along streets in Southern California. Its 8- to 10-inch-long leaves are composed of 5 to 11 leaflets, each 3 to 4 inches long; the variety Majestic Beauty has larger dark green leaves, usually with only seven leaflets.

The shamel ash grows well in Area J. It thrives in full sun in rich moist soil, and will tolerate alkaline conditions. To speed growth, each spring poke a series of holes 6 to 18 inches deep and about 2 feet apart in circles under the trees, beginning 2 feet from the trunk and extending 2 feet beyond the spread of the branches; drop a handful of lawn fertilizer such as 10-6-4 into each hole. Water well after feeding. Prune young trees each spring to develop the shape you desire. Remove lower branches as the tree grows to allow room to walk beneath.

G

GARDENIA
G. jasminoides and varieties (gardenia, Cape jasmine)

Gardenias are 3- to 5-foot shrubs that bear superbly fragrant 3- to 5-inch white flowers and handsome shiny dark green leaves 3 to 4 inches long. They form flower buds only when night temperatures drop below 65°; thus, in the coastal sections of California, where days are warm but nights are cool much of the year, gardenias bloom abundantly from May until November and occasionally at other times. In areas where night temperatures remain above 65° from late spring on, they provide a big burst of flowers in late spring and early summer, and plantings in light shade sometimes continue to blossom into the summer months. Few blossoms are produced in the winter, since the plants become nearly dormant when night temperatures drop below 55°. Three recommended large-flowered varieties are August Beauty, Mystery and Veitchii Improved. A delightful low-growing variety is *G. jasminoides radicans,* the miniature or creeping gardenia; it grows only 6 to 12 inches tall but as much as 3 feet across, and bears fragrant 1-inch white flowers and slender inch-long leaves.

Gardenias grow well in the southern part of Area D and in Areas E and J. They thrive in full sun or light shade in moist soil that is quite acid (either naturally or made so with soil amendments—see page 24); if foliage turns pale with dark veins, add iron chelate or iron sulfate according to the manufacturer's directions. When setting out container-grown plants, plant them at the same depth as they were growing or even an inch higher. Since cultivating around the plants may damage their shallow roots, keep the soil moist and cool by mulching with 2 to 3 inches of wood chips, sawdust or ground bark. Feed the plants every month during the growing season with a light dusting of a rhododendron-azalea-camellia fertilizer, cottonseed meal, or the fertilizer sold especially for gardenias, scattered as far as the branches spread. Prune lightly in early spring to shape plants, and remove deadwood.

GERANIUM, JUNGLE See *Ixora*
GOLD-DUST TREE See *Aucuba*
GRAPEFRUIT See *Citrus*
GUM See *Eucalyptus*

H

HEATH See *Erica*
HEATH, IRISH See *Daboëcia*
HEATHER, CHRISTMAS See *Erica*
HEATHER, IRISH BELL See *Daboëcia*
HEATHER, SCOTCH See *Calluna; Erica*

HEBE
H. andersonii, also called *Veronica andersonii* (Anderson's hebe); *H. buxifolia* 'Patty's Purple,' also called *Veronica buxifolia* (Patty's Purple hebe); *H. speciosa,* also called *Veronica imperialis* (showy hebe)

Hebes, once known as veronicas, are rounded shrubs thickly covered with 1- to 4-inch shiny dark green leaves. They bear 2- to 4-inch-long spikes of tiny white, pink, red, lavender or purple flowers at the ends of their branches in summer. Anderson's hebe grows 5 to 6 feet tall; flowers are bluish violet at the top, fading to white at the base. Patty's Purple grows about 3 feet tall and has deep purple flow-

GARDENIA
Gardenia jasminoides

SHOWY HEBE
Hebe speciosa

For growing areas, see map on page 149.

127

ers on erect wine-red stems. Showy hebe grows 2 to 5 feet tall and bears wine-red or bluish purple flowers.

Hebes grow best in the coastal sections of Areas I and J. They need partial shade in hot inland areas but can tolerate full sun in cooler seaside locations; they withstand salt air. In Area I, where rainfall is plentiful, plant them on the warmest, driest banks. In Area J they do best in moist but well-drained soil. Prune lightly after flowering.

HIBISCUS
H. rosa-sinensis (Chinese hibiscus)

The Chinese hibiscus is a spectacular shrub that comes in a wide range of heights, blossom sizes and blossom colors, and serves most garden uses. Most varieties grow 4 to 8 feet tall, but in frost-free areas some become twice that height. The glossy leaves are 2 to 4 inches in length. The flowers, many of them lushly petaled, are 4 to 8 inches across and range in color from pure white through all shades of pink and yellow to red and orange. The plants bloom the year round where temperatures stay above 70°. But even where the plants might be nipped by frost occasionally, they are so attractive that gardeners simply cut off the damaged growth and await more blossoms in the spring. Most of the flowers last only for a day, but multipetaled types may remain attractive for two to four days.

Chinese hibiscuses can be grown only in Areas E and J. They thrive in hot weather—in full sun or light shade in well-drained soil. Container-grown plants may be set out at any time in the southern parts of Areas E and J, but spring planting is preferable in northern sections. Where frost damage is possible, plant the shrubs where they will be protected from the wind, such as in a sunny nook beside a patio wall. Feed the plants once a month during the growing season, usually early spring to early fall, with a light scattering of 5-10-5 fertilizer. In early spring remove weak branches and cut back the previous season's growth by about one third. Cut back overgrown or frost-damaged plants severely, even as low as 4 inches from the ground; vigorous new flowering stems will grow rapidly.

HOLLY See *Ilex*
HOLLY, FALSE See *Osmanthus*
HOLLY GRAPE See *Mahonia*

HYPERICUM
H. calycinum (Aaron's-beard St.-John's-wort),
H. moserianum (goldflower),
H. patulum varieties (goldencup St.-John's-wort)

The bright yellow 2- to 3-inch flowers of St.-John's-worts bring cheery color to summer and autumn gardens for many weeks, and they could not be easier to grow. Aaron's-beard St.-John's-wort, an excellent ground cover that spreads by underground roots, has 3- to 4-inch leaves turning purplish in the fall in northern areas; it rarely grows more than a foot tall, and blooms much of the summer. Other varieties are taller and have leaves about 2 inches long. Goldflower grows 2 to 3 feet tall and blooms for most of the summer; its stems are reddish when young. Goldencup St.-John's-wort has three varieties that are superb garden plants. *H. patulum henryi,* Henry St.-John's-wort, grows 3 to 4 feet tall and blooms from midsummer until midautumn; Hidcote grows 1 to 4 feet tall and blooms profusely in summer; and Sungold, 2 to 3 feet tall with a spread of 3 feet or more, blooms from midsummer until frost.

Goldflowers grow well in Areas D, E, G, I and J; Aaron's-beard St.-John's-wort and the goldencup St.-John's-worts do well in those areas and also in the southern part of Area C. Plants grown in the colder sections of these areas

CHINESE HIBISCUS
Hibiscus rosa-sinensis

SUNGOLD ST.-JOHN'S-WORT
Hypericum patulum 'Sungold'

often lose their foliage or even freeze to the ground but usually sprout again and bear flowers that same year; however, cold-damaged plants do not become as tall as plants in warmer regions. Most species grow in full sun or light shade, but prefer a bit of shade during midday in hot areas. They thrive in poor sandy soil as long as it is well drained. Small plants are easiest to start; they will grow rapidly, especially if set out in early spring. If plants grow too tall, prune the stems by about one third in early spring. Aaron's-beard St.-John's-wort should be mowed to the ground in early spring to remove old leaves and stems; fresh growth then sprouts quickly.

I

ILEX

I. altaclarensis wilsonii (Wilson's holly), *I. aquifolium* and varieties (English holly), *I. aquipernyi* 'Brilliant' (Brilliant holly), *I. cassine* (dahoon, dahoon holly), *I. cornuta* and varieties (Chinese holly), *I. crenata* and varieties (Japanese holly), *I. glabra* and varieties (inkberry), *I. 'Nellie R. Stevens'* (Nellie R. Stevens holly), *I. opaca* and varieties (American holly), *I. pendunculosa* (long-stalked holly), *I. pernyi* (Perny holly), *I. vomitoria* and varieties (yaupon)

The name holly usually brings to mind the red-berried English and American species used as Christmas decorations. But there are other kinds of hollies, quite different in appearance, that are of equal beauty and serve a variety of garden uses. Some become trees while others rarely grow more than 12 inches tall; berries may be red, black or yellow; leaves may be spiny- or smooth-edged.

The berries are the crowning glory of hollies, especially on the red-berried types, but all hollies do not have berries —in most species male and female flowers are borne on separate plants, and only the females bear fruit. Usually one male tree must be within 100 feet of a female tree of the same species in order for bees to transfer pollen from the male to the female blossoms to start fruit growing. Some species, however, are self-fertile—that is, all plants will produce fruit by self-pollination. In the listing below, both male and female plants are needed to produce berries unless otherwise indicated.

Wilson's holly is a self-fertile hybrid that tolerates wind, drought and sun or shade. It bears heavy crops of red berries and usually grows 6 to 8 feet tall in 10 years, though it sometimes becomes more than twice that height. Its shiny spiny-edged leaves are 3 to 5 inches long.

English holly, considered by many gardeners to be the most beautiful of all hollies, is native to much of Europe and Asia as well as England. It can grow 70 feet tall in 100 years and has 1½- to 3-inch glossy spiny-edged leaves and bright red berries on branches grown the previous season. Among its many fine varieties are Balkans, which is particularly cold resistant; Boulder Creek, James G. Esson and Sparkler, all of whose female plants become heavy with berries; Teufel's Little Bull, a compact male plant that produces abundant pollen; Fructulutea, whose berries are yellow; Aurea Regina, with variegated leaves of green and yellow; and Silver Queen, with variegated leaves of green and white.

Brilliant holly, a self-fertile hybrid variety, grows 8 to 10 feet tall in 10 to 15 years. It has shiny spiny-edged leaves, 2 to 4 inches long and deeply lobed, and produces great numbers of red berries.

Dahoon holly, native to the southeastern U.S., usually becomes a narrowly conical tree 15 to 25 feet tall in 15 to 20 years. Its leaves, much softer than those of most hollies, are 2 to 3 inches long; they have few or no spines.

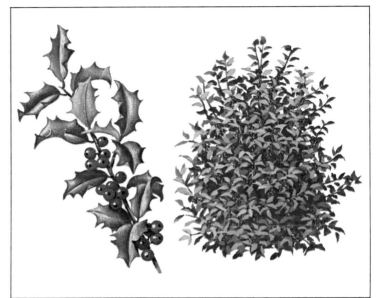

ENGLISH HOLLY
Ilex aquifolium

BURFORD HOLLY
Ilex cornuta burfordii

For growing areas, see map on page 149.

JAPANESE HOLLY
Ilex crenata

CONVEXLEAF HOLLY
Ilex crenata convexa

AMERICAN HOLLY
Ilex opaca

Most plants bear dull red berries on the current season's growth; a few very rare varieties have yellow berries.

Chinese holly has very glossy leaves, 3 to 4 inches long and 2 to 3 inches wide, usually with strong spines at the outer corners and tip. Shrubs grow 6 to 10 feet tall in five to eight years, are self-fertile and bear bright red berries.

I. cornuta burfordii, the Burford holly, is an excellent variety of Chinese holly with spineless, somewhat convex 4-inch leaves and large orange-red berries. Dazzler, a slow-growing compact variety, produces bright red berries. D'Or produces yellow berries.

Japanese holly is a work horse in landscape gardening. A bushy shrub usually growing 8 to 10 feet tall in 10 years, it can easily be kept much smaller with pruning and stands shearing well. It has dark green, finely toothed foliage about 1 inch long and black berries that often pass unnoticed. The Japanese holly has spawned many excellent varieties. *I. crenata convexa,* also called *I. crenata bullata,* the convexleaf holly, is one of the most beautiful of all broad-leaved evergreens. Its densely set, intensely shiny ½-inch leaves are convex, as its name suggests. The plant usually grows no more than 4 feet tall in 10 years, but may become 6 feet or more across if untrimmed; it is ideal for planting beneath windows because it can be kept small with little effort. *I. crenata helleri,* the Heller Japanese holly, usually grows only 12 inches tall but may become 3 feet across in 8 to 10 years if unpruned; a similar variety is Green Island, which grows about 2 feet tall. *I. crenata microphylla,* the littleleaf Japanese holly, develops into a stiff, compact bush about 6 feet tall in 10 years. *I. crenata rotundifolia,* also called *I. crenata latifolia,* the roundleaf Japanese holly, is a fast-growing variety that becomes 10 to 20 feet tall in about 15 to 30 years; it is an excellent plant to use as a hedge.

Inkberry, the most cold-resistant evergreen holly in America, is gradually receiving the recognition it deserves. It usually grows 4 to 6 feet tall in 10 years. Its smooth, nearly spineless glossy leaves are 1 to 2 inches long; its berries —as its name implies—are black. Unlike most hollies, inkberries spread by means of underground stems called stolons. *I. glabra compacta,* the compact inkberry, matures at about half the height of the ordinary species.

Nellie R. Stevens holly, a handsome hybrid, grows 18 to 20 feet tall in 15 to 25 years; conical when young, it becomes more spreading as it matures. It has 2- to 3-inch spiny-edged dark green leaves and is generally loaded with bright orange-red berries. It is somewhat more cold resistant than its parents, English holly and Chinese holly.

American holly, native to the East and Gulf Coasts from Massachusetts to Texas, is broadly conical in shape and usually becomes 8 to 15 feet tall after 10 to 15 years in the garden; old trees may become 30 to 40 feet tall. American holly bears red berries on the current season's growth and has the traditional spiny-edged "holly-shaped" leaves. The leaves are attractive throughout the year but they do not have the deep color and gleam of English holly leaves. Excellent red-berry varieties are Bountiful, Cardinal, East Palatka, Merry Christmas, Mrs. Santa, Old Faithful and Old Heavyberry. *I. opaca xanthocarpa,* the yellow-fruited American holly, bears yellow berries.

Long-stalked holly bears clusters of one to three red berries on long stems (they look like little cherries). The plant is narrowly conical in shape, grows 10 to 15 feet tall in 10 years and has 1- to 3-inch spineless dark green leaves.

Perny holly grows rather slowly to a height of 15 to 20 feet in 15 to 25 years and has spiny-edged leaves and red berries. Both male and female plants must be planted in order to get berries.

Yaupons, native to the southern U.S., are multiple-stemmed plants that grow 20 feet tall in 15 to 20 years with an equal spread, but tolerate shearing well and can be kept at any height. They have 1-inch gray-green leaves and are self-fertile, setting unbelievably large crops of translucent red berries. *I. vomitoria nana,* the dwarf yaupon, grows 1½ to 4 feet tall. It does not bear fruit.

All hollies listed here grow well in Areas D, E, I and J. Wilson's holly and Chinese hollies also do well in Area G and the southern part of Area C; English hollies, Brilliant holly, Japanese hollies, Nellie R. Stevens holly and Perny holly in the southern part of Area C; American hollies and long-stalked holly in the eastern part of Area C; and inkberries in Areas B and C. Yaupons also do well in Area G.

All species thrive in full sun and slightly acid soil, though Wilson's holly will tolerate alkaline soil. They will grow in light shade but bear fewer berries there than in sun. Except for self-fertile types, set out male and female plants within 100 feet of each other, at a ratio of 1 male to every 10 females. Do not cultivate the soil around them; instead, to keep the roots cool and moist, mulch with a 2- to 4-inch layer of wood chips, sawdust, pine needles, ground bark or other organic material. Dust the soil beneath hollies generously early each spring with cottonseed meal or rhododendron-azalea-camellia fertilizer. Keep the soil moist during the summer growing season, but let it become somewhat drier in early fall to allow the season's growth to harden and mature enough to resist winter damage. In northern areas plant hollies where they will have winter shade and protection from the wind.

It is easier to transplant container-grown hollies successfully than those sold balled and burlaped, which must be set in place quickly after they are dug from the nursery ground, or the roots are likely to be injured by drying. Plant newly dug balled-and-burlaped hollies just as they are starting new growth in the spring; in the South they may also be planted in early September. Hollies sometimes drop their old leaves soon after being transplanted, but usually a new crop of foliage quickly follows; however, be careful not to overwater a holly that has lost its leaves.

Most hollies are naturally graceful and require little pruning. If pruning is called for, do it in early spring before new growth begins. To force the development of many side branches for symmetrically formal plants, prune back wayward branches. Use hand clippers on large-leaved types to avoid mutilating foliage; use hedge shears on small-leaved forms to achieve a smooth formal outline and dense growth. The branches of some red-berried hollies are harvested each December to serve as holiday decorations and often this much pruning is all that is necessary to train trees into desired shapes.

INKBERRY See *Ilex*
IRONBARK See *Eucalyptus*

IXORA

I. coccinea (jungle geranium, ixora, flame-of-the-woods)

Jungle geraniums are popular hedge and foundation shrubs in southern Florida. They usually grow 3 to 5 feet tall in four to five years (though some reach as high as 15 feet) and bear 4- to 6-inch globular clusters of bright red, orange, yellow, pink or white tube-shaped flowers, about 1 inch across and 1½ inches long. The flowers, which bloom continuously under ideal conditions, are set among 2-inch leaves that are bronzy when they first appear, then turn a glistening dark green.

Jungle geraniums grow well only in the southern part of Area E. They thrive in full sun in moist but well-drained

YAUPON
Ilex vomitoria

JUNGLE GERANIUM
Ixora coccinea

Illustration by Eduardo Salgado

For growing areas, see map on page 149.

PRIMROSE JASMINE
Jasminum mesnyi

MOUNTAIN LAUREL
Kalmia latifolia

LAUREL
Laurus nobilis

acid soil. They are easily damaged by frost and grow best in hot humid weather. Feed in early spring and midsummer with cottonseed meal or rhododendron-azalea-camellia fertilizer. Prune at any time.

J

JASMINE See *Jasminum*
JASMINE, CAPE See *Gardenia*

JASMINUM

J. humile revolutum (Italian jasmine);
J. mesnyi, also called *J. primulinum* (primrose jasmine)

Evergreen jasmines can be treated either as shrubs or vines. They will grow in graceful mounds with long arching branches, or they can be fastened against a wall or trellis (they will not climb by themselves). As shrubs they grow 6 to 10 feet tall, usually with an equal spread, in four to five years and bear yellow flowers and dark green leaves. Italian jasmine has clusters of up to a dozen fragrant 1-inch flowers from midsummer to fall; its leaves consist of three to seven leaflets. Primrose jasmine bears solitary 2-inch flowers that are lushly petaled and faintly scented from fall until spring; its leaves are divided into three leaflets.

Italian jasmine grows well in Areas D, E and J; primrose jasmine does well only in Areas E and J. Both thrive in full sun or light shade in almost any moist soil. If growth is weak or the leaves are pale, scatter a handful of 5-10-5 fertilizer under the plants in the spring. To encourage lateral branching and greater flower production, nip off the ends of canes that become too long. If plants become overgrown, prune them back as much as desired in early spring.

K

KALMIA

K. latifolia (mountain laurel, calico bush)

Mountain laurels are unusually cold-resistant shrubs that grow 4 to 8 feet high in about 10 years but can easily be kept smaller by pruning. Their 3- to 5-inch lustrous dark green leaves are attractive at all seasons, but they are nearly hidden beneath 4- to 6-inch clusters of small cuplike blossoms in late spring. The flowers range in color from nearly white to a pink so deep as to seem almost red; brownish flecks inside the cups look like freckles or sprinkles of nutmeg. The structure of the flowers is unusual—each stamen is held in a tiny slot under tension until it is released when touched by bees so that it catapults pollen onto them. The plants make handsome ornaments when planted near a foundation or in a shrub border, and can be massed to create a spectacular springtime effect.

Mountain laurels grow well in the extreme southern part of Area B, the northern part of Area E and all parts of Areas C, D and I. They thrive in light shade and moist acid soil. They will tolerate deep shade but bear fewer flowers there than in brighter light. Do not cultivate the soil around the plants to keep roots moist and cool; instead, use a permanent 2- to 6-inch mulch of wood chips, oak leaves or ground bark. If faster-than-average growth is desired, dust the soil under the plants with rhododendron-azalea-camellia fertilizer or cottonseed meal in spring. Remove seed capsules after the flowers fade to ensure an abundance of blossoms the next season *(page 79)*. Pruning is rarely needed, but to lower the height of a plant, prune immediately after flowering; new stems will sprout even from large branches. If an old plant has become too large, cut the plant back so that only 2-inch stubs remain above the ground; it will soon grow into a small, thickly foliaged shrub.

KINNIKINNICK See *Arctostaphylos*
KUMQUAT See *Citrus*

L

LAUREL See *Laurus*
LAUREL, CHERRY See *Prunus*
LAUREL, INDIAN See *Ficus*
LAUREL, MOUNTAIN See *Kalmia*
LAURESTINUS See *Viburnum*

LAURUS
L. nobilis (laurel, sweet bay)

The laurel, whose leaves were once woven into crowns for the conquering heroes of Greece and Rome, is so tough and so amenable to shearing into various shapes that it is the first choice among evergreens for topiary "sculptures" and for smoothly contoured formal hedges in areas where it will thrive; it is also widely grown in tubs. A multistemmed, slender conical shape if unpruned, it grows slowly; although it may become 25 feet in about 30 years in the garden, it is usually kept at 8 to 12 feet by trimming. The aromatic leaves, long used as a seasoning (the bay leaf), are a dull dark leathery green, 3 to 4 inches long and about 1 inch wide. In early spring inconspicuous greenish white flowers appear, to be followed in fall by ½- to 1-inch black berries.

The laurel grows well in Areas D, E, I and J. It thrives in sun or light shade in almost any well-drained soil; keep the soil moist in spring and moderately dry the rest of the year. Prune by removing branchlets in the summer with a knife or hand clippers, or wait until the new shoots are 3 to 4 inches long and then shear them with hedge shears—leaves mutilated by the shears will soon be hidden by new growth.

LAVENDER COTTON See *Santolina*
LEMON See *Citrus*

LEPTOSPERMUM
L. laevigatum (Australian tea tree),
L. scoparium hybrids (New Zealand tea tree)

Though tea leaves come from *Thea sinensis, Leptospermum* leaves have been used to make a different kind of beverage. During his first voyage to New Zealand and Australia in 1769, Captain Cook brewed the leaves of *L. scoparium* to prevent scurvy among his crew. Both species are wind and salt resistant and have very small leaves that are nearly hidden during flowering by masses of small blossoms.

The Australian tea tree usually grows as a large multistemmed shrub but is often pruned to a single-trunked tree, which after 8 or 10 years may become 30 feet tall. Its bark is gray and its graceful drooping branches, lined with leaves, are loaded with white flowers in spring. It may be sheared to a smooth contour to make an airy formal hedge.

Most New Zealand tea trees are 5- to 8-foot shrubs, but some dwarf varieties grow only 2 feet high. All are used in hedges and around foundations. The variety Keatleyi bears pink flowers with single layers of petals in early summer; three varieties with multipetaled blossoms are Pompon, bright pink flowers in summer; Ruby Glow, dark red, early spring; Snow White, white, winter and early spring.

Tea trees grow well along the southern coast of Area I and in Area J. They thrive in full sun in very well-drained acid soil, which should be allowed to become moderately dry in late summer. Prune with hand clippers after flowering.

LEUCOPHYLLUM
L. frutescens, also called *L. texanum*
(Texas sage, Texas ranger, senisa, silverleaf)

Texas sage—the purple sage of the cowboy songs—is a mound-shaped bush, more gray than purple when not in bloom, that grows wild on both sides of the Rio Grande. It grows 3 to 5 feet high under semidesert conditions but may

NEW ZEALAND TEA TREE
Leptospermum scoparium hybrid

TEXAS SAGE
Leucophyllum frutescens

For growing areas, see map on page 149.

become 6 to 8 feet tall—and somewhat straggly—in four to five years in well-watered gardens. The silvery feltlike leaves about an inch long create an illusion of distance when the plants are placed at the far end of a garden vista. In the late spring and summer the shrubs are thickly studded with bell-shaped pinkish purple flowers about ½ inch across. A smaller variety, *L. frutescens compactum,* usually grows about 2½ to 4 feet tall. The subtle color makes the plants a good choice for an accent in borders and around foundations as well as for a hedge, which is attractive whether allowed to ramble naturally or trimmed smooth to a formal contour. Plants grow well in the western part of Area D and in Areas E, G and J and do best in full sun with well-drained soil. For thicker growth and more flowers, water mature plants very little. Cut back long branches in early spring.

LEUCOTHOË
L. fontanesiana, also called *L. catesbaei* (drooping leucothoë)

Drooping leucothoës are moundlike shrubs with arching branches. They grow 3 to 5 feet tall in four to five years, and older plants spread slowly from underground roots. Since leucothoës bear thick foliage on branches that droop almost to the ground, they are excellent for use in front of older, larger shrubs and trees that have become unsightly at the base. They also are useful as a ground cover on a shady bank. New shoots rising from the ground and atop older branches in early spring are a bronzy green; as summer advances and the stems elongate, the glossy 4- to 7-inch leaves become a rich dark green—only to turn to a reddish bronze in northern areas as cool weather arrives. In severe winters the plants may lose some of their upper leaves. In summer small flower buds form at leaf axils (the points where leaves join the stems) on the outer 2 feet of each arching cane. The following spring the buds expand into 2- to 3-inch clusters of tiny white flowers that resemble lilies of the valley. The flowers hang gracefully beneath the canes, accounting for the plant's common name. The leaves, with or without blossoms, make attractive bouquets. The variety Rainbow has leaves marked with creamy yellow; its new growth is pink.

Leucothoës grow well in the southern part of Area B, the northern parts of Areas E and J and all parts of Areas C, D and I. They require light to deep shade and a moist acid soil. They should be planted in spring in Areas B and C but can be set out in either spring or fall in other areas. If fast growth is desired, scatter cottonseed meal or a rhododendron-azalea-camellia fertilizer under the plants in early spring. After plants are well established, cut the biggest and oldest canes to the ground in very early spring; this pruning will keep the plants looking young and healthy.

LIGUSTRUM
L. japonicum (Japanese privet); *L. japonicum texanum,* also called *L. texanum* (wax-leaved, luster-leaved or Texas privet); *L. lucidum* (glossy privet)

Evergreen privets are fast-growing (1 to 2 feet a year), pest-free shrubs that are extensively used in the South and West as screens, shrub borders, hedges, foundation-hiding plants and tub plants for patios. These plants have clusters of pungent white flowers in the summer, followed by small blue-black berries that cling for many months.

Japanese privet usually grows 9 to 15 feet tall in five to six years. Its shiny leaves, 2 to 4 inches long with rounded ends, are dark green on top and pale green underneath. The flower clusters are 3 to 4 inches across; there are few berries. The wax-leaved privet grows compactly to a height of 6 to 10 feet in five to six years. It is notable for its gleaming dark green foliage. The Suwannee River hybrid resists cold

DROOPING LEUCOTHOË
Leucothoë fontanesiana

SUWANNEE RIVER PRIVET
Ligustrum japonicum 'Suwannee River'

exceptionally well and reaches a maximum height of 6 feet in six to eight years. Its shiny leathery dark green leaves are 2 to 4 inches long and shaped like little trowels. It has few flowers and no fruit. The glossy privet may grow 40 feet tall in 15 to 20 years. Its pointed leaves are 3 to 6 inches long and medium green. Despite the name glossy privet, the leaves are not as shiny as those of the Japanese privet. (To confuse matters, some nurseries call *L. japonicum* glossy privet and *L. lucidum* Japanese privet.) Flower clusters 8 or 9 inches across are followed by great masses of berries.

Evergreen privets grow well in the southern part of Area G and in Areas D, E, I and J; Suwannee River can even be grown along the East Coast as far north as Long Island in Area C. All thrive in sun or shade in any soil and are noted for their tolerance of difficult conditions—poor soil, drought and neglect. Fertilizer is seldom needed unless the usually rapid growth seems abnormally slow; in such a case scatter 5-10-5 fertilizer under the plants in the spring. To achieve formal shapes, as in hedges or topiary, shear just as growth starts and again when new shoots are 3 to 4 inches long; the second shearing will quickly be covered by short new growth. Plants that are sheared bear fewer flowers. To keep the plants looking natural indefinitely without letting them grow too large, prune back to side branches at any time.

LILAC, CALIFORNIA See *Ceanothus*
LILAC, WILD See *Ceanothus*
LIME See *Citrus*
LIMEQUAT See *Citrus*
LOQUAT See *Eriobotrya*

M

MAGNOLIA

M. grandiflora and varieties (southern magnolia, bull bay)

Towering 90 feet into the air after 75 to 100 years in the garden and spreading to half that distance if not crowded, the southern magnolia is truly a stately tree. Its gleaming dark green leaves, coated beneath with a tan suedelike covering, serve as foils for some of the largest and most fragrant white blossoms found on any tree. Ordinary seedling trees of the species may take 15 years to blossom and then bear flowers 8 inches across, but grafted varieties such as Majestic Beauty, Russet, St. Mary and Samuel Sommer usually blossom within two or three years and produce 12- to 14-inch flowers. The flowers bloom abundantly in spring and summer, and occasional blossoms appear the rest of the year if night temperatures stay above 40°. Magnolias are practically pest free and are used as shade and street trees; young trees may be espaliered on a wall (*page 77*).

Southern magnolias grow in Areas D and E, the southern part of Area G and all of Areas I and J. They grow best in full sun and moist soil, but will tolerate as little as three hours of sun a day. Move container-grown trees into the garden at any time; balled-and-burlaped trees are best moved in early spring. To spur growth, scatter a rhododendron-azalea-camellia fertilizer or cottonseed meal under young trees each spring. Magnolias rarely need pruning.

MAHONIA

M. aquifolium (Oregon holly grape), *M. bealii* (leather-leaved holly grape), *M. repens* (dwarf holly grape, creeping mahonia)

The holly grapes, which include some of the most cold resistant of the broad-leaved evergreens, have leaves that look like holly leaves and fruit that looks like grapes, but they are related to neither. On most species, the feather-shaped leaves, composed of tough, leathery, spiny-edged leaflets, turn an attractive bronze in cold weather. In the spring holly

SOUTHERN MAGNOLIA
Magnolia grandiflora

OREGON HOLLY GRAPE
Mahonia aquifolium

For growing areas, see map on page 149.

135

grapes bear short clusters of bright yellow flowers at the tops of their stems. The flowers are followed by bluish black edible berries, which can be made into jelly. Holly grapes are excellent for use near foundations and in shrub borders.

The Oregon holly grape usually grows about 2 to 3 feet tall in three to four years and has glossy leaves with five to nine leaflets; *M. aquifolium compacta* is a fine low-growing variety that seldom exceeds 18 to 24 inches in height. The leather-leaved holly grape, which grows 8 to 10 feet tall in five to six years, has horizontal leaves, often 12 to 16 inches long, that are composed of 9 to 15 leaflets, each up to 4 inches long; unlike those of other holly grapes, they usually do not become bronzy in cold weather. The dwarf holly grape, which generally grows only 12 inches tall, spreads vigorously underground, making it a fine evergreen ground cover; its leaves are composed of three to seven leaflets.

All three species grow well in Areas D, E, I and J. In addition, the leather-leaved holly grape does well in the southern part of Area C; and both the Oregon holly grape and the dwarf holly grape grow well in the southern part of Area B, the northern part of Area G and all parts of Areas C and F.

Holly grapes prefer light shade and moist soil but will also grow in the sun except in very hot, dry areas. Set out balled-and-burlaped plants in spring or fall. Holly grapes are rarely bothered by pests but should be planted in a sheltered place in northern areas to prevent winter winds from dehydrating foliage. Growth\ can be stimulated by cottonseed meal or a rhododendron-azalea-camellia fertilizer applied lightly beneath plants in the spring. To control size, prune tall canes to the ground in early spring.

MYROXYLON See *Xylosma*
MYRTLE See *Myrtus*

MYRTUS

M. communis and varieties (myrtle)

Myrtle is widely grown in the Southwest because it tolerates heat so well. A rounded bush suited to most garden uses, it usually becomes 5 to 8 feet tall in four to six years and has thick dark green foliage that can be sheared regularly without damaging the plant. When the 2-inch leaves are brushed against, they are delightfully fragrant and so are the fuzzy ¾-inch white flowers that bloom in summer. Half-inch blue-black berries follow in the fall. Excellent varieties include *M. communis boetica*, the Boetica myrtle, a 4- to 6-foot shrub that tolerates drought as well as heat and has distinctive gnarled branches with 3- to 4-inch leaves; *M. communis compacta*, the dwarf myrtle, a 3- to 4-foot bushy plant with small tightly compressed leaves that make it useful near foundations or in low formal or informal hedges; and *M. communis variegata*, the variegated myrtle, which is similar to the dwarf myrtle but has leaves edged with white.

Myrtles grow well in Areas E, I and J and the southern part of Area G. They thrive in almost any well-drained soil in full sun or light shade. Prune to shape the plants in early spring before new growth begins.

N

NANDINA

N. domestica and varieties
(all called nandina, heavenly bamboo, sacred bamboo)

This shrub, a member of the barberry family, grows slowly and its slender stems become only 2½ to 6 feet tall in three to six years. The stems are topped by graceful 12- to 18-inch fronds subdivided into many 1- to 2-inch tough shiny leaflets that change from bronze in early spring to deep green in summer; in cool areas they become red in the fall and winter. In midsummer each stem bears a 6- to 12-

DWARF MYRTLE
Myrtus communis compacta

NANDINA
Nandina domestica

inch cluster of tiny creamy white flowers, followed by masses of ⅜-inch bright red berries. The variety *N. domestica alba* has white berries. *N. domestica nana purpurea* 'Dwarf' grows only 12 to 18 inches tall and has thick foliage that is especially vivid in the fall. Nandinas are good choices to use near foundations and to add winter color to shrub borders. Setting several plants in a group encourages cross-pollination by bees and increases the production of berries.

Nandinas grow well in the southern part of Area C and throughout Areas D, E, G, I and J. They prosper in full sun or in light shade as long as they have moist soil that has been supplemented with 1 part moss or leaf mold to 2 parts soil. Scatter a small amount of cottonseed meal or a rhododendron-azalea-camellia fertilizer beneath the plants early in spring. At this time cut the older gawky stems back to the ground; the plant will quickly send up new stems.

NERIUM
N. oleander varieties (oleander, rosebay)

From early summer until midautumn oleanders bear large clusters of 2-inch single or lushly petaled double flowers, most of them fragrant. The narrow shiny dark green leaves are usually 4 to 6 inches long. Harmless to touch, all parts of the oleander are poisonous if eaten. Most varieties grow 8 to 12 feet tall in six to eight years in this country. Oleander bushes are grown as lawn ornaments and in informal hedges, screens and windbreaks. Good varieties are Hawaii, single salmon-pink flowers with yellow throats; Isle of Capri, single, light yellow; Jannoch, single, bright red; Mrs. Roeding, double, salmon pink; Sealy Pink, single, pink; and Sister Agnes, single, white.

Oleanders grow well in Areas E and J and the southern part of G. They survive in almost any soil in sun or light shade and will withstand drought, heat, wind, air pollution and salt spray. But they do best in full sun in a moist, well-drained soil that has been mixed with an equal amount of peat moss or leaf mold. For fast growth, dust a small amount of cottonseed meal or 5-10-5 fertilizer beneath the plants in spring. Water infrequently in late summer and fall so the season's growth will mature before cool weather arrives. Cut off the tips of stems after the flowers have faded to encourage branching. In the spring overgrown or cold-damaged bushes can be cut back severely—to the ground if necessary—for new shoots grow rapidly. Single-trunked tree-type oleanders are created by removing side branches. Such specimens can be kept 3 to 5 feet tall with regular pruning if grown in patio tubs; in gardens the trunks of large specimens can be pruned to branch at 7 or 8 feet.

OAK   See *Quercus*

OLEA
O. europaea and varieties (olive)

This staple of Mediterranean farmers grows 1½ feet or more a year when young but slows down later, becoming 20 to 30 feet tall after 30 to 40 years. Its narrow silvery gray leaves, pale beneath, are 1½ to 3 inches long. In summer it bears clouds of tiny white fragrant flowers. Normal olive trees bear great quantities of fruit; the pollen is carried by the wind from blossom to blossom. The familiar olive fruit that ripens in the fall is not edible, however, until it has undergone a curing process *(page 13)*. Unharvested olives stain the terrace and litter the lawn. One way to eliminate that problem is to spray the blossoms with a preparation available at garden centers that inhibits the development of fruit. An even better method is to plant a variety such as Fruitless, which is not quite

OLEANDER
Nerium oleander

COMMON OLIVE
Olea europaea

For growing areas, see map on page 149.

HOLLY OSMANTHUS
Osmanthus heterophyllus

CANBY PACHISTIMA
Pachistima canbyi

as free of fruit as the name suggests but is nearly so. Two fruit-bearing varieties widely grown in home gardens are Manzanillo and Mission.

Olive trees grow well in Areas E and J, but rarely bear fruit in Area E because the soil and air are too moist. They thrive in full sun in well-drained slightly dry soil, but will grow almost anywhere as long as moisture is not too plentiful. Home gardeners often remove some lower branches and thin out higher ones of older trees so the full beauty of the gnarled gray trunks can be appreciated.

OLEANDER See *Nerium*
OLIVE See *Olea*
ORANGE See *Citrus*
ORCHID TREE, HONG KONG See *Bauhinia*

OSMANTHUS
O. fragrans (sweet osmanthus); *O. heterophyllus*,
also called *O. aquifolium, O. illicifolius*
(holly osmanthus, false holly)

The osmanthus, a shrub for general garden use, has hollylike foliage, sweetly fragrant blossoms and bluish black berries. It can also be trained to grow flat against a wall as an espalier (*page 77*).

Sweet osmanthus grows well in Areas E and J. It is delightful set close to a patio or near a window where its exotic fragrance can be enjoyed close at hand. Fragrance is the most noticeable characteristic of the tiny greenish white flowers, which are so small that they are difficult to find. Most appear in late winter and early spring, although some plants produce a few all year. This species may grow 10 feet or more tall in 8 to 10 years if not pruned. It has 2½- to 4-inch leaves, some of which may have scalloped edges. The stems are fine for cutting to bring the fragrance indoors. Holly osmanthus also has spring flowers but they are not as fragrant as those of the sweet osmanthus. It grows well in the southern part of Area C and throughout Areas D, E, G, I and J. This shrub may become 15 feet or more tall in 10 years if not pruned, but it can be kept at 5 or 6 feet. Its shiny 2-inch leaves have spiny edges and dark green color much like those of English holly. Variegated holly osmanthus has leaves edged in white.

Osmanthuses will grow in full sun or light shade but they do better in light shade when the soil is somewhat dry. Ideally, the soil should be moist but well drained and supplemented with 1 part peat moss or leaf mold to 2 parts of soil. Pruning can be done at any time with hand clippers by cutting long branches back to side branches.

P
PACHISTIMA (PAXISTIMA)
P. canbyi (Canby pachistima, ratstripper), *P. myrsinites* (myrtle pachistima, mountain boxwood, Oregon boxwood, false box)

Pachistimas are easy-to-care-for low plants useful as edging for the front of a border or as ground cover, particularly on a rocky slope. They grow only 6 to 12 inches tall and spread to a diameter of 2 to 3 feet in three to four years. The small shiny leaves have squared-off ends; a glistening dark green in summer, they bronze in cool weather. Myrtle pachistima can become 1½ to 4 feet tall, but usually grows about 2 feet tall with a 3- to 5-foot spread in three to four years. Its leaves are about 1 inch long.

Pachistimas grow well in the southern part of Area B and throughout Areas C, D and I. They flourish in well-drained but moist acid soil that has been mixed with 1 part peat moss or leaf mold to 2 parts soil. Canby pachistima does well in full sun or light shade, while myrtle pachistima grows best in light to deep shade with a moist atmosphere. Fertilizer is seldom needed, but weak plants can be given a light application of cottonseed meal or a rhododendron-azalea-camellia fertilizer scattered under them early in the spring. Pruning is not required.

PAXISTIMA See *Pachistima*
PEAR See *Pyrus*
PEPPER TREE See *Schinus*

PHOTINIA
P. fraseri (Fraser photinia), *P. glabra* (Japanese photinia), *P. serrulata* (Chinese photinia)

Evergreen photinias have bold, shiny sawtooth-edged foliage that is bronze or red when new but turns dark green as it matures. In spring they bear small white flowers in flat clusters 4 to 6 inches across; bright red berries follow.

Fraser photinia is suited to Areas D, E, G, I and J. A spectacular shrub that grows 8 to 10 feet tall in five to six years, it bears 2- to 5-inch leaves that are bright red as they appear in spring or after pruning. Japanese photinia thrives in the southern part of Areas D and G and throughout Areas E, I and J. It becomes 6 to 10 feet tall in five to six years and has 3-inch leaves that are bronzy when new. Its red berries turn black when ripe. Chinese photinia grows well in Areas D, E, G, I and J. It may become 20 feet tall in 10 to 15 years, but can be kept smaller by pruning. Its 5- to 7-inch leaves are deeply sawtoothed and reddish bronze when new. *P. serrulata nova (P. serrulata aculeata),* the red twig Chinese photinia, becomes only 6 to 8 feet tall.

Photinias do well in full sun or light shade and tolerate almost any soil, but prefer one mixed with an equal amount of peat moss or leaf mold. Water sparingly in the fall in cooler regions to allow the foliage to mature before winter. Fertilizer is rarely needed, but weak plants can be strengthened with a light application of 5-10-5 beneath them in early spring. To force branching, pinch off the top growth each time the plant adds 18 inches.

PIERIS
P. floribunda (mountain andromeda), *P. formosa forrestii* (Chinese andromeda), *P. japonica* (Japanese andromeda)

In spring andromedas bear 3- to 6-inch clusters of tiny flowers that resemble lilies of the valley. Buds for the following spring form in summer, and are decorative all fall and winter. Andromedas are effective planted in a border or singly on a lawn.

Mountain andromeda grows well in the eastern part of Area B and throughout Areas C, D and I. There plants usually grow 2 to 3 feet tall in four to five years. They have dull green leaves 2 to 4 inches long and white flowers. They thrive in full sun or partial shade. Chinese andromeda, which is suited to Areas D, I and J, is most spectacular because its new 3- to 4-inch leaves are fiery red in spring when the creamy white blossoms are at their prime. The foliage becomes green in summer. The plant needs shade and will become 5 to 10 feet tall in 8 to 10 years. Japanese andromeda grows in the southern part of Area B and throughout Areas C, D and I. It usually grows 4 to 6 feet tall in five to eight years. Its glossy 1½- to 3-inch leaves, bronzy in spring, turn green in summer. The white to blush-white flowers grow in great abundance. It thrives in partial shade, and does well in full sun if the soil is moist.

Andromedas prefer a moist acid soil that has been supplemented with 1 part peat moss or leaf mold to 2 parts soil. Plant them in a place sheltered from the wind. Fertilizer is usually not needed, but weak plants can be strengthened by a light application of cottonseed meal or a

FRASER PHOTINIA
Photinia fraseri

MOUNTAIN ANDROMEDA
Pieris floribunda

For growing areas, see map on page 149.

JAPANESE ANDROMEDA
Pieris japonica

JAPANESE PITTOSPORUM
Pittosporum tobira

CAPE PLUMBAGO
Plumbago capensis

rhododendron-azalea-camellia fertilizer scattered on the ground under them in early spring. A permanent 3- to 4-inch mulch of wood chips, ground bark or chunky peat moss will keep the roots cool and moist. Pruning to shape the plants and to remove seed capsules should be done immediately after the flowers bloom.

PINE, AUSTRALIAN See *Casuarina*
PINEAPPLE GUAVA See *Feijoa*

PITTOSPORUM
P. phillyraeoides, also called *P. angustifolium* (weeping pittosporum, willow pittosporum); *P. rhombifolium* (Queensland pittosporum); *P. tobira* (Japanese pittosporum)

Pittosporums are tough-foliaged evergreen shrubs or small trees with very fragrant blossoms, followed in most species by small yellow or orange fruit. Weeping pittosporum grows well only in Area J. It becomes 15 to 20 feet tall after 15 to 20 years and has deeply drooping branches lined with pale green leaves that may be ½ inch wide and 3 or 4 inches long. In the late winter or early spring tiny yellow flowers appear. Queensland pittosporum also grows well in Area J only. It may become 30 feet or more in height after 20 to 25 years. This species has glossy dark green leaves, diamond-shaped and coarsely toothed, that are 3 to 4 inches long. It bears tiny fragrant white flowers in late spring. Japanese pittosporum grows well in Areas D, E, G and J. Its dense foliage makes a symmetrical mound that is usually 6 to 8 feet tall, with an equal or greater spread after about 10 years. It is excellent close to foundations and in hedges and screens. Its dark green leaves are 2 to 4 inches long. In the spring it bears 2- to 3-inch clusters of creamy white flowers that have an orange-blossom fragrance. The variety *P. tobira variegata,* the variegated Japanese pittosporum, usually grows only 4 to 6 feet tall. Its leaves are pale green edged with white.

Weeping and Queensland pittosporums do best in full sun; Japanese pittosporums also do well in light shade. All will tolerate almost any soil, heat and seaside wind. They can survive some dryness when established, but grow better with average moisture. Fertilizer is not usually needed, but weak plants can be lightly dusted in spring with 5-10-5 on the ground as far as the branches reach. Tree-type pittosporums rarely need pruning. The spreading Japanese pittosporums can be pruned with hand clippers.

PLUM, NATAL See *Carissa*

PLUMBAGO
P. capensis, also called *P. auriculata* (Cape plumbago)

The azure-blue or white flowers of Cape plumbago bring welcome cool colors to warm-climate gardens. Their 1-inch blossoms, borne in 3- to 4-inch clusters above light green 1- to 2-inch leaves, continue to open all year under ideal conditions. In frost-free locations vinelike canes may exceed a height of 10 feet. In most gardens, however, Cape plumbago grows 2 or 3 feet tall in two to three years with a spread of 4 to 5 feet.

Cape plumbago grows well in the southern part of Area G and throughout Areas E and J. It prospers in a warm sheltered position in full sun but will tolerate light shade in hot areas. Almost any well-drained soil is suitable. Plants should be fed in early spring and again in midsummer with a dusting of 5-10-5 fertilizer spread on the ground out as far as the branches reach. Established plants do best if the soil is not constantly moist. When pruned to control size, they make good choices for planting near a foundation and can be shaped into a low hedge or trained to grow up a trellis or wall *(page 77)*. Cape plumbago is sensitive to frost; if it freezes to the ground, cut it back to the soil and usually it will send up new canes. Unless very large plants are desired, prune the oldest and longest canes to the ground each year in early spring. Pinch off the tips of long young canes to stimulate branching.

POINSETTIA See *Euphorbia*
POWDER PUFF See *Calliandra*
PRIVET See *Ligustrum*

PRUNUS
P. caroliniana (Carolina cherry laurel), *P. laurocerasus* and varieties (cherry laurel, English laurel)

Cherry laurels are fast-growing evergreens with tough glossy foliage that is practically pest free. Small clusters of tiny white flowers appear in early spring, followed by ½-inch purplish black berries that cling for months. Because the cherry laurels have dense foliage and many branches close together, they are well suited for use in hedges and privacy screens, for topiary shearing and for training flat against a wall *(page 77)*. Small varieties are often planted near foundations. The berries, leaves and bark are poisonous if eaten.

Carolina cherry laurel grows well in the southern part of Area G and throughout Areas D, E and J. It may become 20 to 40 feet tall but usually grows 8 to 12 feet tall in five to eight years in gardens. Its shiny dark green leaves are 2 to 4 inches long. A recommended variety is Bright 'n Tight. Cherry or English laurel grows well in the southern part of Areas C and G and throughout Areas D, E, I and J. It usually grows about 10 feet tall in five to six years but may become 25 to 30 feet tall under ideal conditions. Its leaves are 4 to 6 inches long. The variety *P. laurocerasus schipkaensis,* Schipka cherry laurel, whose 3- to 4-inch leaves are dark green on top and light underneath, usually becomes 4 to 6 feet tall in three to four years and is much hardier than the species. The variety *P. laurocerasus zabeliana,* Zabel cherry laurel, has narrow leaves 2 to 3 inches long. It has horizontal branches and becomes 3 to 5 feet tall with a spread of 5 to 8 feet in four to five years.

The cherry laurels grow well in full sun but will tolerate partial shade as well as salt air and sea spray. They do best in moist well-drained soil supplemented with 1 part peat moss or leaf mold to 2 parts soil. In late summer the soil should be allowed to become moderately dry to encourage new growth to mature before cold weather arrives.

All cherry laurels will tolerate shearing with hedge shears but it is preferable to shape them by using hand clippers and reaching into the plant to make cuts that will immediately be covered by overlapping foliage.

PYRACANTHA
P. atalantioides varieties (Gibbs fire thorn), *P. coccinea* varieties (scarlet fire thorn), *P. fortuneana* 'Rosedale' (Rosedale fire thorn), *P. koidzumi* 'Santa Cruz' (Santa Cruz fire thorn), *P.* 'Red Elf' (Red Elf fire thorn)

Fire thorns bear many tiny white flowers in the spring, followed by clusters of bright berries in the fall and winter. The berries are relished by birds. One variety of the scarlet fire thorn, called Laland fire thorn, is perhaps the most popular berried shrub in America. All species are fast growing, reaching mature height in only five to eight years. Their sizes range from 2 to 3 feet tall to nearly 20 feet, so that the plants can serve most garden purposes. They can be espaliered against a wall or fence *(page 77)*. The small dark shiny leaves cover sharp spiny spurs, which make a fire thorn hedge a nearly impenetrable barrier.

SCHIPKA CHERRY LAUREL
Prunus laurocerasus schipkaensis

LALAND FIRE THORN
Pyracantha coccinea lalandei

For growing areas, see map on page 149.

Gibbs fire thorn grows well in Areas D, E, G, I and J. Most varieties become 12 to 18 feet tall and have bright red berries, but one, *P. atalantioides aurea,* is noted for its gold berries. *P. coccinea* 'Kasan,' *P. coccinea* 'Lalandei' and *P. coccinea* 'Monrovia' are suited to the extreme southern part of Areas B and F and to all of Areas C, D, E, G, H, I and J. All have orange-red berries and become about 6 to 9 feet tall. P. *coccinea* 'Lowboy' grows in the southern part of Area C and throughout Areas D, E, G, I and J. It is a spreading variety, becoming about 3 feet tall and 6 feet across, and bears orange-red berries. Rosedale fire thorn grows in Areas D, E, G, I and J. It has bright red berries that appear earlier than those of most fire thorns and becomes 7 to 9 feet tall. Santa Cruz fire thorn grows in the southern part of Areas D and G and throughout Areas E, I and J. It has bright red berries and becomes about 3 feet tall. Red Elf is a hybrid fire thorn for the southern part of Area G and Areas D, E, I and J. It has dark red berries and grows to become a mound 2 to 3 feet tall.

Fire thorns will grow in almost any well-drained soil if the site is sunny. Once established, they do best where the soil is relatively dry in summer. They are difficult to transplant balled and burlaped except in early spring. Pruning can be done at any time, but may sacrifice some of the next season's flowers and berries. To encourage branching clip off the tips of long stems in the growing season.

PYRUS

P. kawakamii (evergreen pear)

The evergreen pear, a Japanese species that usually grows 20 to 30 feet tall in 15 years, is blanketed in late winter or early spring with fragrant white flowers. Its deep green glossy leaves, 2 to 4 inches long, are attractive in all seasons. This species is grown entirely for its ornamental value. It has inconspicuous and inedible fruit.

The evergreen pear flourishes in Areas E and J. It needs full sun, but will grow in almost any soil of average moisture content without special preparation or fertilizer. When young, it grows rapidly but weakly, and it must be supported by a stake. In addition, its longest drooping side branches must be pruned short in order to train it into a tree shape; unpruned it will become a large multistemmed shrub. It is easily grown flat against a wall *(page 77)* because of the length and flexibility of its branches, but the close pruning required will lessen flower production.

Q

QUERCUS

Q. agrifolia (California oak, coast live oak),
Q. ilex (holly oak, Holm oak), *Q. suber* (cork oak),
Q. virginiana (live oak)

Evergreen oaks grow 2 to 4 feet a year when young and may reach 40 feet in 20 years. At about that age they begin to fill out, eventually becoming at least as broad as they are tall. Despite their rapid growth they may live for centuries. California oak grows well only in Area J and requires well-drained sandy soil. It becomes 35 to 75 feet tall after 25 to 40 years. It has rough black bark and convex dark green leaves 1½ to 3 inches long with spines around the edges. Holly oak grows well in Areas D, E, G, I and J. It becomes 40 to 60 feet tall in 25 to 50 years. Its 1½- to 3-inch leaves, which are gray-green on top and light green underneath, usually have toothed edges. This species can be sheared regularly and grown as a tall hedge. It does best in well-drained sandy soil and is particularly satisfactory in windy places by the ocean. Cork oak—the source of commercial cork—grows well in Areas G, I and J. It becomes 40 to 60 feet tall after 25 to 50 years and

EVERGREEN PEAR
Pyrus kawakamii

LIVE OAK
Quercus virginiana

142

does best in gravelly soil in hot locations. This species has 3-inch lobed leaves, dark green on top and silvery underneath. Live oak grows well in Areas D, E, G and J and does best if it has moist soil. It becomes 50 to 60 feet tall after about 35 to 40 years and often spreads twice that distance. Its smooth-edged leaves are 1½ to 5 inches long.

Young evergreen oak trees can tolerate some shade, but they do much better in full sun. They benefit from two light feedings yearly, one in early spring, another in early summer. Drop a handful of tree food or a slow-release lawn fertilizer into holes punched 6 to 18 inches deep and 24 inches apart under the branches, starting 2 feet from the trunk. Prune evergreen oaks as little as possible except to guide their growth when they are young.

R

RATSTRIPPER See *Pachistima*

RHODODENDRON, including AZALEA
R. carolinianum (Carolina rhododendron), *R. catawbiense* (Catawba rhododendron), *R. maximum* (rosebay rhododendron, giant rosebay), *R. smirnowii* (Smirnow rhododendron), hybrid rhododendrons, hybrid azaleas

The most impressive flowering shrub in the Northeast and the Northwest is the rhododendron, and the most stunning flowering shrub of the Southeast, Gulf Coast and Southern California is the evergreen azalea (neither survives in the central U.S.). Both are members of the genus *Rhododendron,* and have very similar blossoms. The basic difference is that azalea flowers have five pollen-bearing stamens while rhododendrons have 10 or more.

Most of the rhododendrons and azaleas grown in gardens are hybrids, and their ability to resist cold differs remarkably from one variety to another. For this reason it is best to purchase rhododendrons and azaleas from a local nurseryman who grows his own plants. The descriptions below, listing rhododendrons first, then azaleas, cover types that have proved satisfactory in fairly broad regions.

RHODODENDRONS: The Carolina rhododendron grows well throughout Areas C, D and I. This is one of the most satisfactory species for northern gardens, becoming a thickly branched, rounded shrub that usually grows 3 to 4 feet tall in 10 years. In midspring it is smothered with 3-inch clusters of small rosy pink flowers. The 1½- to 3-inch dark green leaves are brown underneath. A white-flowered variety is *R. carolinianum album.*

Catawba rhododendron grows well in Areas C, D and I. This species grows 6 to 12 feet tall in gardens in 5 to 10 years and has 5- to 6-inch clusters of lilac-purple flowers in the spring. Its dark green leaves are 3 to 5 inches long. The variety *R. catawbiense album* is one of the best white rhododendrons for cold climates.

Rosebay rhododendron does well in Areas B, C, D and I. Because it becomes 10 to 20 feet tall after 15 to 25 years and because its rosy lavender flowers are partly obscured by new growth in late spring, this species is most useful as a background plant. It has slender dark green leaves 5 to 10 inches long and thrives only in the shade.

Smirnow rhododendron grows well in Areas B, C, D, H and I. It becomes 6 to 8 feet tall and equally broad after about 15 years in the garden, and bears 5- to 6-inch clusters of rose or rosy pink flowers with frilled edges in spring. Its 3- to 7-inch-long leaves are dark green on top; the white or tan woolly hairs underneath make it particularly resistant to lace bugs.

The hybrid rhododendrons are immensely varied in color, size, shape and winter hardiness as a result of their complex genetic background. Generally they are classified as

AMERICA RHODODENDRON
Rhododendron 'America'

CAROLINA RHODODENDRON
Rhododendron carolinianum

For growing areas, see map on page 149.

WILSON RHODODENDRON
Rhododendron laetevirens

SMIRNOW RHODODENDRON
Rhododendron smirnowii

DAVID GABLE AZALEA
Rhododendron 'David Gable'

large-leaved, with foliage 3 inches or more in length, and small-leaved, with foliage under 3 inches. The varieties with larger leaves usually have larger flowers, 5 inches or more across, composed of blossoms 2 inches or more in diameter. The individual blossoms of small-leaved types vary from tiny flowers to ones 1½ to 2 inches across, borne in clusters up to 4 inches across. In catalogue listings, the cold resistance of a hybrid rhododendron is indicated by a code that indicates the lowest temperature the flower buds can tolerate during the winter and still open perfectly in the spring. Plants bearing the code designation H-1 survive to −25°, H-2 to −15°, H-3 to −5°, H-4 to 5°, H-5 to 15°, H-6 to 25° and H-7 to 32°. Most varieties grown in this country range between H-1 and H-4 in hardiness. In the hardiest (H-1) group, with flower buds that tolerate −25° in winter, recommended varieties are Boule de Neige, white; Pink Cameo, pink with yellow blotch; Prize, pink with brown blotch; and Tony, cherry red (all 2 to 3 feet tall after 10 years); America, bright red; King Tut, light and deep pink; Pinnacle, pink with citron blotch; and The General, crimson with dark blotch (all 3 to 5 feet tall); Lavender Queen, pale lavender, and Spring Dawn, rosy pink with yellow blotch (both 5 or more feet tall). Recommended in the H-2 group are Cheer, shell pink, and Spring Glory, light pink with crimson blotch (both 2 to 3 feet tall); Blue Peter, violet with dark blotch, and Rocket, coral pink with scarlet blotch (both 3 to 5 feet tall), and Belle Heller, white with golden blotch (5 or more feet tall). Choice varieties in the H-3 group are A. Bedford, pale mauve with dark blotch, 5 or more feet tall; Anna Rose Whitney, deep pink; Britannia, crimson; Crest, primrose yellow; Gomer Waterer, pink buds open white; Jean Marie de Montague, bright scarlet; Mrs. Furnival, pink with maroon blotch; Purple Splendor, royal purple with black blotch; and Scintillation, light pink (all 3 to 5 feet tall). A recommended variety in the H-4 group is Loder's White, white, 3 to 5 feet tall.

The small-leaved, small-flowered hybrid rhododendrons rarely exceed 3 feet in height, and most grow 2 feet tall. They are useful next to foundations, in rock gardens and in front of taller rhododendrons. Recommended varieties in the H-2 category are Blue Diamond, lavender blue; Conestoga, pink; Conewago, rose magenta; Laetevirens, also known as Wilson rhododendron, rose pink; Purple Gem, deep purple; Ramapo, lavender purple; and Wyanokie, white. Choice H-3 varieties are Bow Bells, bright pink; Carmen, dark red; and Moonstone, yellow.

AZALEAS: There are five major groups of hybrid azaleas: Gable azaleas grow well in the southern part of Area C and throughout Areas D, E, I and J. The plants, most of which become 2 to 4 feet tall in four to six years and have 1-inch shiny leaves, bear great numbers of 2-inch blossoms in the spring. Typical varieties are David Gable, rosy pink; Forest Fire, blood red; Louise Gable, salmon pink; Purple Splendor, rich purple; Rosebud, bright pink; Rose Greeley, white; and Stewartstownian, deep red.

Glenn Dale azaleas, which do well in Areas D, E, I and J, may grow upright or spread out; they usually reach 3 to 5 feet in height after about seven years. Individual blossoms range from 1½ to 3 inches across. Of the 400 named varieties the following are recommended: Aphrodite, pale rose pink; Buccaneer, orange red; Cavalier, orange red; Everest, white with chartreuse blotch; Fashion, rose pink; Geisha, white striped red; Glacier, white; and Vestal, white with chartreuse blotch.

The Indica azaleas are divided into two groups according to their hardiness. The Belgian Indicas will grow only in warm parts of Areas E and J; Southern Indicas grow well throughout Areas E and J. Both types may become 6 feet tall and 10 feet or more across after 5 to 10 years in the garden. The flowers, especially of the Belgian Indica type, are apt to be frilled at the edge or many-petaled double blossoms and often are 2 to 3 inches across. Typical Belgian Indica varieties are: Alaska, snow white, two layers of petals; Albert and Elizabeth, white, edged pink, double; Avenir, salmon pink, double; California Sunset, variegated white and pink, double; and Fire Dance, fiery red, double. Typical Southern Indicas, all with single blossoms having one layer of petals, are Brilliant, red; Duc de Rohan, salmon pink; Fielder's White, snow white; Formosa, also called Phoenicia, lavender; Prince of Wales, cherry red; and Southern Charm, deep rose pink.

Kaempferi azaleas grow well in the southern part of Areas C and G and throughout Areas D, E, I and J. Graceful plants that become 5 to 6 feet tall after about five years, they bear many 2-inch flowers in spring. Toward the northern edges of their areas they lose some leaves in cold winters. Typical varieties are Barbara, deep pink; Fedora, deep pink; Herbert, lavender orchid; Holland, deep red; Mikado, bright red; Othello, orange red; Thais, crimson; Wilhelmina Vuyk, white; and Zampa, violet red.

Kurume azaleas grow well in the southern part of Areas C and G and throughout Areas D, E, I and J. After five to eight years in the garden, most Kurume azaleas become dense 18- to 30-inch bushes with small glossy leaves. In spring the foliage is hidden by 1-inch flowers. Typical varieties are Coral Bells, medium pink; Eureka, similar to Coral Bells but hardier; Glory, salmon pink; Hershey's Red, rose red; Hino Crimson, crimson; Hinodegiri, bright red; Lorna, bright pink; and Polar Bear, white.

All rhododendrons and azaleas will grow well in light shade; the Carolina rhododendrons will bloom more abundantly in full sun if the soil is kept moist, but in hot climates or in windy places shade is usually mandatory. Balled-and-burlaped plants may be transplanted in blossom but it is better to transplant them early in spring in areas where their hardiness is questionable, and in spring or fall where there is no likelihood of winter damage.

The most important factor in achieving vigorous growth is an acid soil mixture high in organic content (pages 75-76). Many commercial growers set rhododendrons and azaleas in pure peat moss, or in a 50-50 mixture of peat moss and coarse sand or perlite. A favorite mixture on the West Coast is ½ peat moss and ½ ground redwood, but in such mixtures, plants must be fed regularly.

Because the roots grow near the surface, a bed prepared especially for rhododendrons and azaleas need not be more than 12 inches deep; deep planting keeps the roots from getting the air they need. In fact, it is a good idea to set them about 1 inch higher than they grew at the nursery.

Cultivating the soil around rhododendrons and azaleas would damage their roots. Instead, keep the roots cool and moist with a permanent 2- to 3-inch mulch of wood chips, oak leaves, chunky peat moss or other light organic material. Plants that have been given a soil mixture rich in organic matter probably will not need feeding for several years. Do not stimulate fast growth because it produces long weak stems and few flowers. But if a plant seems weak or sickly, use cottonseed meal or a special rhododendron-azalea-camellia fertilizer, dusted on the soil early in the spring. For maximum flower production, pinch off faded flowers or the seed capsules that follow (page 79).

ROCK SPRAY See *Cotoneaster*
ROSEBAY See *Nerium*
ROSEBAY, GIANT See *Rhododendron*

FEDORA AZALEA
Rhododendron 'Fedora'

HINO CRIMSON AZALEA
Rhododendron obtusum 'Hino Crimson'

For growing areas, see map on page 149.

ROSEMARY
Rosmarinus officinalis

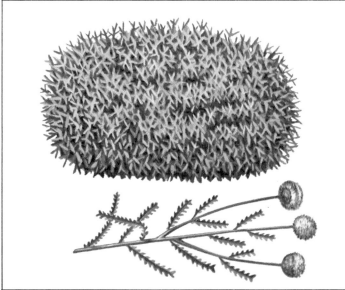

LAVENDER COTTON
Santolina chamaecyparissus

ROSMARINUS
R. officinalis (rosemary)

Rosemary is an aromatic shrub whose leaves have been prized as a cooking and medicinal herb since ancient times. Most plants grow 2 to 3 feet tall in two to three years, but they may become 5 to 6 feet tall. The leaves are ½ to 2 inches long, slender and almost needlelike. Fragrant ½-inch pale blue flowers appear in winter in mild climates, in early spring and occasionally in fall elsewhere. Rosemary makes a good low hedge along the top of a wall, and the variety *R. officinalis prostratus,* creeping rosemary, is an excellent ground cover for a hot dry location.

Rosemary will survive winter outdoors in the southern part of Area C and throughout Areas D, E, G, I and J. It grows best in full sun, but any well-drained soil will do. Abundant moisture shortens the life of this plant; dryness encourages slow, tough growth. No pruning is needed except to nip back a long, errant branch occasionally.

ROSEMARY See *Rosmarinus*

S

SAGE, PURPLE See *Leucophyllum*
SAGE, TEXAS See *Leucophyllum*
ST.-JOHN'S-WORT See *Hypericum*

SANTOLINA
S. chamaecyparissus (lavender cotton),
S. virens (green lavender cotton)

Lavender cotton is an aromatic shrub with ½-inch fernlike leaves that are closer to gray than lavender. Green lavender cotton has dark green foliage. Both bear buttonlike yellow flowers an inch or less in diameter in summer, but most gardeners forgo the flowers, shearing the plants to keep them in a compact formal shape. Lavender cotton is eye catching as a low hedge; even untrimmed plants rarely exceed 2 feet in height. Both types are often used for their foliage color to edge herb gardens, patios and walks.

Lavender cotton grows well in the southern part of Area C and throughout Areas D, E, G, I and J. It needs full sun and will grow in almost any well-drained soil. Plants grown in containers should be set out in the spring in Areas C, D and I, but can be planted at any time elsewhere. In colder climates lavender cotton is treated as an annual.

SCHINUS
S. molle (California pepper tree),
S. terebinthifolius (Brazilian pepper tree)

The name pepper tree was given to these shade trees, which are not true peppers, because the pink or red berries resemble peppercorns in appearance but not in flavor.

The California pepper tree grows well in Area J. It reaches 40 feet in height after 15 to 20 years. With age, the trunk and the larger branches of this tree become gnarled. It has drooping branches, somewhat like those of a weeping willow, and bright green feathery leaves divided into many 2-inch leaflets. This species has separate male and female plants. Both bear tiny yellow flowers in the summer, and female trees produce masses of small rose-colored berries that cling through winter. Though it needs little care and grows rapidly into a handsome specimen, the California pepper tree has far-ranging roots that lift pavements and clog drains, and it often drops twigs or leaves.

The Brazilian pepper tree grows well in the southern part of Area E and throughout Area J. A good shade tree that becomes about 25 feet tall after 30 or 35 years, this species is an excellent choice for lawn or patio. It has stiff horizontal branches; its tough 4- to 8-inch leaves are composed of five to nine leaflets and smell like turpentine when crushed. The 4- to 5-inch cone-shaped clusters of small white flowers at the ends of the branches open in late summer; they are followed, on female trees, by clusters of bright red berries that cling through the winter.

Pepper trees can grow in any well-drained site with full sun. Young trees can be pruned if necessary to shape them.

SENISA See *Leucophyllum*
SHE-OAK See *Casuarina*
SILVER DOLLAR TREE See *Eucalyptus*
SILVERBERRY, FRUITLAND See *Elaeagnus*
SILVERLEAF See *Leucophyllum*

SKIMMIA
S. japonica (Japanese skimmia); *S. reevesiana,* also called *S. fortunei* (Reeves skimmia)

Skimmias are moundlike bushes that are grown for their attractive foliage and their clusters of bright red berries. The berries are often still clinging to plants in spring when 2- to 3-inch clusters of tiny fragrant white flowers appear.

Japanese skimmia becomes 2 to 4 feet tall and 3 to 6 feet across in three to four years. It has shiny 3- to 4-inch leaves crowded onto the ends of the stems. Both male and female plants must be planted if the females are to produce berries. Reeves skimmia grows 18 to 24 inches tall and equally broad in two to three years. Its 3- to 4-inch leaves are dull green. Its berries are not as bright as those of the Japanese skimmia but every plant produces berries.

Skimmias grow well in the southern part of Area C and throughout Areas D, I and J. They must have light shade, and they grow best in moist soil supplemented with 1 part peat moss or leaf mold to 2 parts soil. Pruning is never needed but stems can be cut for indoor decoration.

STRAWBERRY TREE See *Arbutus*

T
TANGELO See *Citrus*
TANGERINE See *Citrus*
TEA TREE See *Leptospermum*
TEXAS RANGER See *Leucophyllum*
TUCKEROO See *Cupaniopsis*

U
ULMUS
U. parvifolia pendens, also called
U. parvifolia sempervirens (Chinese evergreen elm)

The Chinese evergreen elm grows rapidly, often shooting up 5 or 6 feet a year when young. It becomes 40 or 50 feet tall after 25 to 35 years in the garden, but despite its size it is useful even in a small yard because it provides shade for a lawn or patio so quickly. Young growth is so weak that it is necessary to support trees with stakes and to prune parts of heavy drooping branches. As it ages you will also have to prune many of the weeping branches —some as high at their trunk ends as 9 or 10 feet above ground—to keep them from trailing too low. Evergreen elms have 1-inch dark green leaves, sawtoothed on the edges. Drake and True Green are recommended varieties.

The evergreen elm grows well and remains green in winter in the southern part of Area G and throughout Areas E and J; it survives winter but loses its leaves in the southern part of Area C and in Areas D and I. It needs full sun but will grow in almost any soil.

V
VERONICA See *Hebe*

CALIFORNIA PEPPER TREE
Schinus molle

JAPANESE SKIMMIA
Skimmia japonica

EVERGREEN ELM
Ulmus parvifolia pendens

LEATHERLEAF VIBURNUM
Viburnum rhytidophyllum

XYLOSMA
Xylosma senticosa

VIBURNUM

V. odoratissimum (sweet viburnum), *V. rhytidophyllum* (leatherleaf viburnum), *V. suspensum* (Sandankwa viburnum), *V. tinus* (laurestinus)

In mild climates evergreen viburnum provides dark green foliage all year, white flowers in late winter or spring, and red, blue or black berries in summer and fall. The berries are relished by birds. Viburnums are most valuable in hedges and screens.

Sweet viburnum grows well in the southern part of Area G and throughout Areas E and J. Most plants become 8 or 10 feet tall in five to six years and have 5- to 6-inch glossy bright green leaves. The tiny white flowers, borne in 3- to 6-inch clusters, are fragrant and are followed by small berries that turn from red to black as they ripen. Leatherleaf viburnum is recommended for Areas C, D, G, I and J. It becomes an erect 6- to 12-foot shrub in five to six years, with 4- to 8-inch dark green crinkled leaves. It bears 4- to 8-inch clusters of tiny white flowers followed by small berries that turn from red to black. The large leaves make this species susceptible to dehydration by wind; plant it in a protected spot. Sandankwa viburnum grows well in the southern part of Areas D and G and throughout Areas E and J. It becomes 5 to 10 feet tall in five to six years. This species does well in full sun or light shade. It has fragrant white flowers followed by berries that turn from red to black. Laurestinus grows well in the northern part of Area E, the southern part of Area G and throughout Areas D, I and J. It usually grows 6 to 8 feet tall in five to six years. It has 1½- to 4-inch very dark green leaves and rosy white flower clusters followed by blue berries.

Most species grow best in light shade and thrive in well-drained moist soil supplemented with 1 part peat moss or leaf mold to 2 parts soil. They benefit from a permanent 3- to 4-inch mulch of wood chips, chunky peat moss or other organic material to keep the roots cool and moist. Near the northern edges of recommended areas, allow the soil to dry late in the summer so that new branches can mature before cold weather arrives. Clip tall fast-growing stems from time to time to stimulate branching. To lower the height of plants, prune just before new growth starts.

W

WATTLE See *Acacia*
WINTER CREEPER See *Euonymus*

X

XYLOSMA

X. senticosa, also called *X. congestum, Myroxylon congestum* (shiny xylosma)

The shiny xylosma shrub has handsome 2- to 3-inch golden-green leaves that are tinted with bronze when they first appear. It thrives on heat and is a favorite in desert areas. It usually grows 6 to 10 feet tall in five to six years, but may become twice that height; it can be kept at any desired size by pruning. The shiny xylosma is a superb choice for espaliering *(page 77)* against hot south or west walls where few other plants will survive. It also can be grown as a single- or multitrunked 15- to 20-foot tree if it is supported by a stake until it can stand alone.

Shiny xylosma grows well in the southern and western parts of Area G and throughout Area J. It flourishes in full sun or light shade in almost any soil.

Y

YAUPON See *Ilex*
YESTERDAY, TODAY AND TOMORROW See
  Brunfelsia

For growing areas, see map on page 149.

Appendix

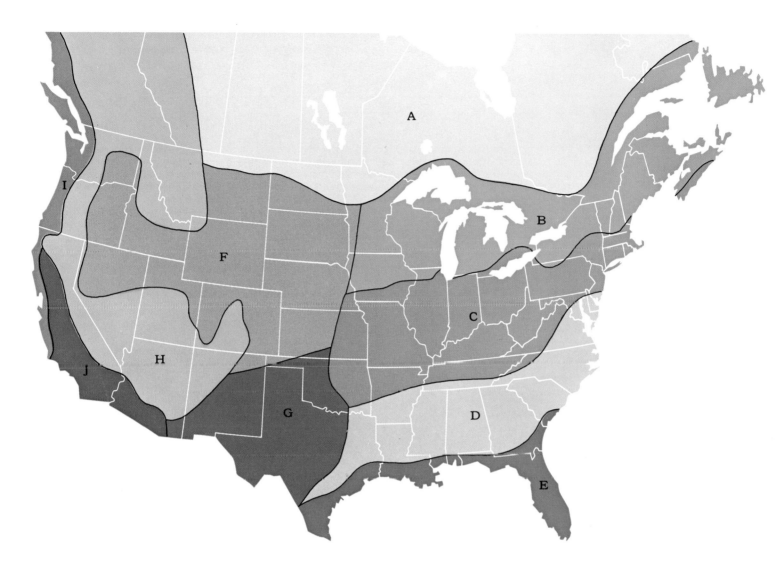

Where to plant recommended evergreens

Evergreens of one kind or another can be grown in all but the sub-Arctic regions of North America, though in general the narrow-leaved cone-bearing types predominate in northern regions and the broad-leaved kinds in the South. The map above, which divides the United States and southern Canada into 10 areas on the basis of temperature, rainfall, altitude and soil, is designed to be used with the encyclopedic entries in Chapter 5; each entry in the encyclopedia indicates by letters keyed to the map the areas in which the plant described grows best. Thus, under *Abies,* you will find that the white fir can be expected to do well in Areas B, C, F, G, H, I and J, but that the Nikko fir is recommended only for Areas B, C, H and I.

Conditions vary greatly within any given area, however, so it is always advisable to consult your nurseryman about the adaptability of a particular plant to your garden before you purchase it. Within Area C, for instance, a broad-leaved evergreen that will thrive near the Atlantic Ocean's shore, where the water serves to moderate wide fluctuations in the temperatures of the atmosphere, may not survive the harsher inland climate of the Alleghenies.

Controlling the pests

Although healthy evergreens are easy to maintain in the right soil and climate, they occasionally need protection against pests. The most common are described on these pages, with specific methods for controlling them. The chemicals recommended are available under various brand names. Since all chemicals are potentially dangerous, follow label directions carefully. Many pests are partially curbed by natural enemies such as ladybug beetles or wasps; insofar as possible avoid chemicals that kill these useful assistants along with the pests.

PEST	DESCRIPTION	METHODS OF CONTROL
	APHIDS These tiny plant lice, seldom longer than ⅛ inch, attack nearly all forms of vegetation, including many evergreens. By sucking the plant's juices they cause leaves and buds to wither and can stunt the growth of the entire plant. On many needled evergreens a toxin they deposit in their nests inside the stems causes swellings called galls. Aphids transmit virus diseases and secrete honeydew that attracts ants. VULNERABLE PLANTS: CITRUSES, DOUGLAS FIR, HIBISCUS, PINE, SPRUCE	Spray in midspring with malathion or nicotine sulfate, taking special care to soak damaged stems, needles and leaves. Galls may be pruned out, provided this does not spoil the shape of the plant. Knock aphids off plants with a stream of water from a garden hose.
	PINE-SHOOT MOTH CATERPILLARS In spring the larvae, or caterpillars (far left near top), of these moths (top left) bore into the tips of new shoots. Gradually the needles yellow, the tips droop downward and resin seeps out where the larvae have bored in. An unchecked infestation of these pests can permanently deform a tree. VULNERABLE PLANTS: AUSTRIAN, MUGO, RED AND SCOTCH PINES	Spray the foliage in spring and midsummer with methoxychlor or dimethoate—chemicals that the plant will absorb and carry with its sap to the shoot tips where caterpillars feed.
	BAGWORM MOTH CATERPILLARS Bagworm caterpillars, as their name suggests, can be identified by the 1- to 2-inch bags they build out of their host's foliage (center left). They carry their needle sacks around on their rear segments while they eat their way through the foliage of those narrow-leaved evergreens that are susceptible to them. VULNERABLE PLANTS: ARBORVITAE, HEMLOCK, LARCH, PINE, RED CEDAR	If possible, pick off bagworm caterpillars by hand and burn them. Spray heavy infestations and those that cannot be reached with malathion or diazinon in late spring, while bagworms are small.
	SAWFLY CATERPILLARS Sawfly larvae (bottom left) attack narrow-leaved evergreens, feeding mostly on full-grown mature needles and working their way from the point toward the base. Their depredations cause a noticeable blunting and yellowing of the needles that leave the foliage thin and make it sickly in appearance. VULNERABLE PLANTS: DEODAR CEDAR, LARCH, PINE	Spray heavily infested trees with carbaryl, methoxychlor or malathion in May or June and again in early fall, the sawflies' second breeding season.
	SPIDER MITES These eight-legged pests are a particular nuisance during hot, dry periods. By feeding on the juices in the foliage of evergreens, spider mites cause discoloration and stunt growth. Tiny, they are hardly visible, but the delicate webs they spin between leaves or needles betray their presence. VULNERABLE PLANTS: ARBORVITAE, AZALEA, CAMELLIA, CYPRESS, EUCALYPTUS, HEMLOCK, JUNIPER, LIVE OAK, SPRUCE	A forceful drenching with a garden hose will clean the cobwebs from infested shrubs and wash away most of the spider mites as well. If any survive this treatment, spray thoroughly in early summer with malathion or one of the miticides such as dicofol or chlorobenzilate.
	SCALES Familiar pests to almost every gardener, scales are known in nearly 200 varieties. Many of these 1/16- to ⅛-inch-long insects are armored with brown oysterlike shells; others simply have tough skins for protection. Short-legged and sluggish, they assemble in dense colonies on needles or leaves and bark, where they sap the plant's strength by sucking its juices. VULNERABLE PLANTS: ARBORVITAE, AZALEA, CEDAR, CITRUSES, CROTON, EUONYMUS, GARDENIA, HOLLY, JUNIPER, PINE, PITTOSPORUM, SPRUCE	Spray infested plants with lime sulfur solution or a so-called dormant oil spray in early spring. (Both are available at garden centers.) Then spray plants with malathion or diazinon in May and June to control the crawler stage. Prune out badly encrusted branches and then burn them.

PEST	DESCRIPTION	METHODS OF CONTROL
WEEVILS	In the larval stage *(far left),* when they are no longer than ⅜ of an inch, weevils live beneath the soil's surface and feed on roots, causing sickly yellow foliage and stunting growth. Later, as mature beetles, they move to the foliage, eating leaves until they have consumed all but the ribs and veins. Left uncontrolled, they can demolish a shrub in a single season. VULNERABLE PLANTS: AZALEA, HEMLOCK, RHODODENDRON, YEW	Spray or dust infested plants and the ground beneath them repeatedly in June and July with chlordane. Take special care to cover the lower branches and their stems with the spray or dust.
MEALY BUGS	A familiar pest to indoor plant growers, mealy bugs also attack many garden evergreens. Close relatives of scale, these ⅛- to ¼-inch-long insects cover their soft bodies with a web of waxy white filaments that cause them to appear as cottony masses on branches and stems. They stunt the growth of plants by sucking their juices; in addition, they secrete honeydew that attracts ants and invites growth of injurious sooty-mold fungi. VULNERABLE PLANTS: AZALEA, CITRUSES, CROTON, EUCALYPTUS, GARDENIA, POINSETTIA, YEW	Ladybug beetles and wasps are natural enemies of mealy bugs. If they do not control them, a spraying with dimethoate or malathion should do the job.
LEAF MINERS	Leaf miners do their damage when they are in the larval stage. The larvae themselves are rarely visible, but their work is readily apparent. By burrowing into the interiors of leaves, where they live and feed, they give the leaves a blistered or tunneled appearance. The infested leaves gradually discolor, shrivel and drop off. After several years under that kind of attack the plant may die from lack of foliage. VULNERABLE PLANTS: ARBORVITAE, BOX, HOLLY, PINE	Spray thoroughly with malathion, diazinon, dimethoate or carbaryl when the leaf miners are in their flying stage in spring; if you wait until the larvae are at work inside the leaves you will be too late.
THRIPS	Thrips, minute flying insects with bristly wings, afflict a variety of broad-leaved evergreens. They are costly pests in regions where citruses are cultivated, since they feed on the leaves and buds, causing leaves to discolor, buds to drop and fruit to be deformed. Discolored foliage and stunting similar to that caused by spider mites can be traced to thrips if the tiny brown flecks of the excrement that they deposit are visible. VULNERABLE PLANTS: AZALEA, CITRUSES, EUONYMUS, GARDENIA, INDIAN LAUREL, RHODODENDRON	Spraying as often as every two weeks during the summer months with malathion or dimethoate may become necessary to control a major infestation of thrips.
WHITE FLIES	These minute insect pests restrict their diet to certain broad-leaved evergreens. As adult flies they lodge themselves on the undersides of leaves and sap the plant of vigor by sucking its juices. Except for a subtle yellowish mottling of the leaves, their presence is difficult to detect until a plant is jostled, when they fly out all at once in a cloud. Their sticky honeydew secretion invites ants and encourages the growth of molds. VULNERABLE PLANTS: AZALEA, CITRUSES, PRIVET, RHODODENDRON	A thorough spraying with dimethoate, diazinon or malathion will control white flies. Pay special attention to the undersides of the leaves.
LACE BUGS	Lace bugs can be identified by the delicate pattern of their wings. Rarely longer than ⅛ inch, they are less apparent than the damage they do; they can be detected by brown sticky spots of excretion they deposit on the undersides of leaves. By sucking sap from broad-leaved evergreen leaves, they cause yellow or white stippling or blotching on the leaves' upper surfaces, sickening foliage and stunting growth. VULNERABLE PLANTS: ANDROMEDA, AZALEA, MOUNTAIN LAUREL, RHODODENDRON	Spray in late spring and again in midsummer with carbaryl or malathion. Take special care to coat the undersides of leaves, where lace bugs feed.

Characteristics of 49 narrow-leaved evergreens

	PLANT HEIGHT						PLANT SHAPE					FOLIAGE COLOR					SOIL NEEDS					USES			
	Under 1 foot	1 to 3 feet	3 to 6 feet	6 to 10 feet	10 to 30 feet	Over 30 feet	Broadly conical	Narrowly conical	Columnar	Bushy	Creeping	Green	Dark green	Yellow-green	Blue-green	Reddish brown	Wet	Average	Dry	Acid	Alkaline	Lawn specimen	Screen	Hedge	Ground cover
ABIES CONCOLOR (white fir)					●			●							●			●		●		●			
ARAUCARIA HETEROPHYLLA (Norfolk Island pine)					●			●					●					●		●					
CEDRUS ATLANTICA GLAUCA (blue Atlas cedar)					●	●									●			●		●					
CEDRUS DEODARA (deodar cedar)					●	●									●			●		●					
CEDRUS LIBANI (cedar of Lebanon)					●		●					●						●		●					
CEPHALOTAXUS HARRINGTONIA (Japanese plum yew)		●							●			●						●		●			●	●	
CHAMAECYPARIS OBTUSA GRACILIS (slender hinoki false cypress)		●						●				●						●		●					
CHAMAECYPARIS PISIFERA FILIFERA (thread sawara false cypress)		●						●		●								●		●					
CHAMAECYPARIS PISIFERA SQUARROSA (moss sawara false cypress)				●	●			●							●			●		●					
CRYPTOMERIA JAPONICA (Japanese cedar)				●	●			●				●				●	●			●					
CUNNINGHAMIA LANCEOLATA (China fir)			●		●			●							●		●	●		●					
CUPRESSOCYPARIS LEYLANDII (cupressocyparis)				●		●						●					●			●				●	
CUPRESSUS ARIZONICA GAREEI (Garee Arizona cypress)				●		●									●			●	●			●			
CUPRESSUS SEMPERVIRENS STRICTA (Italian cypress)				●				●				●						●	●			●	●		
JUNIPERUS CHINENSIS AUREA 'GOLD COAST' (juniper)	●								●					●				●	●	●	●				●
JUNIPERUS CHINENSIS COLUMNARIS (blue column juniper)			●			●									●			●	●	●	●				
JUNIPERUS CHINENSIS 'KAIZUKA' (Hollywood juniper)			●		●					●								●	●	●	●				
JUNIPERUS HORIZONTALIS WILTONII (Wilton carpet juniper)	●										●				●			●		●					●
JUNIPERUS SABINA TAMARISCIFOLIA (tamarix juniper)	●									●					●			●		●					●
JUNIPERUS VIRGINIANA CANAERTII (Canaert red cedar)			●		●							●						●		●	●	●	●		
LARIX LEPTOLEPIS (Japanese larch)				●	●	●		●				●					●			●					
LIBOCEDRUS DECURRENS (California incense cedar)				●	●			●				●					●			●	●				
METASEQUOIA GLYPTOSTROBOIDES (dawn redwood)				●	●			●						●	●		●			●					
PICEA GLAUCA CONICA (dwarf Alberta spruce)		●			●			●				●						●	●	●		●	●		
PICEA OMORIKA (Serbian spruce)				●	●			●				●						●	●	●		●	●		
PICEA PUNGENS MOERHEIMII (Moerheim Colorado spruce)				●	●			●							●		●	●		●		●	●		
PINUS CEMBRA (Swiss stone pine)			●		●			●				●						●	●		●				
PINUS DENSIFLORA UMBRACULIFERA (Tanyosho pine)			●						●				●	●				●	●		●				
PINUS HALEPENSIS (Aleppo pine)				●	●			●				●						●	●		●				
PINUS MUGO MUGO (mugo pine)	●								●			●						●	●		●			●	●
PINUS RESINOSA (red pine)				●	●			●				●				●		●	●						
PINUS STROBUS (eastern white pine)				●	●			●				●				●		●	●		●	●		
PINUS THUNBERGII (Japanese black pine)			●	●				●				●				●		●		●				
PODOCARPUS MACROPHYLLUS (yew podocarpus)			●				●					●					●			●	●	●	●		
PSEUDOLARIX AMABILIS (golden larch)				●	●			●					●				●			●	●				
PSEUDOTSUGA TAXIFOLIA (Douglas fir)				●	●			●				●					●			●		●	●		
SCIADOPITYS VERTICILLATA (umbrella pine)			●		●			●				●					●			●	●				
SEQUOIADENDRON GIGANTEUM (giant sequoia)					●	●								●				●		●					
TAXODIUM DISTICHUM (bald cypress)				●	●			●				●				●	●			●					
TAXUS BACCATA REPANDENS (spreading English yew)		●							●				●					●		●				●	
TAXUS BACCATA STRICTA (Irish yew)			●			●						●						●		●			●	●	
TAXUS CUSPIDATA CAPITATA (upright Japanese yew)			●		●							●						●		●			●	●	
TAXUS MEDIA HICKSII (Hicks yew)			●				●					●						●		●			●	●	
THUJA OCCIDENTALIS DOUGLASII PYRAMIDALIS (Douglas arborvitae)			●		●							●					●			●			●	●	
THUJA ORIENTALIS AUREA NANA (Berckman's golden arborvitae)		●							●		●						●			●			●	●	
THUJA PLICATA (giant arborvitae)				●				●				●					●			●			●	●	
TSUGA CANADENSIS (Canada hemlock)				●	●			●				●					●			●	●		●	●	
TSUGA CANADENSIS PENDULA (Sargent's weeping hemlock)		●								●		●					●			●					
TSUGA CAROLINIANA (Carolina hemlock)					●	●						●					●			●	●	●	●		

Characteristics of 83 broad-leaved evergreens

	PLANT HEIGHT						FLOWER COLOR				FLOWER SEASON				LEAF SIZE			SOIL NEEDS				USES			
	Under 1 foot	1 to 3 feet	3 to 6 feet	6 to 10 feet	10 to 30 feet	Over 30 feet	White	Yellow-orange	Pink-red	Blue-purple	Spring	Summer	Fall	Winter	Under 1 inch	1 to 3 inches	Over 3 inches	Wet to average	Dry	Acid	Alkaline	Lawn specimen	Hedge	Ground cover	Fruits or berries
ABELIA GRANDIFLORA (glossy abelia)		●							●			●	●	●		●									
ACACIA BAILEYANA (Cootamundra wattle)				●	●			●					●	●		●			●			●			
ARBUTUS UNEDO COMPACTA (compact strawberry tree)				●	●								●	●		●			●	●					●
ARCTOSTAPHYLOS UVA-URSI (bearberry)	●								●		●			●					●	●				●	●
AUCUBA JAPONICA PICTURATA (Japanese aucuba)			●	●						●			●			●	●	●		●					●
BAUHINIA BLAKEANA (Hong Kong orchid tree)				●					●	●		●	●	●	●			●			●				
BERBERIS JULIANAE (wintergreen barberry)		●				●			●			●			●	●						●			●
BRUNFELSIA CALYCINA FLORIBUNDA (yesterday, today and tomorrow)		●	●		●				●	●	●	●	●		●	●									
BUXUS SEMPERVIRENS SUFFRUTICOSA (edging box)	●												●		●								●		
CALLIANDRA INAEQUILATERA (pink powder puff)		●	●						●		●		●	●		●						●			
CALLISTEMON CITRINUS (lemon bottle brush)			●	●					●		●	●	●	●		●			●	●	●				
CALLUNA VULGARIS 'H. E. BEALE' (heather)		●							●			●	●		●				●					●	
CAMELLIA JAPONICA (common camellia)			●						●		●		●	●		●	●		●	●				
CARISSA GRANDIFLORA 'GREEN CARPET' (Natal plum)	●			●				●	●	●	●	●	●		●	●		●	●					●	●
CASUARINA EQUISETIFOLIA (horsetail beefwood)				●									●		●	●	●		●		●				●
CEANOTHUS THYRSIFLORUS (California lilac)		●	●						●	●	●			●		●									
CINNAMOMUM CAMPHORA (camphor tree)				●	●				●			●	●	●	●	●			●		●			●	
CITRUS SINENSIS (sweet orange)			●		●			●			●	●	●	●		●	●			●				●
CODIAEUM VARIEGATUM (croton)			●	●											●	●				●				
COTONEASTER DAMMERI (bearberry cotoneaster)	●								●		●			●	●				●	●				●	●
CUPANIOPSIS ANACARDIOIDES (carrotwood)				●											●	●			●		●				
DABOËCIA CANTABRICA (Irish heath)		●					●		●	●	●	●		●		●			●	●					
DAPHNE CNEORUM (rose daphne)	●								●		●			●	●				●						
ELAEAGNUS PUNGENS (thorny elaeagnus)			●	●		●								●	●	●	●	●	●		●		●		●
ERICA HERBACEA (spring heath)	●								●		●	●	●	●		●			●	●				●	
ERIOBOTRYA JAPONICA (loquat)			●		●								●	●		●	●		●	●	●	●			●
ESCALLONIA FRADESI (pink princess escallonia)		●	●						●		●	●	●	●	●		●					●			
EUCALYPTUS FICIFOLIA (red flowering gum)			●	●					●			●	●	●		●			●						
EUONYMUS FORTUNEI 'EMERALD 'N GOLD' (winter creeper)		●													●	●		●	●		●			●	
EUPHORBIA PULCHERRIMA (poinsettia)		●	●						●					●		●	●			●					●
FATSIA JAPONICA (Japanese fatsia)		●	●		●									●		●	●			●					●
FEIJOA SELLOWIANA (pineapple guava)			●	●	●				●	●	●			●		●			●						●
FICUS BENJAMINA (weeping fig)				●											●	●				●				●	
FRAXINUS UHDEI 'MAJESTIC BEAUTY' (shamel ash)				●											●	●			●		●	●			
GARDENIA JASMINOIDES (gardenia)		●			●				●			●	●	●		●	●			●					
HEBE SPECIOSA (showy hebe)		●	●						●			●		●	●	●				●					
HIBISCUS ROSA-SINENSIS (Chinese hibiscus)			●	●					●			●	●	●		●	●					●	●		
HYPERICUM PATULUM 'SUNGOLD' (Sungold St.-John's-wort)		●			●			●				●	●	●		●			●	●					
ILEX AQUIFOLIUM (English holly)				●									●			●	●	●		●			●		●
ILEX CORNUTA BURFORDII (Burford holly)			●											●		●	●	●	●				●		●
ILEX CRENATA (Japanese holly)			●										●			●	●	●		●			●		
ILEX CRENATA CONVEXA (convexleaf holly)		●											●			●	●	●		●			●		
ILEX OPACA (American holly)			●	●	●									●		●	●	●		●			●		●
ILEX VOMITORIA (yaupon)			●											●		●	●	●		●			●		●
IXORA COCCINEA (jungle geranium)		●	●						●		●	●	●	●	●		●			●					
JASMINUM MESNYI (primrose jasmine)		●			●			●			●	●	●			●			●		●	●			
KALMIA LATIFOLIA (mountain laurel)		●	●						●		●			●		●	●			●			●		
LAURUS NOBILIS (laurel)			●	●	●							●			●	●	●			●			●		●
LEPTOSPERMUM SCOPARIUM HYBRID (tea tree)		●	●						●		●		●		●	●	●			●		●			

153

	PLANT HEIGHT						FLOWER COLOR				FLOWER SEASON				LEAF SIZE			SOIL NEEDS				USES			
	Under 1 foot	1 to 3 feet	3 to 6 feet	6 to 10 feet	10 to 30 feet	Over 30 feet	White	Yellow-orange	Pink-red	Blue-purple	Spring	Summer	Fall	Winter	Under 1 inch	1 to 3 inches	Over 3 inches	Wet to average	Dry	Acid	Alkaline	Lawn specimen	Hedge	Ground cover	Fruits or berries
LEUCOPHYLLUM FRUTESCENS (Texas sage)		●	●						●	●	●			●	●				●				●		
LEUCOTHOË FONTANESIANA (drooping leucothoë)		●			●		●				●				●	●		●						●	
LIGUSTRUM JAPONICUM 'SUWANNEE RIVER' (privet)		●			●		●				●				●	●	●	●	●	●	●		●		
MAGNOLIA GRANDIFLORA (southern magnolia)				●	●		●				●	●	●			●	●	●				●			
MAHONIA AQUIFOLIUM (Oregon holly grape)	●							●			●					●		●	●						●
MYRTUS COMMUNIS COMPACTA (dwarf myrtle)		●			●		●				●				●	●		●	●						●
NANDINA DOMESTICA (nandina)	●	●			●		●				●				●			●							●
NERIUM OLEANDER (oleander)			●	●			●		●			●	●		●			●	●						
OLEA EUROPAEA (common olive)			●	●			●				●				●			●	●						●
OSMANTHUS HETEROPHYLLUS (holly osmanthus)			●	●			●						●	●		●		●	●				●		
PACHISTIMA CANBYI (Canby pachistima)	●												●		●			●						●	
PHOTINIA FRASERI (Fraser photinia)		●			●		●				●				●	●	●	●	●				●		●
PIERIS FLORIBUNDA (mountain andromeda)	●	●			●		●				●					●		●		●				●	
PIERIS JAPONICA (Japanese andromeda)		●	●		●		●				●					●		●		●					
PITTOSPORUM TOBIRA (Japanese pittosporum)			●		●		●				●				●	●		●	●				●		
PLUMBAGO CAPENSIS (Cape plumbago)	●							●	●	●	●	●	●		●			●							
PRUNUS LAUROCERASUS SCHIPKAENSIS (Schipka cherry laurel)		●			●		●				●					●	●	●					●		●
PYRACANTHA COCCINEA LALANDEI (Laland fire thorn)			●		●		●				●		●		●	●		●	●				●		●
PYRUS KAWAKAMII (evergreen pear)				●	●		●				●			●	●	●		●	●						●
QUERCUS VIRGINIANA (live oak)					●										●	●	●	●				●			●
RHODODENDRON 'AMERICA' (America rhododendron)		●							●		●					●	●	●		●					
RHODODENDRON CAROLINIANUM (Carolina rhododendron)		●							●		●				●	●		●		●					
RHODODENDRON LAETEVIRENS (Wilson rhododendron)	●								●		●				●	●		●		●					
RHODODENDRON SMIRNOWII (Smirnow rhododendron)		●							●		●					●	●	●		●					
RHODODENDRON 'DAVID GABLE' (David Gable azalea)	●	●							●		●			●		●		●		●					
RHODODENDRON 'FEDORA' (Fedora azalea)		●							●		●			●		●		●		●					
RHODODENDRON OBTUSUM 'HINO CRIMSON' (Hino Crimson azalea)	●								●		●			●		●		●		●					
ROSMARINUS OFFICINALIS (rosemary)	●	●							●	●		●	●	●	●			●	●			●			
SANTOLINA CHAMAECYPARISSUS (lavender cotton)	●				●			●				●			●			●	●			●			
SCHINUS MOLLE (California pepper tree)				●	●							●			●			●	●						●
SKIMMIA JAPONICA (Japanese skimmia)	●	●							●		●					●		●							●
ULMUS PARVIFOLIA PENDENS (evergreen elm)					●										●			●				●		●	
VIBURNUM RHYTIDOPHYLLUM (leatherleaf viburnum)			●	●		●					●			●			●	●						●	●
XYLOSMA SENTICOSA (xylosma)			●	●									●		●	●	●	●	●			●			

Acknowledgments

For their help in the preparation of this book, the editors wish to thank the following: Blair Adams, Extension Horticulturist, Univ. of Wyoming, Laramie, Wyo.; American Association of Nurserymen, Washington, D.C.; Timothy E. Anderson, Fairchild Tropical Garden, Miami, Fla.; James R. Aninag, Jimmie's Interior Planting Studio, Los Angeles, Calif.; Woodbury Bartlett, Landscape Architect, Hamilton, Mass.; Albert S. Beecher, Professor of Horticulture, Virginia Polytechnic Institute and State Univ., Blacksburg, Va.; Conley Tree Surgeons and Garden Center, Inc., Boothbay Harbor, Maine; Cooperative Extension of Nassau County, Agricultural Division, Mineola, N.Y.; Coorlis Brothers, Inc., Ipswich, Mass.; A. E. Cott, Extension Horticulturist, Iowa State Univ., Ames, Iowa; Mrs. Edith Crockett, Librarian, The Horticultural Society of New York, Inc., New York City; Mrs. Muriel C. Crossman, Librarian, Massachusetts Horticultural Society, Boston, Mass.; William B. Davis, Extension Environmental Horticulturist, Univ. of California, Davis, Calif.; Professor A. F. DeWerth, Floriculture Section, Texas A&M Univ., College Station, Texas; Professor R. D. Dickey, Department of Ornamental Horticulture, Univ. of Florida, Gainesville, Fla.; Robert J. Dingwall, Chief Horticulturist, Missouri Botanical Garden, St. Louis, Mo.; Dr. John Fogg, Barnes Foundation Arboretum, Philadelphia, Pa.; Daniel B. Franklin, Landscape Architect, Atlanta, Ga.; Gable Nurseries, Stewartstown, Pa.; Mr. Fred Galle, Director of Horticulture, Callaway Gardens, Pine Mountain, Ga.; Miss Marie Giasi, Librarian, Brooklyn Botanic Garden, Brooklyn,

N.Y.; Eric V. Golby, President, American Hibiscus Society, Bradenton, Fla.; Mary Gordon, Landscape Architect, Palo Alto, Calif.; Cornell Green, Visual Aids Specialist, Texas Agricultural Service, College Station, Texas; Dr. Gordon Halfacre, Horticultural Service Department, North Carolina State Univ., Raleigh, N.C.; Miss Elizabeth Hall, Senior Librarian, The Horticultural Society of New York, Inc., New York City; Dr. C. Gustav Hard, Landscape Specialist, Univ. of Minnesota, St. Paul, Minn.; Allen C. Haskell, Landscape Architect, New Bedford, Mass.; Keith Hellstrom, Landscape Architect, Spokane, Wash.; Dr. A. C. Hildreth, Director Emeritus, Denver Botanic Garden, Denver, Colo.; Horticultural Printers, Mesquite, Texas; Milford C. Jorgensen, Extension Agent, Horticulture, Hillsborough County, Fla.; Miles C. Labrun, Director, The State Arboretum of Utah, Univ. of Utah, Salt Lake City, Utah; Leslie Laking, Director, The Royal Botanical Gardens, Hamilton, Ontario; Jaul J. Mitchell, Extension Ornamental Horticulturist, Oklahoma State Univ., Stillwater, Okla.; Monrovia Nursery Company, Azusa, Calif.; Musser Forests, Inc., Indiana, Pa.; The New York Botanical Garden Library, Bronx Park, N.Y.; Charles O. O'Brien, President, Agricultural Division, Geigy Chemical Corporation, Ardsley, N.Y.; Dr. Neil G. Odenwald, Specialist, Landscape Architecture, Louisiana Cooperative Extension Service, Louisiana State Univ., Baton Rouge, La.;

Raymond E. Page, Landscape Architect, Beverly Hills, Calif.; Dr. Norman Pellett, Department of Plant and Soil Service, Univ. of Vermont, Burlington, Vt.; Rear Admiral Neill Philip, U.S.N. (ret.), Upperville, Va.; Dr. Pascal P. Pirone, Senior Plant Pathologist, The New York Botanical Garden, Bronx Park, N.Y.; Rose K. Rice, Bernardsville, N.J.; Dr. Victor H. Ries, Professor Emeritus of Ornamental Horticulture, Ohio State Univ., Columbus, Ohio; Dr. Robert H. Ruf, Associate Professor of Horticulture, Univ. of Nevada, Reno, Nev.; Dr. Charles Sacamano, Extension Horticulturist, Univ. of Arizona, Tucson, Ariz.; Harvey S. Sadew, Monkton, Md.; Ralph D. Smith, Communications Specialist, Univ. of California, Berkeley, Calif.; Stribling's Nurseries, Inc., Merced, Calif.; Sweeney, Krist & Dimm, Portland, Ore.; Mr. and Mrs. Leland E. Swett, Los Angeles, Calif.; C. Powell Taylor, Rosedale Nurseries, Hawthorne, N.Y.; U.S. Department of Agriculture, National Arboretum, Washington, D.C.; Ted Van Veen, Van Veen Nursery, Portland, Ore.; Gil Whitten, County Extension Director, Pinellas County, Fla.; Professor Fred B. Widmoyer, Department of Horticulture, New Mexico State Univ., Las Cruces, N.M.; Professor Donald Williams, Agriculture Extension Service, Univ. of Tennessee, Knoxville, Tenn.; Hermann A. Wirth, Horticultural Tools, Sayville, N.Y.; Joseph Witt, Assistant Director, Univ. of Washington Arboretum, Seattle, Wash.

Picture credits

The sources for the illustrations that appear in this book are listed below. Credits for the pictures from left to right are separated by semicolons, from top to bottom by dashes. Cover—Costa Manos from Magnum. 4—Keith Martin courtesy James Underwood Crockett. 6—Costa Manos from Magnum. 11—Drawings by Matt Greene. 18—Farrell Grehan. 23,25,27,29—Drawings by Matt Greene. 33—Ralph Crane. 34,35—Ralph Crane; Costa Manos from Magnum. 36,37—Enrico Ferorelli; Costa Manos from Magnum—Fred Lyon from Rapho Guillumette. 38,39—Leonard Wolfe. 40,41—Costa Manos from Magnum except top Nicholas Foster. 42,43—Costa Manos from Magnum. 44,45—Ralph Crane; Fred Lyon from Rapho Guillumette—Enrico Ferorelli. 46,47—Ralph Crane. 48—Fred Lyon from Rapho Guillumette. 50 through 54—Drawings by Matt Greene. 57 through 60—Richard Meek. 62—Drawings by Matt Greene. 67—Malak, Ottawa. 68—Map by Robert Ritter—Dean Brown. 69—Sebastian Milito; Robert Walch—Maps by Robert Ritter. 70—Map by Robert Ritter—Dr. John W. Davis Jr. 71—Ralph Crane; Phil Brodatz; Helen Kittinger —Maps by Robert Ritter. 72—Courtesy Mr. and Mrs. Lawrence Pierce; Nicholas Foster—Maps by Robert Ritter. 73—Map by Robert Ritter—Gottlieb Hampfler. 74—Dean Brown. 77,78,79—Drawings by Matt Greene. 81 through 84 —C. Harrison Conroy courtesy Brooklyn Botanic Garden, drawings by Adolph E. Brotman. 86—Drawing by Matt Greene. 88—Illustration by Don Moss. 90 through 148—Illustrations by Rebecca Merrilees and John Murphy except where otherwise indicated next to illustration. 149—Map by Adolph E. Brotman. 150,151—Drawings by Davis Meltzer.

Bibliography

Bailey, L. H., *The Cultivated Conifer in North America*. The Macmillan Company, 1933.
Bowers, Clement Gray, *Rhododendrons and Azaleas*. The Macmillan Company, 1960.
Brooklyn Botanic Garden, *Broadleaved Evergreens*. Brooklyn Botanic Garden, 1967.
Brooklyn Botanic Garden, *Conifers*. Brooklyn Botanic Garden, 1969.
Brooklyn Botanic Garden, *Flowering Trees*. Brooklyn Botanic Garden, 1967.
Brooklyn Botanic Garden, *The Hundred Finest Trees and Shrubs for Temperate Climates*. Brooklyn Botanic Garden, 1959.
Cloud, Katharine M-P, *Evergreens for Every State*. W. H. and L. Collingridge, 1952.
Curtis, Charles H. and W. Gibson, *The Book of Topiary*. John Lane, 1904.
Flemmer III, William, *Shade and Ornamental Trees in Color*. Grosset & Dunlap, Inc., 1965.
Harrison, Richard E. and Charles R., *Know Your Garden Series, Trees and Shrubs*. Charles E. Tuttle Company, 1965.
Hull, George F., *Bonsai for Americans*. Doubleday and Company, Inc., 1964.

Hyams, Edward, *Ornamental Shrubs for Temperate Zone Gardens*. A. S. Barnes & Company, 1965.
Kumlien, L. L., *The Friendly Evergreens*. Rinehart & Company, Inc., 1954.
Lee, Frederic P., *The Azalea Book*, D. Van Nostrand Company, Inc., 1968.
Ouden, P. Den and Dr. B. K. Boom, *Manual of Cultivated Conifers*. Martinus Nijhoff, 1965.
Sunset Magazine and Sunset Books, *Sunset Western Garden Book*. Lane Magazine & Book Company, 1967.
Taylor, Norman, *The Guide to Garden Shrubs and Trees*. Houghton Mifflin Company, 1965.
Van Veen, Ted, *Rhododendrons in America*. Sweeney, Krist & Dimm, Inc., 1969.
Watkins, John V., *Florida Landscape Plants*. University of Florida Press, 1969.
Welch, H. J., *Dwarf Conifers*. Charles T. Branford Company, 1966.
Wyman, Donald, *Shrubs and Vines for American Gardens*. The Macmillan Company, 1969.
Wyman, Donald, *Trees for American Gardens*. The Macmillan Company, 1965.
Wyman, Donald, *Wyman's Gardening Encyclopedia*. The Macmillan Company, 1971.

Index

Numerals in italics indicate an illustration of the subject mentioned

156

PRINTED IN U.S.A.

XXXX
PRINTED IN U.S.A.

160

XXXX